Local Education Policies

Comparing Sweden and Britain

Edited by

Christine Hudson
Assistant Professor of Political Science
Umeå University, Sweden

and

Anders Lidström
Associate Professor of Political Science
Umeå University, Sweden

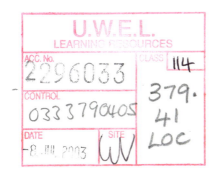
palgrave

First published 2002 by
PALGRAVE
Houndmills, Basingstoke, Hampshire RG21 6XS and
175 Fifth Avenue, New York, N. Y. 10010
Companies and representatives throughout the world

PALGRAVE is the new global academic imprint of
St. Martin's Press LLC Scholarly and Reference Division and
Palgrave Publishers Ltd (formerly Macmillan Press Ltd).

ISBN 0–333–79040–5

This book is printed on paper suitable for recycling and made from fully managed and sustained forest sources.

A catalogue record for this book is available from the British Library.

Library of Congress Cataloging-in-Publication Data
Local education policies : comparing Sweden and Britain / edited by Christine Hudson and Anders Lidström.
    p. cm.
    Includes bibliographical references and index.
    ISBN 0–333–79040–5
    1. Schools—Great Britain—Decentralization. 2. Schools–
–Sweden—Decentralization. 3. School management and organization—Great Britain. 4. School management and organization—Sweden. 5. Education and state—Great Britain. 6. Education and state—Sweden. 7. Comparative education. I. Hudson, Christine, 1950– II. Lidström, Anders, 1953–

LB2862 .L63 2001
379.41—dc21
                                            2001032730

10   9   8   7   6   5   4   3   2   1
11   10 09 08 07 06 05 04 03 02

Printed and bound in Great Britain by
Antony Rowe Ltd, Chippenham, Wiltshire

Local Education Policies

Also by Christine Hudson

AGAINST ALL ODDS: Local Economic Development Policies and Local Government Autonomy in Sweden and Britain

SKOLA I FÖRÄNDRING (Schooling in Transition) (*with Anders Lidström*)

THE UNIVERSITY AND REGIONAL RECIPROCITY

Also by Anders Lidström

DISCRETION – AN ART OF THE POSSIBLE

HANDLINGSUTRYMME I SKOLANS VÄRLD (Scope for Action in Schooling) (*with Gunnel Gustafsson*)

KOMMUNSYSTEM I EUROPA (Local Government Systems in Europe)

SKOLA I FÖRÄNDRING (Schooling in Transition) (*with Christine Hudson*)

*To Kathleen and Ingrid, mothers and educationalists,
and Anton and Stefan, sons and pupils*

Contents

List of Tables

xi

List of Figures

Preface

In the Western world, education policy has increasingly become a local matter. Localities and schools construct their own systems, develop their own particular profiles and adjust the content of education to meet specific local needs. Even if economic, political and cultural globalization, and the increasing emphasis on knowledge in society have, to some extent, contributed to a streamlining of education across different countries, these tendencies have also promoted fragmentation, diversity and the development of specific local features in education.

These changes require a new understanding of education policy. The national education system is only a part of the context in which local education policies are created. The ideas and preferences of local policy makers need to be explored. The relationship between education on the one hand and local economic, political, social and demographic conditions on the other, has to be examined. However, local education must also be investigated against the background of wider global and transnational changes.

At present there is a gap in the literature concerning the ways in which education is created in the intersection between the global and the local. Our edited volume tries to go some way towards filling this gap. The book brings together a collection of papers, which analyse different aspects of local education policy-making. In order to establish a broader base for our conclusions, a comparative perspective is used. Scholars from Great Britain and Sweden investigate various aspects of these policies in the two countries. We hope that the book will provide new knowledge and additional insights into the conditions of local education policies.

The book is the result of a research project, which developed in two phases. It started as a pilot study of consequences of the decentralization reforms in Swedish primary and secondary education during the beginning of the 1990s. This was published in Swedish, in our common book *Skola i förändring* (Schooling in Transition). On the basis of this, we applied for, and received, a research grant from the Swedish National Agency for Education (project no. 15001).

xv

Parts of our studies have also been supported through the national Political Science Research Programme 'Democracy in Transition', financed by HSFR, the Swedish Social Sciences Research Council. Individual chapters in the book have been financed by separate sources. We are grateful to the National Agency for Education and the HSFR, for making this research possible.

Three of the chapters in this volume have previously been published by academic journals. Chapter 3 appeared in *Scandinavian Political Studies*, 22 (2), 1999; Chapter 4 is a revised and extended version of an article published in the *Oxford Review of Education*, 24 (4), 1998; and Chapter 5 was originally published in Swedish as 'Utbildning och kommunal utvecklingspolitik', in *Kommunal Ekonomi och Politik*, vol. 2 (2), 1998. We acknowledge that the publishers of these journals have kindly accepted that the articles are also published in this book. We also express our gratitude to the Open University Press, which has agreed to the reproduction of Table 2.1 in this book.

Valuable comments concerning the different contributions in this volume have been received from a number of sources. In particular, we would like to express our thanks to fellow researchers, at the Department of Political Science, engaged in education policy studies whose active discussion of our work has provided a welcome stimulus. We also acknowledge the helpful comments and suggestions from colleagues at the Centre for Principal Development at Umeå University, Sweden.

CHRISTINE HUDSON   ANDERS LIDSTRÖM
Umeå University, Sweden

Notes on the Contributors

Sue Cara is Associate Director of the National Institute for Adult and Continuing Education. She has undertaken case studies of a number of learning cities published in *Learning Cities* (1997) and, with S. Ranson, *Practice, Progress and Value: The Learning Community, Assessing the Value They Add* (1998).

Sharon Gewirtz is a Lecturer in Social Policy at the Open University. Her research is on markets, managerialism and social justice in education. She is co-author of *Specialisation and Choice in Urban Education* (1993) and *Markets Choice and Equity in Education* (1995) and author of *The Managerial School: Essays on Post-Welfarism, Social Justice and New Labour* (forthcoming).

Christine Hudson is an Assistant Professor in Political Science at the Department of Political Science, Umeå University, Sweden. She has undertaken research on local government, regional policy and comparative politics. She is co-author of *Skola i förändring* (1995) and has recently published *The University and Regional Reciprocity* (2000).

Olof Johansson is an Associate Professor of Political Science and Chair of the Centre for Principal Development and Director of the National Head Teachers Training Programme at Umea[o] University, Sweden. His research interest has focused on political culture, public policy making and administration, but during recent years mainly on educational leadership. Among recent publications are 'Value Orchestration by the Policy Community for the Learning Community: Reality and Myth' (with P.V. Bredeson), in Begley, P. (eds), *Values and Educational Leadership* (1999) and 'The Values of School Administration: Preferences, Ethics and Conflicts' (with P. Begley), in *The Journal of School Leadership*, vol. 8, 1998.

Charles Landry is Director of the Research Consultancy COMEDIA. He has recently concluded a series on *The Richness of Cities: Urban*

Policy in a New Landscape with L. Greenhalgh, W. Solesbury and K. Worpole. He is also author with F. Bionchini of *The Creative City* (Demos/Comedia).

Anders Lidström is an Associate Professor at the Department of Political Science, Umeå University, Sweden. His research interests are local government, education policy and comparative public administration. Among recent publications are *Kommunsystem i Europa* (Local Government Systems in Europe; 1996), and 'The Comparative Study of Local Government Systems – a Research Agenda', in *Journal of Comparative Policy Analysis*, vol. 1, 1998.

Leif Lundberg is Director of Studies for the Head Teacher Training Programme at Umeå University, Sweden. He has a background as a school psychologist and has been working with school improvement and school leader development for 20 years. His main research interests are learning organizations, learning communities, learning cultures and leadership that fosters learning within and between organizations. He is also involved in comparative research projects within that field.

Stewart Ranson is a Professor of Education in the School of Education at the University of Birmingham. His research has examined the changing governance and management of education. Since the mid-1980s the focus of his work has been on analysing the value, purposes and conditions of a democratic learning society. His publications include *Inside the Learning Society* (1998) and *A Framework for Evaluating Learning Communities: Assessing the Value They Add* (1998).

Part I
Introduction

1
Introduction

Christine Hudson and Anders Lidström

We are living in a time of considerable change and uncertainty; processes of restructuring are taking place within the economy, society and politics at the international, national and local levels. Countries are becoming more inter-linked as political, economic, cultural and technological activities increasingly span the boundaries of states. Non-governmental actors, such as transnational companies, are playing an increasingly significant role in these transactions. Transnationalization challenges the traditional role of the nation state. The globalization of the economy, the spread of 'mass culture' through the mass media, environmental problems, the growth of supra-national political structures such as the EU mean that it is increasingly difficult for countries to isolate their domestic political institutions, behaviour and policy from international influences.

However, while there are certain common global problems and developments, not all countries are affected in the same way or to the same extent. There are not only differences between countries but there are also differences within countries concerning the effects of these broader changes. Thus at the same time as there have been trends towards greater integration there have also been moves towards disintegration (Rosenau, 1994; Robertson, 1995; Clark, 1997). One consequence has been a reassertion of the importance of difference and of the salience of the local territory. Regions and localities have increasingly exerted their right to be independent actors.

Throughout most of the Western world, education is in the midst of these changes. National decentralization policies have resulted in a transfer of responsibility for primary and secondary education to the local level during the last 10–20 years. This has made education, to a greater extent, a local matter and a primary concern for local policy-makers. However, at the same time, major exogenous forces, often referred to as economic, political and cultural globalization (Waters, 1995), are increasingly affecting policy-making. The question in focus in this book is how the new local education systems can be under-stood in the balance between the global and the local. Are they shaped according to a common, international format, or is the local policy vacuum, which decentralization policies created, filled differ-ently in different localities, both within and between countries?

One argument is that the developments taking place at the local level can be understood within the framework of the general econ-omic restructuring and social, political and ideological changes occurring in the Western world. As this forms a common context, we would expect a considerable degree of similarity in the changes taking place and hence, a general tendency towards convergence. However, a counter-argument is that these broader trends are medi-ated through national and local contexts, which means that their effects vary. This would assume that there are significant and increasing divergences between different countries and/or between different localities – municipalities and schools.

The *purpose* of the book is to analyse local education policies in Sweden and Britain. Its focus is on how these policies have taken shape and how this process can be understood in relation to global transformations and specific local conditions.

Even if our theoretical interest is broader, our empirical field of investigation is limited to Sweden and Britain. In many ways, these countries have much in common in terms of culture, political institu-tions and economic systems. However, they are also different. Not least educational restructuring has followed different paths, albeit within a similar framework. In both countries, space has opened up at the local level as a consequence of decentralization reforms. However, these have taken different shapes in the two countries. In Sweden, powers have been transferred mainly to local government and to schools, whereas in Britain it has been away from local government and to schools and the market. Nevertheless, schools and/or local government have been given increased decision-making indepen-dence and an increased ability to structure their activities themselves.

The theme underlying this study of changes in the school systems in Britain and Sweden is the *governance of learning*. However, we limit our focus to three interlocking aspects of this broader theme. These arise from the wider changes taking place in society and all relate to the development of the knowledge society, but are also linked to notions of globalization and to the spread of market values and management ideas across borders. The first sub-theme is freedom of choice and market policies at local level. This concerns the influence of ideologies promoting parental choice and individualization and how schools and municipalities meet and adjust to the demands placed by the new, well-educated, middle class. The second sub-theme deals with education's role in local economic development (*the (l)earning economy*). At national as well as local levels, education is seen as a key resource in a world open for international competition. The localities are – to varying extents and with differing focuses – adjusting educational content to business needs and the interests of economic growth. Both these developments raise challenges to democracy. Freedom of choice policies highlight concerns over the right for those who are well-educated and vocal to exert a disproportionate influence over the shaping of a major welfare institution. Local government adjustment of education to accommodate business interests raises important issues concerning democratic accountability and responsibility.

However, the book also emphasizes the practical side of local schooling. Our third sub-theme focuses on the practice of learning and the ways in which the major changes taking place represent a new reality for local education decision-makers. At school level, the leadership task has attracted renewed attention. How do school leaders cope with the new challenges and opportunities? At the city level, the practice of learning also involves broader questions of how a learning community can be created and how learning can be used as a means of revitalizing a locality.

Most chapters are studies of either Swedish or British conditions, although a number aim at integrating perspectives and experiences on a comparative basis. On the whole, there is an attempt to keep a rough balance between contributions reflecting the Swedish situation and those concerning the British. The material included represents a mixture of methodologies. Some chapters are based on quantitative analysis whereas others adopt a qualitative approach.

There is no ambition to obtain any sort of rigorous methodological matching. Instead we are concerned with presenting pictures from both countries which can form the basis for a more summarizing, reflective type of comparative analysis.

Our starting-point is a framework for analysis, consisting of a number of assumptions about general tendencies of change, the importance of context and the interplay between the general and the specific. We do not expect there to be a common logic in terms of capitalism, culture or technological development, through which everything can be explained. Instead, we present our framework as a summary of tendencies, sometimes interrelated, sometimes conflicting, but which are all relevant for an understanding of contemporary educational changes.

Framework for analysis

Common tendencies of change

A number of contemporary changes with political consequences are common for most countries in the Western world. The trends are summarized under four headings; globalization, the emergence of the knowledge society, the challenged polity and demographic changes. However, these trends are mediated through specific national and local contexts and thus, in themselves, contain the seeds of fragmentation. Therefore, a more complete picture requires the recognition that the particular responses differ not only *between* but also *within* countries, that is between localities. Our intention here is simply to paint a broad picture of these changes and, while acknowledging that they are interrelated in many ways, we do not focus on the forms or working of these interrelationships.

1   Globalization

The thesis of *a globalized economy* stresses the increasing rate and speed of economic exchange and interdependency in recent decades. Markets and competition have been extended to a world scale. Investments and units for production are being moved from one country to another in search of better returns and quicker profits. Transnational corporations, with no commitment to any specific country, are major actors (Sally, 1996). Particularly significant is the globalization of finance and the exponential growth in transnational economic activity spurred on by the liberal-ization of market controls, both nationally and internationally, and the deregulation of international markets and financial institutions. These developments have facilitated the mobility of capital across the world, as finance capital is more easily transferred across borders. (Cerny, 1996; Eatwell, 1998). This has been accompanied by the global organization of production and the new international division of labour. The market for unskilled labour is becoming increasingly globalized and production is becoming more differenti-ated with manufacturing located to low labour cost countries and research and development to high technology countries. These developments have been underpinned by the rate of technological change. In particular, the widespread effects of generic or carrier technologies such as information and communication technologies that enable a faster spread of economic information. The breakdown of communism has meant that neo-liberalism and other market-friendly ideologies have developed, largely unchallenged, into a global ideology and acquired a hegemonic position. Although, econ-omic gobalization can be regarded as a logical step in the develop-ment of capitalism, it is has also been seen as marking a move from organized to disorganized capitalism or post-Fordism (Jessop, 1994). This is coupled to changes in production methods with short-run, batch production and niche marketing; a growing division of the workforce into a highly-skilled, flexible and permanent core and a unskilled, low-paid, insecure periphery; declining national control over markets and a reduction in the power of national labour market organizations. This is leading capitalism to become increas-ingly disorganized and mobile (Crow, 1997).

However, globalization is not an uncontested concept. First, and not surprisingly, is has been understood and defined in various ways. It has been seen as predating enlightenment and the modern society (Robertson, 1992), connected with modernity (Giddens, 1990) or a phenomenon which replaced imperialism in the 1960s (Tomlinson, 1991, cp. Nederveen Pieterse, 1995). Some writers are taking globalization to mean a general integration and uniformiza-tion of the world, pointing towards convergence (Mishra, 1999), whereas others emphasize globalization as the compression of time and space, meaning that different parts of the globe are increasingly related to each other, without necessarily becoming more similar

(Robertson, 1992). Indeed, a number of discourses of globalization may be identified; between different parts of the world, different disciplines, different ideologies and from different gender perspectives (Robertson and Khondker, 1998).

Second, sceptics such as Hirst and Thompson (1996), argue that the globalization thesis is over exaggerated. No overall increase in trade relations can be detected. Instead, the concept has a Western, or perhaps a triad focus (North America, Europe and East Asia), and tends to exclude the rest of the globe. It has been criticized for being hegemonic and deterministic, presenting the processes of globalization as something inevitable that actors can only react to and not influence.

In our way of using the concept, we explicitly limit our focus to processes taking place in the Western world. Nevertheless, globalization highlights the unevenness of the world, the differences of wealth and resources, and indeed how these differences are increasing. Even if integrating economic activities are mainly limited to the triad, the rest of the globe is also affected. A third world country may experience this process through a demand for unskilled labour. Less powerful states are 'rule-takers', as they adjust to rules set by others (Hurrell and Woods, 1999).

However, globalization does not just concern the economy, *culture* is also being globalized. Indeed, Waters (1995) argues that the spreading of signs and symbols is in the forefront of globalization. This is perhaps most obvious in the gradual expansion of an Americanized consumer culture (Tomlinson, 1991), sometimes sarcastically labelled McWorld or Hollyworld. Chains of consumer goods and fast food are represented all over the world. McDonald restaurants are now established in 116 countries. Brand names and products are the same in different countries leading to a 'coca-colarization' of indigenous cultural values. Fashion changes occur simultaneously. Advertising campaigns present similar arguments and images. These tendencies, supported by strong economic interests, mainly focus on lifestyle and entertainment.

Cultural globalization also implies a standardizing of news flows, films and TV programmes. Transnational TV networks have emerged (CNN, MTV). Programmes with basically the same content are broadcasted in culturally very different countries. Technological innovations have facilitated the emergence and the global spread of this 'mass culture', through for example satellite and cable TV. Linked to this is also an easier access to information through the Internet.

However, cultural globalization refers to more than a mere spreading of similarities across the globe. In the same way as with economic globalization, it also includes an aspect of relativization. The time-space compression, inherent in globalization, opens up for instant and closer impressions of other cultures, ethnical groups and religions. Each cultural expression has to relate itself to others, which may foster an awareness of differences, but also of similarities. This also includes a deterritorialization of culture (Tomlinson, 1999). Ankie Hoogvelt (1997) suggests that people can now have social and community relationships regardless of space and the territory they share. She argues that this enables the emergence of 'imagined' communities and cultures that cross borders. In this sense, globalization can be regarded as shared phenomenal worlds.

Finally, globalization also contains a *political* element. Supranational political institutions are increasing in number and importance. These include both inter-governmental organizations and international non-governmental organizations (NGOs, for example the International Labour Organization, ILO). In Europe, the stronger position of the EU *vis-à-vis* its member states, and the suggested extension of its membership base to include east and central European countries is, of course, particularly significant. The EU may be regarded as a way of improving the competitiveness of Europe in the world economy, but has also been presented as a project aiming at preventing mass destruction through wars. Closely linked to this are the attempts by the union itself to create a common European identity. Political globalization may also be a response to the transnational nature of many environmental problems, such as global warming and pollution, which cannot be solved in one country or by countries acting alone.

It is a debated matter what the consequences are likely to be for the nation state. It has been argued that the transfer of powers from the nation state to inter-governmental organisations, together with a strong tendency towards regionalization and decentralization, and the general globalization of the economy, would result in its decline. A global government would be necessary (Held, 1991). However, others claim that the nation-state, on the contrary, retains or even strengthens its position, as strong regulative forces are necessary for a functioning market economy (Hirst and Thompson, 1996). There is also a tendency for one form of government, liberal democracy, to spread across the globe. The number of states with, at least in a formal sense, liberal democratic systems of government, has gradually increased during the 20th century, and very rapidly during the last decade. However, under this label there is still considerable variation with regard to, for example, respect for human rights, treatment of ethnical minorities and openness and transparency. This aspect of globalization can also be conceived of in relativizing terms. For example, all nations are faced with requirements to comply with the UN charter of human rights and have to relate to ideas of liberal democracy.

2 *The emergence of the knowledge society*

In the knowledge society, *education and research* are seen as the keys to the future. The move from manual to non-manual employment, from the dominance of manufacturing industry to service sector and knowledge-based employment has meant a major transformation of the Western societies of the late 20th century. Even previously, great expectations have been placed on scientific knowledge, but this is now penetrating all spheres of society. Knowledge is seen as a productive force and professional knowledge of all kinds is valued (Bell, 1973; Böhme and Stehr, 1986). Scientific research is emphasized as a means for enhancing the knowledge base of a society and for improving its competitiveness.

This transformation is expected to require a much better educated work force. As knowledge increases in importance, both private business and public organizations emphasize their human resources. Relevant knowledge is a major competitive advantage. Thus, the level of education is increasing throughout the Western world. The role of higher education is stressed, but the quality and content of primary and secondary education are also given prominence. In a rapidly changing society where old skills become obsolete and new skills are required, where learning includes the building of competencies and affects all sectors of society, education needs to be a life-long process.

A more *flexible workforce* is emerging. New organizational models have developed in the wake of economic globalization and increasing pressure for competitiveness. These emphasize flexibility and the ability to adapt to rapidly changing market conditions. Strategic management, decentralized responsibilities, quality awareness and just-in-time-deliveries are a few features of these new models. The consequences for the labour market are profound. Employees are expected to be flexible with regard to their wages, tasks and forms of employment. Various forms of short-time employment are becoming increasingly common. Corresponding changes are taking place within the public sector.

This transformation reflects more general changes in the Western economies, often characterized as a transition from Fordist to post-Fordist forms of production (Burrows and Loader, 1994). Under Fordism, which prevailed during most of the 20th century, standardized mass production for a mainly national market, dominated. The Ford motor company and the assembly line symbolized this form of production. Workers' tasks were clearly specified and rigid. However, during the 1960s and 1970s, this form of production lost its momentum, and entered a crisis stage. It was regarded as necessary to re-create dynamism in society and the economy.

Hence, from the early 1970s, more agile, post-Fordist, forms of production replaced previous static forms. The production of more individually adjusted consumer goods was emphasized. This required the establishment of a more flexible labour market. In the typical post-Fordist enterprise, a distinction is made between the core employees – management, experts and key workers – and those with more peripheral positions. The core employees are given high wages and opportunities to retrain and develop, whereas those with peripheral employment are hired on a short-time basis, receive lower wages and are laid off when necessary. These relatively unskilled workers oscillate between unemployment and temporary jobs.

However, despite these general changes, there is still scope for other models, or deviations from this pattern. For example, specific national labour market models remain important. These include an American model, with limited employment protection and considerable wage differences, a Nordic model with an extensive public safety net and a Japanese model where labour rights are still closely tied to specific enterprises (Glimstedt, 1998).

Another implication of the knowledge society is *the development of a broad middle class*. At the same time as the traditional working class is declining in number, a new middle class is expanding. The new middle class is defined mainly through its educational resources (cp. Giddens, 1981). Indeed, the members of this class have typically reached their positions because of their education. They have usually attended a university or college and now have a professional status through their knowledge and expertise. Compared to the old working class, the new middle class is less distinct in terms of how it may be delimited (Crompton, 1993), but also in terms of the values and the nature of its activism. However, its members tend to promote individualism and they prefer individual or *ad hoc* means of influencing political decisions. The increasing levels of education will result in a further growth of the middle class in most Western countries, well into the 21st century.

Finally, there are also signs of *increasing social problems*. The knowledge society is not necessarily more equal than its predecessors. On the contrary, access to knowledge is unevenly distributed in society and post-Fordist flexibility and division of task on the labour market opens up for widening gaps between different strata of the society.

In terms of income distribution, cleavages have been increasing (Stewart and Berry, 1999). This is a general trend during the 1980s in the Western world, as well as in the developing countries and the transition economies. In the OECD countries, this is mainly linked to increasing wage differences and unemployment. In particular among immigrants, young people and those with short education, unemployment has stabilized on a high level. These social problems have coincided with and been reinforced by a dismantling of public welfare systems.

3   *The challenged polity*

The liberalization and de-regulation of markets together with new regulation by supra-national institutions has *reduced the scope for political decision-making vis-à-vis* private business. States are less able to pursue independent economic policies and are more inclined to adjust to market needs. They are sensitive about creating conditions that would disadvantage their own economy, for example, by restricting private investments or by accepting a higher rate of inflation than in other countries. There is considerable pressure to homogenize constraints on the economy, such as specific national regulations and tax systems (Cerny, 1996).

Areas of national policy-making, not directly linked to economic policies, have been regarded as less affected by the global economy. These include education and health policy. However, the need to adjust national welfare systems to global economic pressures has been used as an argument for a general downsizing of the public welfare commitment (Mishra, 1999). This is sometimes conceived of as a 'race to the bottom' (Moran and Wood, 1996). Nevertheless, there is still scope for public decision-makers in nations and localities to create better conditions for private business, as long as these are limited to the general social and physical infrastructure of the country. This may include measures to improve telecommunications, education systems or transport.

There has been *a questioning of the public commitment to welfare*. During the post-war period, an extensive public responsibility for welfare was developed. This is now being questioned (Mishra, 1999). The public sectors are either not growing any longer or they are downsized, or are at least facing problems of austerity (Mouritzen, 1992). Tasks and responsibilities have been transferred from the public sector to private firms and civic organizations (Moran and Prosser, 1994). Sometimes families (women) and individuals are expected to take on more responsibility. Several public monopolies have been dismantled, particularly in areas where technical development has made previous natural monopolies obsolete.

The distinction between the public and private sectors is also blurred, as public–private co-operation and partnerships have become more common. The concept of governance summarizes this tendency towards network building and unclear lines of responsibility, through which non-public actors are also brought into the public decision-making and implementation process (Rhodes, 1997). Direct state interventions in private business have been reduced. Public subsidies to private firms and nation-specific regulation are not accepted as these are seen as obstructing market principles and fair competition. However, indirect support, through the provision of infrastructure and the establishment of partnerships, is favoured. These changes are linked to an increasingly globalized economy, but also to the spread of neo-liberal and market oriented ideas.

The inner working of the public sector has also been transformed. *Market principles have been introduced into the public sector*, replacing previous Weberian ideals. These new ideas are aimed at improving administrative efficiency and flexibility. Constrained by tighter economic conditions, and influenced by policies developed under Thatcher and Reagan, the private firm has been seen as an ideal of efficiency. The notions behind the New Public Management are widely accepted among various political parties. These ideas include the establishment of market-like conditions within the public sector, a concern with performance and results, an emphasis on incentives, a stronger role for management, decentralized responsibility and private provision of publicly financed services (Lane, 1997; Hughes, 1998).

There has been a *questioning of traditional democratic actors and institutions*. Throughout the Western world, there is a general decline in public support for important democratic institutions, such as parliament, the legal system and the civil service and there is a tendency for citizens to have less trust in politicians. Whilst support for democracy as a principle remains high (Dalton, 1999), forms of participation regarded as important in a representative democracy, for example, voting in elections and membership of a political party, are declining (Inglehart, 1997). Established political parties are challenged in several ways: their membership base is eroding at the same time as newly established, often temporary, single-issue or protest parties are competing for votes. In sum, these changes represent a challenge to representative democracy.

New social movements, often with communitarian ideas, have developed in the wake of post-industrialism and the new knowledge society. Increasingly, political activism is channelled through such movements, for example through green and feminist organizations and *ad hoc* interest groups. These changes in the pattern of participation reflect a more profound value shift. Although neo-liberalism has promoted individualism, many of these movements involve a new collectivism based on values of community and non-materialism. Beliefs in traditional authorities have also been challenged. These new values have a particular stronghold in the younger generation and among professionals and those who are well educated (Inglehart, 1990).

4 Demographic changes

Finally, a set of demographic changes characterizes Western societies. There is *an increase in life expectancy*. This is putting additional pressure on the welfare systems, as particularly those above 80 years of age demand much more health and social care than the rest of the population. The care needs of an 80-year-old are estimated at between 5 and 10 times those of a 60-year-old. At the other end of the continuum, there is a tendency for birth rates to decline (OECD, 1998a). The combination of low fertility and longer life expectancy is leading to burdensome dependency ratios. The pension system is now a big issue in most countries, since a smaller share of the working population will, in the future, have to finance longer periods of pension payments. Demographic changes also involve an alteration in the family structure, for example through an increase in the number of single parent families and one-person households, and a less linear and standard lifecycle.

Nations in the western world are becoming *less ethnically and religiously homogenous*. This is partly a result of voluntary migration but also reflects refugee flows from troubled areas. The foreign or immigrant population has been increasing in practically all OECD countries during the last decade. In addition, the national origins of the immigrants have become more diversified (OECD, 1998b). Linked to this general tendency towards heterogeneity, segregation within nations and localities is also increasing.

Finally, patterns of migration in the Western world suggest that *urban and sub-urban areas are growing at the expense of the rural countryside*. The difficulties in earning a living in rural communities have resulted in a general urbanization tendency during most of the post-war era. Present changes, linked to the knowledge society, have reinforced this trend and university towns or cities with universities are often contemporary centres of growth. There are also an increasing number of well-educated couples who need a large labour market within easy commuting distance to safeguard employment for both.

However, the post-war period has also witnessed a move from urban centres to sub-urban areas or villages within commuting distance. In some countries, significant parts of the population have migrated to middle-size towns. This represents an escape from high-priced, overcrowded and congested cities to more peaceful towns. Modern technology and IT have enabled distant work and facilitated this tendency. Nevertheless, the overall pattern of urban change is mixed: it contains booming global cities and declining industrial centres; recreated and revitalized old cities; expanding university towns, sub-urbanisation and the growth of middle-size towns and villages in semi-rural areas (Hall, 1998).

Fragmentation

The full picture does not only contain common trends but also tendencies towards fragmentation (Mlinar, 1992). Apart from the general patterns of change, each nation and locality has its own specific characteristics, which influence how the particular outcomes are being shaped. Historical traditions and culture, established institutions and the demographic, social and economic structure of an area make one locality different from another. Further, there is a process of interplay between the broader trends and the specific national and local contexts. On the one hand, the general trends are mediated in ways that modify, reinforce or divert their influence in each nation, locality or setting. On the other hand, local and national conditions contribute to the long-term creation and transformation of broader trends. Specific national and local conditions of importance may be the following:

1. *National conditions*: There are certain experiences and events that may be common for a nation as a whole, for example its general history, the emergence of democratic institutions or the position of popular movements. Language and education may also have been used in the process of unifying and building the nation state and thus, may also be a shared feature. Structures of privilege, acceptable ways of behaving, the unspoken rules of the game and taken-for-granted meanings are all embedded in a society. Factors such as these form part of a collective history, a common social and cultural heritage. This is not to argue that these are shared equally by all or that all have the same relationship to them. Nevertheless, even if the nation-state were to decline, it has still made a lasting imprint on history.
2. *Local conditions*: Conditions also vary between localities. A locality, in this sense, is a sub-national territory, including anything from municipalities to regions. Localities have their own particular histories and identities as well as shared national ones. Each local area has its own special occupational history, conditions of existence, experience, culture, traditions, patterns

of social relations and political structures (Hudson, 1995). There are differences between localities/regions in terms of the state of the local/regional economy and its specific characteristics such as the industrial and employment structure. Local political, social and economic institutions have been built which may limit future choices and mediate the impact of broader trends.

Hence, globalization simultaneously consists of homogenizing and heterogenizing forces, of complementary global and local logics, which are dialectically related to each other. A common theme in contemporary globalization theory is the criticism of the assumption of convergence, the idea that the world is increasingly becoming more similar. Instead, it is frequently argued that there also exist parallel tendencies towards divergence and the creation of a global mosaic.

Theories have developed which support the notions of disintegration in terms of how society can be understood. Lyotard (1984) has criticized attempts to develop meta-narratives, or over-arching, general theories and argues that the post-modern society cannot be captured in general categories. Instead he stresses the chaotic *hyper-differentiated* character of the globalized culture. A different concept on the same theme is *hybridization*, which refers to the situation where a general model meets specific conditions and becomes recreated as something new (Nederveen Pieterse, 1995). Many writers prefer to discuss these phenomena in terms of the general concept of *fragmentation* (for example Clark, 1997). However, in order to emphasize the combination of fragmentation and integration, Rosenau (1994) has suggested the concept of *fragmegration*. A similar idea underlies Robertson's (1995) concept of *glocalization*, which captures the dual character of globalization and localization, but with a more explicit focus on the territorial aspect.

As previously noted, the general and seemingly homogenizing trends in themselves contribute to disintegration and specific local responses. This underlines the dialectics and complexity inherent in concepts such as globalization and glocalization. A few examples can illustrate how, in this way, the global and the local may come together.

First, one may conceive of *economic differentiation*. In an increasingly globalized economy, with worldwide competition, it is particularly important for business as well as local and regional authorities to identify and develop niches, in order to be successful. Attempts to find comparative advantages promote specialization, which is often linked to local conditions and competences. However, some areas are advantaged by, or can take advantage of the changes in the economy whereas others are disadvantaged. Despite strong global economic forces, economic life is still closely connected to specific localities. Cox (1997) suggests that there persist tendencies towards the territorialization of economic life. Localities and regions are beginning to take greater responsibility for their own development and are increasingly important as arenas for competitive struggle for economic development (Hudson, 2000a).

Second, there is also an on-going *cultural differentiation*. Uniform Americanized mass culture and attempts to create a common European identity foster counter-tendencies. Indeed, it has been suggested that 'globalization stimulates forces of opposition which may just as readily lead to an increasingly fragmented world' (McGrew, 1992, p. 23). Strong needs are expressed for seeking roots in a world characterized by a superficial, commercialized culture and considerable migration. Many of these tendencies emphasize the importance of place and the local territory, its specific features, such as its history, culture and traditions. Identity, representation and sense of place are important in the construction and reconstruction of uniqueness (Hudson, 2000b). In a period of rapid change when many of the 'old certainties' have been questioned we increasingly need 'placed identities for placeless times' (Harvey, 1989). Attempts to strengthen ethnical and religious identities also figure here. Although, it is important to emphasize that cultural differentiation may also take non-territorial forms. The interconnection of religious or cultural enclaves in various parts of the world is facilitated by new and improved means of communication.

Finally, differentiation coincides with *political decentralization*. In most Western countries, political reforms have been implemented which give the local authority level or the regional level of political decision-making a stronger position. Powers and functions have been transferred, specific grants have been merged into block grants and detailed regulations replaced with general goals (Batley and

Stoker, 1991; Sharpe, 1993; Loughlin *et al.*, 1999). The emphasis on regions has also been supported by the EU and corresponds to the notion of subsidiarity. Even if there are also tendencies towards a re-centralization through an increasing emphasis on output control, decentralization remains significant. Decentralization reforms have opened up a greater scope for local variation and for local and regional decision-makers to develop policies in order to enhance local profiles and niches.

General consequences for education

Most of the general tendencies outlined above have, in one way or another, affected education. Not only do they concern its role in society but they also have consequences for the ways in which it is governed and for the content of educational programmes. Indeed, these tendencies verify that education is a core policy area in the on-going transformation of Western societies. However, fragmentation and variation are also features of the educational arena.

Among these general trends, two stand out as particularly important. One is the tendency towards globalization and the other the emergence of a knowledge society. These are interrelated and can, to a large extent, be seen as two sides of the same coin. In a sense, education is situated in the cross-section between them, constantly under pressure to adjust and to perform.

Throughout the Western world, there is today a stronger emphasis on education and research. Education is seen in instrumental terms, as a key to the future. Through an educated population, the competitiveness of a nation, a region or a locality can be enhanced. Education is, together with knowledge development through research, the Western strategy for economic prosperity in a globalized economy, where competition with low wages is out of the question. This requires closer co-operation between public education authorities and private business interests. It also puts pressure on the work force to constantly train and retrain in order to keep its skills up to date.

To some extent, there are also tendencies towards a standardization of the content of education. As English is increasingly establishing itself as a world language in business, politics and mass culture, it is gradually being accepted as a *lingua franca* even in countries whose own languages are strong internationally. Courses explicitly aimed at preparing students for wider labour markets, rather than just a national, are emerging. These may include education programmes conducted entirely in English (in non-English speaking countries) and courses with a mainly non-country specific content.

Social changes are closely linked to the increasing emphasis on education: a broad, well-educated middle class is gradually emerging. Middle-class parents are putting pressure on education systems, for example, by demanding quality and choice for their children. Private educational institutions have become more common, even in countries where education traditionally has been a public task. At the same time, the knowledge society fosters new, and enhanced, social cleavages. Considerable sections of society, particularly those with limited education and a peripheral position in an increasingly flexible labour market, risk being marginalized.

Finally, education has also been affected by new approaches to the governing of public affairs. This includes decentralization measures, with a transfer of powers to local authorities and schools. Attempts have been also made to create market-like conditions for schools by, for example, subjecting them to targeting, league-tables and competition. Accordingly, the traditional role of the head teacher has changed to a new one as manager. Decentralization has opened up opportunities for other interests to make themselves heard. Parents are increasingly involved in school decision-making and private firms exert influence through school–business partnerships.

However, the picture does not only consist of these general traits, but also of a multitude of specific local responses. Hence, in practice, these trends are mediated by specific national and local conditions and, therefore, they take different shapes in different places. For example, there are likely to be differences between municipalities and schools depending on whether they are situated in a deprived urban area, a wealthy suburb or in the rural countryside. National education policies vary, which also affect local schooling. For example, some countries emphasize a comprehensive, others an elite approach to education. Private schools may be more or less common. In several countries, sub-national identities are consolidated through separate languages and systems of education.

As previously mentioned, contemporary trends contain, in themselves, an emphasis on features which are locally specific. Even if education is increasingly used as an instrument for economic growth, each locality finds its own way and specific niche. The general need to reconnect with the local territory, its history, culture and traditions is even likely to affect schools' educational content, but is, by necessity, different in different places. Political decentralization has made it possible for schools to develop their own profiles and courses, partly with the aim of competing for students. Choice opportunities have further increased variation and fragmentation within the systems.

Hence, each local education system and each school is affected simultaneously by general comprehensive tendencies and by specific local responses and features. This balance between the general and the particular is a recurring theme throughout the book.

The structure of the book

The book consists of nine chapters, divided into five parts: after the introductory section, the three sub-themes of the book relating to the governance of education are discussed: policies concerning freedom of choice and markets; the role of schools in a local development strategy; and the practice of learning at school and municipal levels. The concluding chapter ties together the threads and discusses implications of the findings. In the following, the content of each chapter is briefly presented.

Chapter 2, written by Christine Hudson and Anders Lidström, provides a comparative discussion of national school policy changes in Britain and Sweden. The two school systems are described and compared with particular focus on the post-1970 development. This is discussed with reference to the framework of the book, that is how this can be understood in the balance between general trends and specific conditions. Finally, a set of ideal typical education systems are developed as a tool for analysing education policy changes in a comparative perspective.

The next two chapters are studies of *freedom of choice and market policy*. In chapter 3, Anders Lidström analyses local government school choice policies in Sweden. During the 1980s and the beginning of the 1990s, a national policy of school choice was established. Several local authorities decided to develop these policies further, for example, by stimulating parents to select other local

authority schools than the one closest to the home and by supporting the establishment of independent schools.

Chapter 3 analyses how this pattern can be understood. The con-
ventional wisdom is that it reflects the strength of the Moderate
(Conservative) party in the local council, since it has been the major
proponent of these policies. However, this hypothesis is tested
against three other explanations: The size of the middle class, the
ethnic diversity in the locality and whether the local authority is
located in any of the major urban areas. The empirical analysis is
based on data from all Swedish local authorities.

Chapter 4, by Sharon Gewirtz, presents a study of consequences of
the market orientation of British education. According to public
choice theorists, the introduction of parental 'choice' and market
force policies in education will lead to the raising of standards. This
crude formulation ignores the complex, varied and sometimes
subtle interplay between schooling, local politics and history and
the socio-geographical and economic contexts within which schools
operate. In practice, these factors combine with choice policies to
contribute to a re-acculturation of state schooling, within which different kinds of schools and different kinds of children are differen-
tially affected. On the basis of interview and observational data, the
chapter explores some of these differences by focusing on two
inner-London secondary schools, Beatrice Webb and John Ruskin.

The next pair of chapters concerns the *new role of education in local
development policies*. Chapter 5, by Anders Lidström, analyses this
development among Swedish municipalities. It is argued that the
decentralization of the Swedish school system, together with a shift
of focus of Swedish regional policies, have made it possible for local
political leaders to use schools as a means to promote growth.

Different measures used by local authorities to adjust schooling to
business needs are investigated in the chapter. However, the main
task is to analyse how these local strategies vary between municipalities. Some are only making marginal adjustments whereas others
have developed extensive policies. Two types of explanations are
investigated; the amount of educational resources available and the
presence of serious local problems.

The role of schools in British local development strategies is investigated in Chapter 6, written by Christine Hudson. In the transition
from the industrial to the knowledge society changes are taking

place in the structure of work and education and in the relationship between education and work. Partnerships between schools and industry are becoming increasingly common. This chapter considers the relationship between business and education and how this can be understood in the local context. It builds on two case studies carried out in the City of Birmingham and in the County of Cheshire. Both these local authorities are bringing education and economic development closer together and are encouraging partnerships between schools and business. Birmingham, for example, has given education an important role in promoting the development of the city through the image of the learning city. Cheshire County Council is forming a corporate development strategy based on a broad range of its services. The high educational standard of both its workforce and its schools figure prominently in this strategy.

Two chapters represent the third sub-theme of the book, *the practice of learning*. Chapter 7, written by Olof Johansson and Leif Lundberg, discusses the changing role for principals and superintendents in Sweden. The decentralized responsibility for schooling has put new demands on school leaders. They are expected not only to function as pedagogical leaders, but also as managers of semi-autonomous units. These pressures have been reinforced by the fact that there is a gap between the local school system and political decision-makers in terms of educational values and norms. The chapter analyses how the new role of the school leader varies between localities. Drawing on evidence from a survey of Swedish municipal education superintendents, important differences between municipalities of different sizes are detected. The chapter also explores the implications of these finding for the school leaders.

In Chapter 8, Sue Cara, Charles Landry and Stewart Ranson provide an overview of the learning city movement in Britain, its theoretical foundations and practical applications. A learning city is a place where individuals and organizations are encouraged to learn about the dynamics of where they live and how it is changing. This is used strategically in order to revitalize a city and create a new basis for the development of individuals, institutions, the economy and the whole city. Learning is a much broader concept than education and takes place outside, as well as inside the formal education system. However, the notion of learning also provides valuable lessons for how education and schools can be used more strategically.

In the final chapter of the book, the editors bring together the threads from the previous chapters. The main theme of the book, the balance between general tendencies of change and the role of the locally specific, is further elaborated on the basis of the studies presented in the earlier chapters. Conclusions are drawn, with regard to the results of the comparisons, but also in terms of the usefulness of the perspective as a research agenda.

References

Batley R. and Stoker, G. (eds) 1991. *Local Government in Europe: Trends and Developments*. Basingstoke: Macmillan Press – now Palgrave.
Bell, D. 1973. *The Coming of the Post-Industrial Society*. New York: Basic Books.
Burrows, R. and Loader, B. (eds) 1994. *Towards a Post-Fordist Welfare State*. London: Routledge.
Böhme, G. and Stehr, N. (eds) 1986. *The Knowledge Society: The Growing Impact of Scientific Knowledge on Social Relations*. Dordrecht: D. Reidel.
Cerny, P.G. 1996. 'International Finance and the Erosion of State Policy Capacity', in Gummett, P. (ed.), *Globalization and Public Policy*. Cheltenham and Brookfield: Edward Elgar.
Clark, I. 1997. *Globalization and Fragmentation. International Relations in the Twentieth Century*. Oxford: Oxford University Press.
Cox, K.R. 1997. *Space and Globalization. Reaserting the Power of the Local*. New York: The Guilford Press.
Crompton, R. 1993. *Class and Stratification. An Introduction to Current Debates*. Cambridge: Polity Press.
Crow, G. 1997. *Comparative Sociology and Social Theory: Beyond the Three Worlds*. Basingstoke: Macmillan Press – now Palgrave.
Dalton, R.J. 1999. 'Political Support in Advanced Industrial Democracies', in Norris, P. (ed.), *Critical Citizens: Global Support for Democratic Governance*. Oxford: Oxford University Press.
Eatwell, J. 1998. 'The Liberalisation of International Capital Movements: The Impact on Europe, West and East', in Swedish Ministry for Foreign Affairs, *Understanding Globalisation*. Stockholm.
Giddens, A. 1981. *The Class Structure of Advanced Societies*, 2nd edn. London: Hutchinson.
Giddens, A. 1990. *The Consequences of Modernity*. Cambridge: Polity Press.
Glimstedt, H. 1998. 'Contending Visions of the World: Deciphering and Reinterpreting Uncertainties of Industrial Globalization', in Fleming, D., Kettunen, P., Søborg H., and Thörnqvist, C. (eds),*Global Redefining of Working Life*. Copenhagen: Nordic Council of Ministers. Nord p. 12.
Hall, T. 1998. *Urban Geography*. London and New York: Routledge.
Harvey, D. 1989. *The Condition of Postmodernity: An Enquiry into the Origins of Cultural Change*. Basil Blackwell: Oxford

Held, D. 1991. 'Democracy and the Global System', in Held, D. (ed.), *Political Theory Today*. Cambridge: Polity Press.

Hirst P. and Thompson G. 1996. *Globalization in Question*. Cambridge: Polity Press.

Hoogvelt, A. 1997. *Globalization in the Post Colonial World: The New Political Economy of Development*. Basingstoke: Macmillan Press – now Palgrave.

Hudson, C. 1995, 'Does the Local Context Matter?: The Extent of Local Government Involvement in Economic Development in Britain and Sweden; in Walzer, N. (ed.), *Local Economic Development: Incentives and International Trends*, Boulder, Colorado: Westview Press.

Hudson, C. 2000a. *The University and Regional Reciprocity*. CERUM Working Paper no 18. Umeå University: Centre for Regional Science.

Hudson, C. 2000b. *The Role of the University in Region-Making*, paper prepared for Habitus 2000 Conference, Perth, Australia, 5–9 September 2000.

Hughes, O.E. 1998. *Public Management & Administration*, 2nd edn. Basingstoke: Macmillan Press – now Palgrave.

Hurrell, A. and Woods, N. (eds) 1999. *Inequality, Globalization and World Politics*. Oxford: Oxford University Press.

Inglehart, R. 1990. *Culture Shift in Advanced Industrial Society*. Princeton: Princeton University Press.

Inglehart, R. 1997. *Modernization and Postmodernization: Cultural, Economic and Political Change in 43 Societies*. Princeton: Princeton University Press.

Jessop, B. 1994. 'The Transition to Post-Fordism and the Schumpeterian Workfare State', in Burrows, R. and Loader, B. (eds), *Towards a Post-Fordist Welfare State?* Routledge: London.

Lane, J.E. 1997. *Public Sector Reform: Rationale, Trends and Problems*. London, Thousand Oaks, New Delhi: Sage.

Loughlin, J. Aja, E., Bullmann, U., Hendriks, F., Lidström, A. and Seiler, D. 1999. *Regional and Local Democracy in the European Union*. Luxembourg: Committee of the Regions.

Lyotard, J.-F. 1984. *The Postmodern Condition*. Manchester: Manchester University Press.

McGrew, A. 1992. 'Conceptualizing Global Politics', in McGrew, A. *et al.*, *Global Politics*. Cambridge: Polity Press.

Mishra, R. 1999. *Globalization and the Welfare State*. Cheltenham: Edward Elgar.

Mlinar, Z. (ed.) 1992. *Globalization and Territorial Identities*. Aldershot: Avebury.

Moran, M. and Prosser, T. 1994. *Privatization and Regulatory Change in Europe*. Buckingham and Philadelphia: Open University Press.

Moran, M. and Wood, B. 1996. 'The Globalization of Health Care Policy', in Gummett, P. (ed.), *Globalization and Public Policy*. Cheltenham and Brookfield: Edward Elgar.

Mouritzen, P.E. (ed.) 1992. *Managing Cities in Austerity: Urban Fiscal Stress in Ten Western Countries*. London: Sage.

Nederveen Pieterse, J. 1995. 'Globalization as Hybridization', in Featherstone, M., Lash, S. and Robertson, R. (eds), *Global Modernities*. London: Sage.

OECD 1998a. *Maintaining Prosperity in an Ageing Society*. Paris.

OECD 1998b. *Trends in International Migration: Annual Report*. Paris.

Rhodes, R.A.W. 1997. *Understanding Governance: Policy Networks, Governance, Reflexivity and Accountability*. Buckingham: Open University Press.

Robertson, R. 1992. *Globalization*. London: Sage.

Robertson, R. 1995. 'Glocalization: Time–Space and Homogeneity-Heterogeneity', in M. Featherstone, S. Lash and R. Robertson (eds), *Global Modernity*. London: Sage.

Robertson, R. and Khondker, H.H., 1998. 'Discourses of Globalization: Preliminary Considerations', *International Sociology*, 13 (1): 25–40.

Rosenau, J.N., 1994. 'New Dimensions of Security: The Interaction of Globalizing and Localizing Dynamics', *Security Dialogue*, 25 (3): 255–81.

Sally, R. 1996. 'Public Policy and the Janus Face of the Multinational Enterprise: National Embeddedness and International Production', in Gummett, P. (ed.), *Globalization and Public Policy*. Cheltenham and Brookfield: Edward Elgar.

Sharpe, L.J. (ed.) 1993. *The Rise of Meso Government in Europe*. London: Sage.

Stewart, F. and Berry, A. 1999. 'Globalization, Liberalization and Inequality: Expectations and Experience', in Hurrell, A., and Woods, N. (eds), *Inequality, Globalization and World Politics*. Oxford: Oxford University Press.

Tomlinson, J. 1991. *Cultural Imperialism*. Baltimore: John Hopkins University Press.

Tomlinson, J. 1999. *Globalization and Culture*. Cambridge: Polity Press.

Waters, M. 1995. *Globalization*. London and New York: Routledge.

2
National School Policy Changes in Britain and Sweden

Christine Hudson and Anders Lidström

In both Britain and Sweden, responsibility for schools is shared between the central and local levels of government. Local policy-making is largely dependent on the decisions taken centrally, and these form a general context for local education policies. National education policies establish goals, set rules, provide resources and specify how outcomes should be evaluated. This context may be both constraining and enabling for local decision-makers, that is, it may limit some choices, but at the same time provide opportunities. The national policy context undergoes constant change, and it varies between countries, even if there may be similarities. Further, even if it forms a common context for all the local education authorities within a country, the national policy context must always be interpreted and applied in particular local situations.

In this chapter, principal changes in national school policies in Sweden and Britain are discussed. Initially, a brief historical back-ground describes how the school systems became what they were in the middle of the 1970s. This is followed by a more in-depth analysis of the post-1975 changes. Both Sweden and Britain entered a formative stage at this point, during which education policies found new directions, partly similar and partly different. Reforms have taken place in both countries that have fundamentally altered many of the basic principles on which education has been provided in terms not only of what and how it is delivered, but also who delivers it. Here we focus on two directions of change which we have labelled: *the political way* and *the market way*.

The last section of the chapter summarizes the analysis in two respects. First, conclusions are drawn about differences and similarities between national education policies. The question of how these can be understood in the balance between general trends and specific conditions is addressed. Secondly, a framework, consisting of ideal typical education systems, is developed and this is used as a way of classifying education policy changes in the two countries.

Education before the 1970s

In order to understand the differences and similarities in the British and Swedish school systems, it is important to examine the context in which they have developed. This includes the different traditions, expectations and ideologies that have prevailed concerning the role of education at different periods. A brief examination of their respective histories shows that, although there were some basic similarities, there were also important differences. In both countries, the church played an important role in the development of education prior to the establishment of a national school system. However, there were variations when it came to the role of the state, with national government becoming active in education much earlier in Sweden than in Britain. Thus, although local government was given responsibility for school education when the general systems of education were being established in both countries, important aspects such as the school curriculum, syllabuses and teachers remained centralized in Sweden. Further, while an élitist view of education dominated during the establishment of the Swedish and British educational systems, a democratic ideology embodying the idea of 'a school for all', fostering support for democratic values and emphasizing equality of opportunity appeared earlier in Sweden and became much more prevalent than in Britain. The needs of business and the economy also played an important role in influencing the type and content of education in both countries, albeit in differing ways and degrees.

Pre-Second World War education

In Britain, the task of education was left to the churches and private individuals until 1870 when universal elementary education was introduced and local school boards were set up to supplement the churches' provision. This can be seen as marking the beginning of the history of local government involvement in education. As the level of state intervention in education grew from the 1870s onwards, local authorities became the chosen agents for implementing government policy, 'albeit with a latitude of local discretion' (Sheldrake, 1992, p. 83). The Elementary Education Act 1870 introduced national government financing for education and empowered local authorities to provide elementary schools where no voluntary (mainly church) schools existed. The expansion of schools was rapid and, by 1876, attendance was compulsory for children up to the age of 10 who lived within two miles of a school (Robins, 1987), although there was opposition among the working classes to compulsory state education until fees for state schooling were abolished in 1891. The role of local authorities was expanded further under the Education Act 1902 making them the cornerstone of the education system (Peele and Adonis, 1990) and giving them the power not only to provide elementary education but also to assist or provide secondary and technical education. Thus the provision of public education became almost solely the property of local government, with national government often lacking the statutory power or ability to compel local education authorities (LEAs)[1] to act in particular ways or to lay down what should be taught in schools (Sullivan, 1996).

By the end of the 19th century, education had been accorded an important role in improving the nation's competitive position in the world market. Britain was an expanding industrial and commercial nation and society was in a process of change. Many of the developments in education at this time could be described, in part, as a response to the demands of the new technology of the period, in particular to the needs of industries based on the new chemical technology (Glass, 1961). Industry required a better-educated workforce if it was to compete on the world market and schools needed to provide the kind of instruction necessary to meet these demands. Thus general education of a utilitarian, practical nature was emphasized for the children of the working class. At the same time, another force for change was exerting pressure for a different more academic type of education. The middle classes were demanding better education and qualifications for their children to meet the raised standards of entry and educational attainments being imposed by the professions and thereby enable them to improve their position in society. This encouraged the establishment of more élitist grammar and independent schools with an academic-oriented curriculum. From this arose an education system divided into 'superior' secondary schools (for the middle class) and 'inferior' elementary schools (for the working class).[2] This division continued despite the opposition of, for example, the trades union movement which had been campaigning not only for free secondary education but also for a 'common' school for all since the 1890s (Simon, 1974). Nevertheless, during the inter-war years support grew to move beyond elementary education for all to secondary education for all. By the 1920s and 1930s, the Labour Party, the teachers unions and the wider trades union movement were also pushing for a secondary school for all. However, this went 'against the status consciousness of the British educational establishment' (Sullivan, 1996, p. 45), which favoured a differentiation of post-primary education into high prestige secondary schools, following a literary or scientific curriculum, and general, more practically orientated, schools.

In Sweden, the State played an important part in developing the educational system from an early stage. This is not to deny the dominant role of the Church, which was a major actor and ran the earliest schools, dating from medieval times. Nevertheless, there is also a long tradition of state involvement in schooling dating from the 17th century. During this period Sweden was developing as an important country in Europe, and it was considered necessary to educate administrators (civil servants) for the developing national and local administration. Accordingly, the state made money available to establish and maintain thirteen upper secondary schools (*gymnasia*) in various parts of the country. The setting up of these schools, together with other educational reforms financed by the state, facilitated the establishment of a stable educational system. However, this was largely education for an elite, as it was mainly middle-class children who attended the schools (see Fägerlind and Saha, 1989).

In 1809, following the adoption of a new constitution, a proposal was put forward in parliament for the introduction of a school for all (*en allmän bottenskola*) and a reform of the education system. A school attended by children from all social classes was advocated as the way to unite and weld together the nation, to develop democratic values and protect the new constitution (see Isling, 1980). There was, however, a great deal of conflict over these ideas and it was not until 1842 that a four-year common elementary school (*folkskola*) was established for children from all social classes. Although schooling was not compulsory, every parish had to provide and maintain at least one school and it had to have a qualified teacher. The Church retained an influence, as the head of the local education committee was to be the parish priest (Fägerlind and Saha, 1989). Progress was slow and it was first at the end of the 19th century that one could speak of an elementary school for all. Even then there was not a single common school system, but rather a parallel school system with separate schools for the children of the wealthy. This tendency was strengthened after the introduction of junior secondary schools (*realskola*) in 1905, which has been called the middle classes' school reform (Isling, 1980). The elementary school was formed primarily as a school intended for the working class. Thus in common with Britain, the Swedish school system was adapted to the class society emerging after the agrarian and industrial revolutions.

Post-war developments

A basic difference exists between the British and Swedish traditions of secondary education in the period following the Second World War up until the end of the 1970s. This can be related to the differing impact and strength of social democratic ideology in influencing the shape of the education system in the two countries. The British system continued to be largely characterized by segregation or streaming (élitism), whereas the Swedish system was moulded by the idea of solidarity and equality in the form of a comprehensive system. Britain, having in wartime 'idealism' proclaimed secondary education for all, nevertheless instituted a 'segregated' tripartite system consisting of a grammar school, a technical, and a secondary modern school, the latter attended by the majority. In Sweden, the government led by the Social Democratic Party (more or less continuously in power since the early 1930s in a country untouched by the effects of war) was concerned to promote secondary education for all. It was eager to achieve social equality and regarded education as one means of achieving a fair society. Accordingly, in contrast to Britain, it opted to introduce a comprehensive system covering all compulsory education and replacing a 'parallel' school system similar to that found in Britain and other countries.

Britain

The experiences of the Second World War led to demands for change in British society and this included the reform of the education system. The 1944 Education Act established the framework of the post-war British education system, which tried to achieve an uneasy synthesis between order and liberty; voluntary agency and the state; the private life of the school and the public life of its district; and manual and intellectual skills (Barber, 1994). The Act embodied a number of democratic values in that the aim was to secure a happier childhood and a better start in life for children and equality of opportunity. Education was organized into a national system based on three successive stages: primary, secondary and further. The number of LEAs was reduced making the county councils and the borough councils (mainly the larger towns and cities) the sole education authorities. While it provided for free, compulsory secondary education for all children up to the age of 15,[3] the Act did not introduce a common secondary school for all. Instead a tripartite, selective system of secondary schools (based on selective examinations at age 11) was set up designed to meet varying aptitudes. This comprised: secondary grammar schools for more academically orientated children; secondary technical schools for children interested in applied science and applied art; and secondary modern schools with a more vocational orientation for 'non-academic' children. The 'dual system' of maintained schools was also retained with, on the one hand, schools directly provided by the LEA and, on the other, voluntary schools (mainly attached to churches), which received grants from the LEA. It should be pointed out that the Act did not deal with the extensive network of independent or other private schools.

Another feature of the 1944 Act was that it increased the role of central government in education by establishing the first Ministry of Education with a senior member of government as its minister. Local government was made a 'partner' with the Education Minister and the teachers (Peele and Adonis, 1990). National policy was to be secured by the LEAs under the control and direction of the Secretary of State for Education. This was often known as the post-war settlement in which central government provided the broad policies, which were then administered and interpreted by the local education authorities which in turn entrusted curriculum decision-making and pedagogy largely to professionals on the ground (Whitty, 1990). There was a deliberate avoidance of a national curriculum in the aftermath of Fascism. Thus the British system could be described as a locally administered, national system of education.

There was a bi-partisan acceptance of the 1944 Act (Sheldrake, 1992), which nurtured a consensus over education in the period after 1945 that lasted until the 1970s. This is not to argue that education was not politicized during this period. The Labour Party emphasized greater provision from public funds whereas the Conservative Party advocated private funding and the benefits of the market. Nevertheless, the consensus meant that similar problems were identified and similar policies pursued, albeit with distinctive points of party political emphasis (Dale, 1989). However, there was already growing criticism of the education system during the 1950s and 1960s, particularly from the Left. One of the main problems was the tripartite secondary school system described earlier. Many in the Labour Party and the unions had been opposed to this system and advocated a single secondary school (Sullivan, 1996). Further, despite the original intention that all three types of schools should have equal status, this had not been the case in practice. Very few technical schools were built and secondary modern and grammar schools were never seen as being equal by parents, teachers or pupils. Grammar schools had a much higher prestige because of their strong links with higher education and the professions. Secondary modern school pupils, on the other hand, were generally expected to leave school at 15 and enter manual occupations. Only 20 per cent of 11-year-olds could go to grammar school and a system that failed 80 per cent of its pupils each year was seen as undesirable. Many primary schools became geared to preparing their pupils for the 'eleven-plus' rather than developing all the aspects of the children's ability and personality. Working-class children were still disadvantaged. Those who were selected for grammar school tended to do less well than their middle-class peers. Educational theorists began to question the possibility of measuring intelligence in the way attempted in the eleven-plus.

The idea of comprehensive schools began to gain ground. The 1944 Education Act had given central government the power to promote comprehensive schools, but not many were established under the Labour government of 1945–51. A few were set up in London, a Labour stronghold. Ironically, many more were initiated in Conservative controlled rural counties, where scattered populations made a single type of secondary school an attractive solution. Concerns emerging during the late 1950s and early 1960s about the capacity of the selective system to produce the sort of technologically flexible workforce needed to improve Britain's competitive position also fuelled the demands for a reorganization of the education system (Sullivan, 1996). The Labour Government elected in 1964 adopted a policy urging LEAs to abandon selective examinations and reorganize their schools into single status comprehensive schools. Between 1960 and 1970, the number of comprehensives increased from 130 to 1,145 and by 1970 they were educating over 30 per cent of secondary-school pupils (Chitty, 1992). However, the issue gradually became more controversial and party-polarized with the Conservatives opposing the comprehensive schools and defending the selective system (see Heidenheimer *et al.*, 1983) and the Labour Party promoting reform. The comprehensive school policy was also resisted by many parents, teachers and LEAs who sought to preserve grammar schools and, in their eyes, the standard of education. In 1974, the Labour government legislated for universal comprehensive education, but the Conservative government elected in 1979 allowed grammar schools to continue. Thus, by the end of the 1970s, a patchwork of provision existed at secondary level in England and Wales with variations occurring according to the political complexion and the policy of the local education authority (Sheldrake, 1992).

Sweden

During the years immediately after the Second World War, the Swedish education system was still underdeveloped in comparison with other Western countries. It continued to be a parallel or dual system (Richardson, 1983), with in-built social tensions. Most children only received a six or seven-year education, which provided them with basic skills in counting, reading and writing. Secondary and higher education were reserved for a minority, which typically came from the wealthier classes and aimed at forming an elite. A distinction has been made between the socializing function of the basic elementary school and the qualification function of the elite schools (Isling, 1988). However, a function common to the school system as a whole was the cultural reproduction of society. Classical languages, national heritage, moral standards and hierarchical relationships were emphasized. The system was also highly differentiated with, for example, the seventh school year being offered by at least 19 different types of schools (Marklund, 1980).

Later, in the 1950s, the Social Democratic aim of 'A School for All' gained broad acceptance in Swedish society and equality of opportunity was given greater importance. Indeed it has been suggested (Husén *et al.*, 1992) that, in the post-war period, equality of opportunity in education has always been accorded greater importance in Sweden than, for example, Britain. During the 1960s, the parallel system was replaced by a uniform nine-year comprehensive school (*grundskola*), providing publicly supported education for all children of mandatory school age in a given catchment area. No organizational differentiation or grouping practices such as, for example, academic, technical and vocational were employed which would direct children's educational careers in a specific direction from an early age.

A number of factors have been seen as contributing to Sweden's decision to introduce a comprehensive system. One of these was the popular movements characteristic of Swedish society after the turn of the century, particularly the workers educational organization (*ABF*) and the labour movement. These movements were concerned to achieve structural reform in order to provide increased equality not only between social classes but also between urban and rural areas. Another was the growth of the Swedish welfare state. There was broad support for the comprehensive school reform. It was accepted by most interest groups and by a majority in Parliament and by local government. It was seen as a self-evident consequence of society's democratization and the development of the welfare society.

At the beginning of the 1970s, the educational agenda was still dominated by the recent implementation of the comprehensive school. To a large extent, the emphasis of this reform had been on the educational needs of working class children, thereby giving them a better starting position in life. During the 1970s, the reform movement continued with a transformation of upper secondary education, mainly through an integration of vocational and academic courses into the same organization. This was also a period when great expectations were placed on education as a vehicle for social change. Olof Palme, the Minister of Education at that time, had introduced the idea of schools as a 'spearhead towards the future, an initiator of increased equality and democracy in society' (Hildebrand, 1969, p. 23). Education was regarded as a key instrument in the social engineering reform movement. By promoting values of democracy, citizenship and social consciousness, education would contribute to a gradual change in society.

In common with Britain, the role of education in achieving economic growth has been given prominence in Sweden, although the strength of this role has varied both between the countries and over time. For example, upper secondary and university education have been more directed towards the needs of industry for longer in Sweden than in Britain. The Swedish 1946 School Commission included the need for a better educated workforce in order to achieve economic growth, as one of the three main reasons for reforming the school system (see Isling, 1980). The modern industrialized society was seen as requiring a skilled workforce to be able to compete in the international market. Existing vocational education was regarded as insufficient, of shifting quality and too limited in availability so that a considerable proportion of youngsters did not receive any vocational education at all. The introduction of the comprehensive school was seen as providing an opportunity to rectify this situation.

Education after 1975: central control, decentralization and marketization

In both Sweden and Britain, the latter part of 1970s represents a formation period in education. Previous solutions were reconsidered in the light of earlier experiences and under pressure from new developments in society. For example, the growth of the middle class, a more individualized value pattern, the increasing importance of knowledge in achieving economic development and attempts to bring education closer to the needs of business challenged traditional forms of education. However, these changes were mediated through political decision-makers with different ideologies and value systems. Hence, in Sweden, the mid-1970s were the starting point for more than a decade of decentralization reforms and a strengthening of the municipal level in education. They also marked a shift from a strong belief in comprehensive values to an acceptance of greater variation. Similarly in Britain, the late 1970s mark a peak in the debate about the comprehensive school and a return to greater emphasis on selection and variation in education. It also marked the beginning of one of the most extensive and far-reaching processes of educational reform in Europe which, in contrast to Sweden, involved stronger central control over education and a weakening of the role of local government.

A common feature of the education reform process in both Britain and Sweden is that they simultaneously seem to follow two different paths. One is a more traditional *political way* of governance, based on hierarchy, control and regulation. This is targeted towards local politicians, local government officers, and the teaching profession. The other represents a *market way* of governance, with emphasis on user choice, vouchers and independent schools. Here the demand from parents and pupils meets the supply offered by private and public providers in the education market. These two paths will be further explored below.

The political way

Britain

The 1970s and 1980s saw concern over the standard of education replace the comprehensive versus selective schools debate at the top of the political agenda. This was a period marked by public and political discontent concerning education. Both parents and industrialists began to question the nature and quality of education being offered in schools (Ranson *et al.*, 1986) and there was a call for its fundamental redirection. Debate concerned low standards, lack of parental say in schooling and the need to make education more relevant to the requirements of industry. The existence of private school alternatives in Britain meant that an increasing number of dissatisfied parents, who could afford to pay for schooling, were choosing to educate their children outside the public sector. The radical right emerged emphasizing choice, competition and parental control of schools. Several Conservative 'think-tanks' (for example, the Centre for Policy Studies) produced highly critical reports on the education system, and stressed the need for reform. Tendencies towards greater central control over education also began to make themselves felt under the guise of needing to raise the standard of qualifications and skills if the UK was to improve its competitive position in the global economy. It also marked the beginning of a change in the governance of education with a growing emphasis on partnership between different educational stakeholders, both public and private, in the formulation of policy and service provision.

Increasing attention began to be given to education's role in improving national economic competitiveness. In 1976, the then Labour Prime Minister, James Callagan, in a now famous speech given at Ruskin College, Oxford, stated that schools should pay greater attention to preparing pupils for the world of work; reconsider the curriculum and the teaching methods used; encourage greater parental involvement and increase lay influence through school and college governing bodies. His suggestions included a number of strong centralizing features, for example, a core curriculum and enhanced roles for the central government Department of Education and Science and the schools inspectorate (Her Majesty's Inspectorate). The 1977 Green Paper *Education in Schools* saw a connection between Britain's relatively poor economic performance and the education system, which led to an increasing concern for education to provide the technical skills required by industry and to the introduction of greater instrumentalism and commercialism in education (Kelly, 1990).

The return of a Conservative Government to power in 1979 did not alter the general thrust of this policy. National government increased its efforts to direct the education system making it more centralized than ever before (Ranson *et al.*, 1986) and to promote links between education and business. However, it was not until after the mid-1980s that the Conservatives began to make radical changes in education policy. These culminated in the 1988 Education Reform Act (ERA) which has been regarded as marking the beginning of a new era in education policy, one that involved a comprehensive and deep-going transformation of the education system making it more subject to market forces and causing a profound change in the balance of power between central government, local government and schools (Riley, 1990). The partnership relationship, established by the 1944 Education Act between the Department of Education and Science, the LEAs and the teachers, was effectively broken, with the LEAs and the teachers being put into an agency relationship with central government. The Secretary of State for Education gained new powers to directly control much of the policy-making, management and supervisory functions previously the preserve of the local education authority (Peele and Adonis, 1990). ERA 'unleashed a flow of legislation which has changed the education system of England and Wales almost beyond recognition' (Convey and Merritt, 2000, p. 377).

The LEA's monopoly on the provision of state education from pre-school to tertiary level (with the exception of the universities) was broken during this period and education was transformed from one of the most expensive and prestigious of local government services into little more than a co-ordinating function (Sheldrake, 1992, Blackledge, 1994). Service provision was opened up to competitive tendering and private purchase and many former LEA responsibilities were dispersed to schools and other bodies, including private companies. This dispersal of power has meant that LEAs must co-operate with other actors who may have different or even conflicting interests. These changes have also raised questions concerning local democracy; LEAs are directly elected and publicly accountable, private companies are not.

National government significantly increased its own powers over local education through the introduction of a centrally controlled, compulsory National Curriculum, the first ever in British history. It consisted of 'core subjects' (English, mathematics, science) to which were added 'foundation subjects' (technology, history, geography, art, music, PE and a modern foreign language)[4] and was characterized by instrumentalism (preparing for adult life and employment); commercialism (imagery of 'providers' and 'consumers'); and élitism (assessment and testing) (Kelly, 1990). The original curriculum met with such strong criticism that a 'slimmed down', revised version was introduced in August 1995. Nevertheless, it still specifies subjects in much more prescriptive detail than is found in most other countries' curricula (Convey and Merritt, 2000). Assessment is integral to the National Curriculum and a centrally prescribed system for testing pupils in state schools in a range of subjects at 7, 11, 14 and 16 has been introduced. Standard Assessment Tasks (SATs) have been implemented as a form of national external testing to enable pupils' progress to be measured against national standards and provide pupils, parents and teachers with a measurable achievement. All National Curriculum and assessment matters are overseen

by a central independent statutory body: the Qualifications and
Curriculum Authority in England and the Curriculum and
Assessment Authority in Wales.

ERA continued earlier efforts, such as the Technical and
Vocational Education Initiative (sponsored by the Manpower
Services Commission) to modernize the curriculum, make it more
relevant to the needs of industry and develop and enhance work
skills. As part of the emphasis on technology, a number of centrally
funded City Technology Colleges (CTCs) for 11–18 year olds were
set up to provide broadly based secondary education with a strong
technological element. These colleges were to be 'beacons of excellence' (Convey and Merritt, 2000), increase choice and compete
with local authority secondary schools (see Burns *et al.*, 1994). The
intention was that they should be heavily sponsored by industry
and were promoted as a way of pushing up standards in the state
sector. However, the support from business proved to be lukewarm
and only 15 CTCs were created. Nevertheless, the present Labour
government has recently revived this concept in its proposal for
City Academies to replace some failing inner city comprehensives.
Other curriculum initiatives aimed at developing vocational and
occupational competences have included the introduction from the
mid-1990s onwards of General National Vocational Qualifications,
for pupils aged 14 to 16, in business manufacturing, health and
social care, art and design, information technology, leisure and
tourism and engineering.

A further consequence of ERA was that local authorities also lost
power through the decentralization of responsibilities to schools and
increased parental choice. School admission regulations were altered to
provide greater flexibility (open enrolment) to support choice. The
introduction of the local management of schools (LMS), gave school
governing bodies much greater managerial discretion, control over the
school budget and the appointment and dismissal of staff. They
became responsible for the main policy decisions within schools,
including academic matters. The involvement of business expertise in
school governance to provide financial and managerial assistance was
encouraged. (Schools can now appoint up to four 'sponsor governors'
from the business world). LMS also changed the role of head teachers
from predominately educationalist to increasingly managerial. They
were given responsibility for the internal organization, management
(including the budget) and control of the school.

The LEA´s role was reduced to estimating the total resources available to schools according to centrally determined formulae, but with little influence over how these should be utilized by the schools. Most of the delegated budget was to be allocated on the basis of the number of pupils. The LEA was not allowed to earmark the resources for specific uses. Schools were given the discretion to decide how their budgets should be spent and their staff deployed (John, 1991), in other words, the local education authorities were constrained to delegate the bulk of the day-to-day running of education to the schools themselves. This meant they were forced to reorganize around an entirely new role with a shift towards a school-driven system in which there was maximum feasible decentralization to schools (Young and Mills, 1993). Schools were also given the right, on a vote of the parents, to opt out of local authority control entirely and become free-standing, *grant maintained* (GM) schools, receiving their funding directly from national government and with a greater degree of independence over their admission policies.

The position of LEAs was further undermined by the introduction under the 1993 Education Act of a new funding quango, the Funding Agency for Schools (FAS), with the power to take decisions affecting all schools both within both the local authority and the grant maintained sectors. The legislation envisaged a progressive erosion of LEA powers, with FAS replacing the role of the LEA in relation to primary and secondary schools. Thus by the early 1990s, the delivery of education provision in Britain had become characterized by a complex pattern of organization (Butcher, 1995), consisting of a complicated network of LEAs, grant maintained schools, CTCs, various funding bodies[5] and the School Curriculum Assessment Authority (now the Qualifications and Curriculum Authority). By the mid-1990s it appeared as if the abolition of the LEAs was likely. However, the Conservative Government softened its stance slightly and the 1996 White Paper *Self-Government for Schools* saw them as having a role to provide services and undertake functions which the schools could not carry out themselves and which no other agency was better placed to carry out. However this role was to be 'tightly specified to the minimum consistent with the efficient and effective operation of the education service' (DfEE 1996, p. 49). In effect, the LEA's function was reduced to largely one of planning the supply of school places; co-ordinating school networks; supplying optional support services and special educational needs; and allocating and monitoring budgets and performance standards.

The return of a Labour Government to power in 1997, committed to putting education issues at the very top of the agenda, has not, however, altered the general direction of change in education. Many of the reforms introduced in the last couple of years have maintained and even reinforced both the centralizing tendencies and the decentralization to schools and the market initiated by the Conservatives. Despite paying lip service to the significance and continuing role of LEAs in education, many of the changes have continued to undermine the role of local government. For example, funding reforms have still left schools controlling the vast majority of resources, unfavourable Office for Standards in Education (OFSTED) inspections of LEAs have led to privatization of some educational services and the introduction of Education Action Zones, involving a partnership of businesses, community organizations, schools and LEAs, give business a lead role. There is an emphasis on diversity of provision, specialization and excellence, with centrally steered testing, target setting and standard raising even for the very young. For example, since September 1998, four- and five-year-olds starting school in England are tested on their reading, writing and use of number. However, the publication of skill levels that should be achieved by three- and four-year-olds met with considerable criticism for putting unnecessary pressure on the very young.

Initially some of the more recent reforms seemed to offer potential for local government to reassert its role in education. The 1997 White Paper *Excellence in Schools*, spelling out the Government's proposals for raising standards in compulsory education through the twin strategies of pressure and support, was the subject of the first ever joint consultation exercise between local and national government on a piece of legislation. However, in July 1998 the Government issued a consultation paper *Fair Funding: Improving Delegation to Schools* setting out its proposals for the reform of the local management of schools. It outlined new funding arrangements, known as devolved funding, that meant far greater funding was to be delegated to schools.

The School Standards and Framework Act 1998, for example, whilst giving LEAs an important role in education, still embraces a significant level of central coercion and of decentralization to schools and the market. A system of intervention in schools causing concern was set up to allow LEAs to intervene before a crisis point is reached. A new framework of schools[6] was established that removed the 'opted-out' grant-maintained sector and brought all types of publicly maintained schools back under LEA control, at least to an extent. LEAs were also given a statutory responsibility to promote high standards in education and to produce three-year Education Development Plans containing clear targets, a programme for improving standards, as well as methods for auditing performance, and strategies for monitoring and evaluating progress. LEAs and schools are to co-operate in this process, but their relationship is regulated by a code of practice issued by the DfEE in 1999. This defines, among other things, the general principles informing LEA-school relations.

The Act also provides for a system of monitoring of LEAs performance with powers for the Secretary of State to intervene directly if necessary and a statutory framework was introduced in 1999 regulating the inspection of LEAs. Under the Act, Education Action Zones could be introduced in areas where schools are in need of additional focused support. The creation of special forums to manage the schools within the zones has been criticized for weakening the LEA's role by permitting organizations other than the LEA to be responsible for management (Convey and Merritt, 2000). Provision was also made in the Act for greater parental representation on governing bodies of schools and for at least one parent governor representative on the education committee of each LEA, with two or three in larger LEAs.

The need to build a new culture of lifelong learning to meet the demands of the information and knowledge based economy and to combat problems of social exclusion have led to reforms in both pre-school and post-16 education. The UK has lagged behind countries such as Sweden in the provision of pre-school education which is currently a patchwork of places provided by state, voluntary and private nurseries, childminders and playgroups. However, there are proposals to expand and improve the quality of pre-school education and all four year olds are now promised a place and a target has been set of providing a place for two-thirds of three-year-olds by 2002. Particular measures have been introduced to help young children in disadvantaged areas and improve their life chances through, amongst other things, better access to early learning.

Concern about too few young people continuing in education and the consequences this will have for the UK's competitive position in the global economy have led to a number of proposals for reforming post-16 education. Criticism has been directed at the lack of coherence and the absence of a common sense of purpose in this sector. Considerable dissatisfaction has been expressed with the existing system which has been criticised for the complexity of its funding, for its plethora of different types of qualifications, for its lack of flexibility, for making it difficult to combine academic and vocational routes, for too many providers competing for the same students and for failing to meet the demands of a changing world of work and the future skill needs of the knowledge economy. A number of reforms have been introduced and others are proposed aimed at modernizing the framework for post-16 education and raising quality. All have in common an emphasis on partnerships between stakeholders in education and business.

Initially some of these reforms gave local government an important role in promoting lifelong learning. The 1998 Government Green Paper *The Learning Age*, introduced the concept of local learning partnerships as part of its lifelong learning strategy to widen participation in learning, increase attainment, improve standards and meet the skills challenge. Local government was given a key role in these partnerships which were intended to improve the planning and coherence of local post-16 education. Local authorities are required to produce Lifelong Learning Development Plans showing how they are going to develop adult learning provision and proposals for new learning initiatives. The 1999 White Paper *Learning to Succeed,* which aimed at transforming post-16 education, proposed the establishment of a central Learning and Skills Council for England supported by a system of local Learning and Skills Councils to bring greater coherence and responsiveness to local learning needs. These local Learning and Skills Councils will not, however, coincide with existing local government boundaries and the proposals have been criticized for introducing yet another layer of bureaucracy and reducing local accountability through the transference of responsibility for planning and funding adult and community education from local authorities to a new non-elected agency.

Sweden

During the middle of the 1970s, as the reforms of the comprehensive school had been fully implemented, attention was shifted towards the inner working of schools. It was generally recognized that policies improving the internal situation could not be centrally imposed according to a streamlined format, but required adjustment to specific local problems and conditions. Hence, the new era of school reforms implied a decentralization of powers from central to local government and to the schools (Lindensjö and Lundgren, 1986).

The tendency to decentralize powers and responsibilities has also characterized the educational reform movement in other countries (cp. Boyd, 1992; Daun, 1993; OECD, 1995), as well as other policy areas. Hence, explanations are likely to be found not only in specific Swedish conditions. Decentralization may equally well be regarded as a way for the state to handle a welfare system that has become increasingly difficult to govern, partly as a result of its size, but partly also because of the new pattern of more individualized demands on public welfare (Gustafsson and Lidström, 1996).

However, contrary to changes in many other Western countries, the Swedish reforms had a distinctive emphasis on transferring powers to the municipal level (Whitty *el al.*, 1998). It was mainly a process of gradual steps, but nevertheless included some more distinctive leaps. For example, in 1991, municipalities took over employer responsibility for teachers from central government. They were also permitted to decide how to organize the political leadership and the management of their schools. The right to decide themselves whether to provide upper secondary education was added to municipal powers in 1992. Prior to this, only municipalities authorized by the central government education agency had the right to run such schools. By 1995, a third of the municipalities previously without an upper secondary school had taken the opportunity to start one. Small- and medium-sized municipalities dominate among the newcomers.

The system of central government funding of local schooling was reformed accordingly. In the beginning of the 1990s, a number of specific grants for detailed purposes were merged into just one overarching grant for primary and secondary education, but this was later amalgamated with practically all central government funding to municipalities into a general block grant. One effect is that schools are now more vulnerable to resource decisions taken locally, and hence, have to present arguments for schooling which convince the political leadership of the municipality. This could be seen as one reason why schools tend to emphasize what they can do to promote local economic development.[7] Another consequence is that it has become more difficult for central government to use resources to stimulate educational provision. There have been a few attempts to increase central government financial support to education during the late 1990s. However, as this is now included in the block grant, the municipalities themselves decide how they want to use the new money they receive. Local priorities may not be the same as those expressed centrally.

Even if powers have been transferred to the local level, central government retain significant control over schooling. However, the means of governing have changed. Traditionally, schools were regulated in detail, but this has been replaced, to a considerable extent, by governing through national goals and objectives. These are expressed as general aims, but also as more specific objectives, for example about expected pupil achievements. The objectives are supposed to be sufficiently concrete to make evaluations possible. In addition, the new way of governing education has an emphasis on rhetorical competence (Municio-Larsson, 1999).

Connected to the launching of a new system of governing education, the central agency for education and its regional organization was abolished and, in 1991, replaced by the Swedish National Agency for Education. The previous organization had been closely associated with the task and culture of detailed regulation whereas the Agency's functions are related to the new way of governing education. Its role is not to set national standards, but to provide support to schools and municipalities so that they can fulfil their new responsibilities. In addition, it is to evaluate the extent to which schools and municipalities reached the national goals and objectives (Skolverket, 1997). During its first years, the Agency emphasized its supportive role, but after receiving criticism from the Government and Parliament, it has put increasing stress on evaluating results and on examining compliance with goals and remaining rules. For this purpose, educational inspectors have been appointed to carry out regular quality controls of schools (Regeringens skrivelse, 1996/97:112).

The decentralization tendency was strongest in the late 1980s and early 1990s, but it still retains some of its momentum. For example, the Government has recently initiated a programme in which a number of municipalities will be exempted from the rules in the national curriculum which specify a fixed number of hours for each subject to be taught. This will further the development towards distinctive local curricula. However, there has in recent years also been a tendency for national government to try to regain some of its lost powers by strengthening its control over local schooling. For example, attempts by municipalities to introduce a charge for school meals were stopped by the government through a new law, which in 1998 made free school meals obligatory in comprehensive schools. This is one example, where the value of equal treatment has been given higher priority than decentralization.

The new ways of governing education have also resulted in a changed pattern of control at local level in Swedish education. As previously mentioned, much of the emphasis in the decentralization reforms has been on the municipalities. However, at the same time, the lack of resources has been a serious problem and put limits on what municipalities have been able to do during much of the 1990s. The leading education employee, the Chief Education Officer, has also moved from being an anonymous administrator to a holder of power. His/her tasks are now more explicit, with a greater emphasis on leadership.

In recent years, the process of decentralization has continued one step further, with the transfers of powers from municipalities to schools. However, the pace of reform has been slower than expected by the Government. At school level, the tasks of headmasters and school leaders have changed. After the decentralization reforms, they have tended to become local managers even if they retain their role as pedagogical leaders. This emphasis on managerialism corresponds to international trends as well as to changes in other policy sectors (Whitty *et al.*, 1998). School leaders now tend to have a different background than before. It is more common to employ someone without the previously practically obligatory teacher background. The number of female school leaders has also increased (Lindvall and Ekholm, 1997).

Decentralization and management by objectives were expected to enhance the position of the teacher in the classroom. Policy-makers regarded the teachers' professional status as a prerequisite for the successful implementation of the reforms (SOU, 1992, p. 94). However, recent empirical studies suggest that the independence of teachers has instead been constrained, for example, by attempts to involve parents and pupils in everyday school decision-making

(Falkner, 1997). In addition, the traditional authority of teachers is challenged by increasingly better educated parents (Lindblad, 1994).

The influence of parents over schools is undergoing a change. In particular, the expanding middle class has put pressure on schools, but has also been keenly involved in school activities. New forms of decision-making bodies have been introduced. From 1996, governing boards with a majority of parents may be established at schools. In 1997, there were 93 such boards, mainly in municipalities with less than 50 000 inhabitants. A large proportion of these were in schools threatened with closure. Their powers are specified by the local municipal Education Committee and include dealing with programmes against bullying, school-parent co-operation and the profile of the school. This form of parental influence is basically a copy of a Danish model.

There has been an on-going debate about how to strengthen pupil influence in schools. Class forums, where pupils regularly discuss matters affecting them, are now frequent. Where a school is governed by a board, pupils are represented on it. Recently, the Government has suggested that governing boards with a pupil majority can be set up in upper secondary schools. This way of providing parental and pupil influence through representation on governing boards has been both suggested and tried in various forms. A major problem has concerned how the links between parents and pupils and their representatives should be organized. Recently focus has shifted towards providing choice options as a way of enhancing influence. By establishing market-like conditions, it is expected that the choices made by each individual will make an impact.

Finally, it should be underlined that a closer relationship between school and business has been established during the period, which has given local business interests a greater influence in schools. Municipalities and schools increasingly try to adjust local courses in upper secondary and vocational schools to the needs of existing firms and to enterprises which are expected to develop in the future. Business interest in the content of education and the use of instructional material has increased (Landell, 1996). This has not only come from firms themselves, but has also been encouraged by central government (Proposition 1997/98:169). These changes are clearly in line with the new role of education the 1990s, which emphasizes its use as instrument for economic growth.

On the whole, Swedish primary, secondary and adult education expanded significantly during the last three decades of the 1900s. At the upper secondary level, different courses of various lengths have been merged into an integrated three-year upper secondary school. Of those leaving comprehensive school in 1997, 98 per cent continued in upper secondary education, compared with 75 per cent in 1971 (Svenska Kommunförbundet, 1998). Hence, in practice, Sweden now has a 13–year primary and secondary school.

These changes correspond to a massive increase in financial resources to primary and secondary education, which were doubled in real terms between 1970 and 1990 (Ds, 1994, p. 56). This changed during the 1990s, when primary and secondary education suffered a reduction in resources, in line with the general shrinking of public services taking place in Sweden in this period. In 1997, the teacher–pupil ratio at the comprehensive schools was back to the 1979 level, with approximately 7.5 teachers per 100 pupils (Svenska Kommunförbundet, 1998). Costs for instruction suffered most, whereas spending on school buildings actually increased (Skolverket, 1996). However, by the end of the 1990s, resources for education were once again increasing. Despite the budget cuts, Sweden remains a high spender on education. Expenditure on primary and secondary education represents 4.5 per cent of GDP, which is the highest per cent in the whole OECD area (OECD, 1997).

The market way

Britain

Since the beginning of the 1980s, reforms in line with the market way have had a considerable impact in Britain. Egalitarianism's already weakened position in education was further undermined by the introduction of a market forces philosophy emphasizing consumer choice, competition, privatization, differentiation and accountability in education. Performance controls, league tables and other forms of assessment were seen as means to increase efficiency and effectiveness in schools. The 1980 Education Act started this process, permitting increased parental choice, introducing competition between schools and requiring LEAs to publish examination results. Subsequent legislation has continued this trend. The 1988 Education Reform Act, for example, sought to make schools more responsive to market forces by permitting open enrolment to schools in accordance with parental preference (Whitty, 1990). Compulsory school prospectuses were introduced providing information (including examination results) for parents, both present and potential. School governing bodies were given greater powers and responsibilities, which were intended to decentralize power from the LEAs to local parents.

Greater choice has also been encouraged by promoting diversity in provision. As mentioned earlier, all secondary and primary schools were eligible to apply for grant-maintained status, and thus opt out of LEA control. The 1992 White Paper *Choice and Diversity: A New Framework for Schools* continued the discussion on diversity and parental choice. Schools were to be able to choose to specialize in, for example, music, languages or technology. A scheme was pioneered under the Conservative government in which schools could be designated as Centres of Excellence for science, arts, modern languages and sports and receive extra funding. These were to provide an example of good practice and improve standards in the state sector. This idea has been developed further under the Labour Government and at the beginning of 2000 there were 480 specialist schools with plans to increase the number to 800 by September 2003. These schools are expected to share their expertise with neighbouring schools and the wider community, and receive extra funding to enable them to provide advanced teaching in their specialisms. However, to qualify for these additional resources, they must raise sponsorship funds from the private sector, present a development plan and higher targets for pupil achievement.

The tendency to remove responsibility for education from local government and to extend the application of the market idea has continued under subsequent Conservative, and even Labour, education legislation. The changes embodied in the Education Acts passed during the 1990s have marked a significant alteration in the governance of education. 'The strategies of increasing both the powers of state regulation and the forces of market choice have served to erode institutions designed to support educational opportunity and local democracy' (Ranson, 1995, p. 119). The market mechanisms set in place by this legislation have had the effect of increasing inequality and reinforcing the selectiveness in the system.

In Britain, to a larger extent than in Sweden, evaluations of educational results have been linked to a market way of education. A prime example is the privatisation of the inspection of schools under the 1992 Education (Schools) Act. Prior to this, schools were subject to occasional examination by local authority inspectors and the national inspectorate, Her Majesty's Inspectors of Schools (Convey and Merritt, 2000). The 1992 Act set up an independent agency, OFSTED, to organize a system of more rigorous and regular school inspections and to judge the 'failure' of schools (see Hill, 1994). Freelance teams are contracted to undertake school inspections according to a rigorously defined framework.

Failing schools can be placed on special measures and required to produce an improvement plan. They are subject to re-inspections until they have reached an adequate standard or, if they fail to improve, the LEA or the DfEE can appoint new governors and place the school under new management (including private companies). Where no progress is made, schools can be closed. Under a scheme known as 'fresh start', 'new' schools can be opened on the site of failed ones, usually with a new name, headteacher and staff. All failing schools must be turned round within two years, closed or given a fresh start. Since January 2000, when a revised set of guidelines was introduced, OFSTED operates according to the principle of intervention in proportion to need. Successful schools will be inspected less frequently and be subject to a 'short' inspection, whereas other schools will receive a 'full' inspection. The inspections examine the educational standards achieved and the quality of education provided, the efficiency of financial management and the spiritual, moral and cultural development in the school.

In 1999, a new framework for inspecting LEAs was introduced and OFSTED now check the quality of services they deliver. This led to a series of highly critical inspection reports that resulted in a number of interventions from central government and the appointment of private contractors to run education services in some local authorities. The continued erosion of local government involvement in education has led to the emergence of an education service industry. Private companies are taking over the running of state schools, careers services, teacher recruitment and other educational services previously the exclusive responsibility of LEAs. This development is raising questions for local democracy.

Sweden

Even if marketization reforms have been extensive in Britain, in one sense they represent a more profound change in Sweden, as the starting point was a highly streamlined and uniform comprehensive system. The critics claim that this system contained strong paternalistic tendencies, as the policies assumed that the state knew what was best for everyone. In primary and lower secondary schools, every age group read the same courses, as specified by the national curriculum. Basically, pupil choices were limited to the selection of a third language and whether to follow easier or more difficult courses in English and mathematics. Streaming was otherwise forbidden, including the creation of more informal ability groups. Remedial teaching and special education were integrated into the ordinary classrooms, which made the system even more comprehensive. The options were, however, greater at upper secondary level. Nevertheless, the idea of uniformity had a strong influence on the system.

This uniformity has been eroded by a number of policies, mainly in the last 15 years. The right for parents to choose a school for their children was introduced in the 1989 School Act. As previously, children are automatically allocated to the nearest public school, but parents may now select a different one or even an independent school. Municipalities are also allowed to encourage parental choice through voucher schemes. The obligatory school age is seven but parents may now let their children start school the year of their sixth birthday, if they so wish.

Another important change concerns the steady growth in private/independent schools. Traditionally, Sweden has been dominated by public education and private schools have been virtually non-existent, only for a wealthy few. At the end of the 1980s, however, a system of public funding was introduced that provided greater opportunities to establish independent schools. Initially, this was politically controversial and was mainly promoted by the Moderate (Conservative) Party. Today, independent schools are accepted by the Social Democrats, even if this party has a more restrictive view on how public funds should be used to support these schools. Nevertheless, private schools are still unusual in Sweden compared with other countries. In 1997, only 2.7 per cent of the children in primary and lower secondary education and 3.1 per cent of upper secondary pupils attended independent schools. However, the figures are considerably higher in and around the three largest cities (Skolverket, 1998).

There are also an increasing number of choices to be made within schools. Already at primary level, pupils and parents make selections between course alternatives. At upper secondary level, students can choose between 16 national programmes, and often also specific local programmes. Student preferences, rather than the needs of society or the labour market, have been given priority. In principle, students are entitled to a place in the programme of their choice, but in practice, not all municipalities are able to provide the requested places (Skolverket, 1998). An increasing number of upper secondary schools are adopting a course-orientated approach, which gives students further scope for choosing their own set of courses.

The introduction of choice is matched with an ambition to develop more distinctive local profiles. This characterizes the independent schools, which tend to have a specific pedagogy or religious basis. Public schools are starting to establish their own profiles, such as a focus on environment, music or languages. In addition, school classes may have distinctive features. Parents may for example choose to place their child in a mixed age class or in a specialized music class. Taken together, this has lead to greater variation within the Swedish school system.

Finally, variation has also been enhanced as a result of the multicultural challenge. With immigration and more refugees, schools have – with varying success – adjusted to a reality in which other mother tongues than Swedish is spoken, other religions than protestant Christianity is practised and other cultures than the traditional Swedish is present.

Concluding analysis

Between general trends and specific conditions

The above discussion revealed a number of national policy differences between Sweden and Britain. It is obvious that, despite the relative closeness and similarity in cultural and political life, there are distinctive national features of the two countries' education systems and policies. First, there are some traditional differences which still exert an influence on present conditions. The British system has a stronger emphasis on promoting the development of an élite. Class distinctions are reinforced through a dual education system and streaming and selection are accepted and encouraged to a much greater extent. In Sweden, post-war education ideals have been more strongly influenced by ideas of egalitarianism and an emphasis on the equal value of different kinds of education, academic as well as vocational.]

Secondly, the educational reforms occurring during the last few decades are also characterized by distinctive differences. Britain has been out of step with the rest of Europe with regard to developments concerning local government (Blair, 1991). In Sweden, as in many other European countries, there are numerous instances of the decentralization of powers and transfer of functions from state administrations to local authorities. In Britain, on the other hand, there has been a general reduction of local government responsibilities and powers through increased centralization (Wolman, 1988) or through privatization or transfer to appointed bodies (that is, decentralization to market and NGOs, see Bennett, 1990).

This difference is reflected in their national education policies. In Sweden, local government has been given an increased role in education and the previously closely regulated national curriculum has acquired a more framework character, setting general goals. This can be contrasted with the situation in Britain where local government's role in education has been strongly curtailed. The national framework of legislation, policy and procedure within which British LEAs operate has been transformed and they have lost an 'empire' where they had controlled the provision of education from pre-school (nursery) to tertiary level (the polytechnics) with the exception of the universities. This has been done both by increasing central government's control over education (for example, through the introduction of a national curriculum and centrally prescribed examination systems) and by devolving functions away from local government to schools (through, for example, the introduction of the local management of schools) and to the market (through the privatisation of schools and educational services).

Evaluations of educational results are more clearly linked to a market ideology in Britain. They are primarily used as a way of assessing educational achievements, and provide the basis for comparative school league tables. Schools are in competition with each other and parents are expected to choose a school on the basis of this information. Whereas in Sweden, evaluations focus on whether schools and pupils reach the national standards and goals, and are the basis for assessments of whether resources should be redirected in order to ensure that as many pupils as possible reach the minimum requirements before leaving school. Further, there has been an outright privatization of significant components of the education service in Britain (for example schools inspection) placing them outside local government control, which has not been matched in Sweden.

While there are differences between Britain and Sweden when it comes to the position of local government, the emphasis on the market and privatization of key functions, there are some similarities in other areas. In both countries, schools have been given an increased responsibility to manage their own affairs (although budget responsibilities have not been devolved on such an extensive scale in Sweden as in Britain). There are similarities in terms of the greater involvement of parents and parental choice, voucher systems, the encouragement of independent schools and the introduction of market forces (see Miron, 1996). In addition, the experiments with governing boards for schools composed of representatives of parents, teachers and pupils which have been set up in recent years in Sweden bear some resemblance to the British school governors. Competition between schools has become a feature of the reforms in both countries, although it is stronger in Britain. Schools are being encouraged to develop their own profiles and differences between them are increasing. The development of closer links between education and business is another common characteristic. In both countries education has been seen as crucially important in increasing the nation's competitiveness in the global economy. There have been pressures to make the school curriculum more relevant to the needs of industry and business, and to use education and training as part of a local strategy to develop the local economy.

Recent developments in both countries have illustrated how a previously fairly closed sector has been opened up to external influences. Business, parents and, in Sweden, municipal leaders have put new pressures on schools. Ideas and values about adjustment to meet local needs, efficiency and performance have influenced everyday life in schools. Together, these influences have challenged the policy community of the education sector. It has been transformed from a fairly closed, relatively insulated network of local and central actors, held together by stable and restrictive relationships (cp. Rhodes and Marsh, 1992) into one that is more open, less tightly meshed and incorporates previously excluded influences.

Chapter 1, a number of general trends in western education policies were detected. Many of the similarities between the national education policies in Britain and Sweden can be understood in terms of these trends. Both countries have been affected by globalization and the emphasis on the knowledge society. Education is increasingly measured on the basis of its ability to develop human capital. Business is involved is course design and work place training. Choice policies, voucher systems and market forces are emphasized in both countries, which partly can be seen as responses to a growing, more individualistic middle class. New ways of managing schools, influenced by new public management ideas, are spreading.

However, there are also major differences between the systems, which may be understood in the light of specific national conditions – the history, institutions and culture of both countries. Obviously, in Britain traditional educational élitism is still very influential, which is reflected in the way the school system functions, whereas it is far less prevalent in Sweden. Further, recent British education policy has more strongly emphasized schools' individuality and the competitive relationship between them. This has been enhanced by the extensive system of evaluation and by choice policies. Market policies for education seem to have been easier to develop and accept in a society with élitist traditions. Nevertheless, similar tendencies can be found in Sweden, and the changes compared with the uniform comprehensive era are profound. However, market adjustment is still not as extensive as in Britain. The strong role of local authorities in Sweden has worked as a barrier against the development of considerable differences between schools.

Cleavages in post-war education policy

Apart from providing a summary of similarities and differences between the education policies of Britain and Sweden, this overview has also illustrated how these policies have undergone significant changes. Earlier reforms such as the establishment of a comprehensive school system were challenged during a formative period in the mid 1970s. Later, in the 1990s, policies of marketization and choice were emphasized. Together, these and other policies have reshaped the education systems of both Britain and Sweden during the post-war period.

In this final section, we address the question how these changes can be understood as transformations of a more principal kind. We make use of two dimensions: the *instrumentality of education* and *the value basis of education*, which represent major cleavages in the post-war debate on education policy.

The instrumentality of education concerns where emphasis is put – by policy-makers and in the general debate – with regard to the question of the usefulness of education. This may concern not only how it can benefit the individual child and give him/her a good start in life but it also how it can produce what society needs in terms of the competence of its workforce, and its cultural and social development (cf. Ranson, 1994). Of course, education may have other functions, for example, to handle social problems, to provide an activity for the unemployed and to reduce the effects of business cycles. Education has, however, a largely two-sided character, focusing on both individual and collective needs. This is highlighted in the theoretical discussion about the nature of education as a public good. Education is neither a simple private, nor a clear public good, but because it is both an asset for society and for the individual it can be thought of as a merit good.

At one end of this dimension, the *social/cultural instrumentality* of education is emphasized. Here education is viewed as a way of promoting cultural reproduction or social change. It becomes a vehicle for implanting traditional values among the young or for promoting the development of new ideas. Cultural reproduction and social change may easily conflict, but they both emphasize non-economic values. At the other end, the *economic instrumentality* of education is stressed. Its economic usefulness, for individuals and society, is the guiding principle. Education is expected to contribute to growth and economic development and is seen as a means for enhancing a nation's or individual's competitive position. This brings education closer to the sphere of production. Over time, education systems have leaned more towards one or other of these positions.

The second dimension concerns the value basis of education as it is reflected in the post-war debate on the choice between values of comprehensiveness and elitism. In a recent book by Gewirtz *et al.*

(1995), these two approaches are conceptualized in terms of as comprehensive versus market values. A tendency towards 'decomprehensivization' has been identified in British education, which has emerged in the wake of the introduction of markets and choice. Table 2.1 summarizes the two positions.

Some of the features presented, for example, the reference to school uniforms, are specific for the British context. On the whole, however, the characteristics of these two value sets mirror the positions in the debate more generally. It is striking how closely the market values, perhaps with the exception of competition between schools, correspond to values that were dominant in previous élite school systems. Accordingly, comprehensive versus market/élite values are used to represent the two ends of the scale on this dimension.

In order to arrive at the analytical model, the two dimensions are combined. Thus, four ideal-typical education systems are generated (Figure 2.1).

It must be emphasized that these alternatives do not exist in their pure form in real life. In practice, previous and existing education systems contain components from all four types. Nevertheless, real-

Table 2.1   Values drift in education

Comprehensive values	Market values
Led by agenda of social and educational concerns	Led by agenda of image/budgetary educational concerns
Oriented to serving community needs	Oriented to attracting 'motivated' parents/'able' children
Emphasis on student need	Emphasis on student performance
Resource emphasis on 'less able'	Resource emphasis on 'more able'
Mixed ability	Setting
Integrationist	Exclusive
Caring ethos	Academic ethos
Emphasis on good relationships as basis of discipline	Emphasis on extrinsic indicators of as discipline, e.g. school uniform
Co-operation among schools	Competition between schools

Source: Based on Figure 5.1, Gewirtz *et al.* (1995).

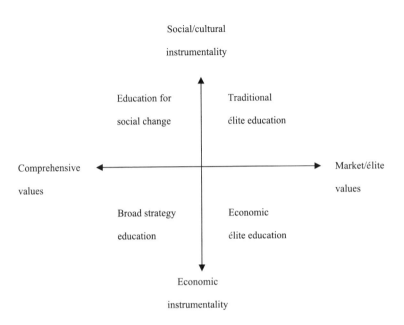

Figure 2.1   Four ideal typical education systems

life systems give prominence to certain aspects and the ideal types capture variations in this respect.

Hence, *traditional élite education* corresponds to pre-modernized education systems in both Sweden and Britain, whereas *education for social change* has its major empirical representation in the comprehensive school. Their common trait is a social/cultural instrumentality, but they are markedly different with regard to their value positions. Indeed, this corresponds to the previously identified conflict between tradition and change. The two remaining ideal types represent contemporary policy choices, where instrumentality increasingly concerns whether education is economically beneficial. *Broad strategy education* emphasizes that (practically) everybody needs to be better educated in order for society to benefit most. *Economic élite education*, on the other hand, has a different perspective. Economic development is seen as primarily élite-driven. The differentiation of the labour market is underlined and it is argued that the main function of the education system is to promote the emergence and development of a highly skilled élite able to compete in the global economy. It is claimed that, in the long run, this will benefit society as a whole. Basic education is sufficient for people who are likely less to be employed in qualified occupations.

In both Britain and Sweden, post-war education policy has moved from traditional élite education to education for social change and is now confronted with a choice between broad strategy education and economic élite education. As was concluded earlier in this chapter, the principal difference between the two countries lies in the focus on the élite: Britain, both now and previously, has been closer to the market/élite end of the scale, whereas Swedish education policy has been more influenced by comprehensive ideas.

Contemporary choices made by Swedish policy-makers seem to be in the direction of broad strategy education. An extension of upper secondary schooling, and in particular its vocational courses, is in line with this alternative. Adult education has also grown, for example, through a recent programme targeted at improving education skills among low educated adults (*kunskapslyftet*). Values of equal treatment and a school for all remain strong among all major political parties. A distinctive feature in comparative evaluations of educational achievements is that there is less variance in test results between Swedish pupils, that is, extremely good or bad results are more unusual (OECD, 1994; Svenska Kommunförbundet, 1998). Schools are still overwhelmingly public and even the independent schools are financed through public means.

However, despite the continued prevalence of comprehensive values, there are also strong tendencies towards the market value alternative. There is a move away from the ideal of a uniform comprehensive school towards greater variation, and even private provision of education. Previously, the school system emphasized redistribution, but today, after a few years of cuts in public spending on education and as a result of schools facing increasing social cleavages in society, this is no longer so certain. However, it remains to be seen whether these tendencies will more fundamentally alter the focus of Swedish education policy in the new millennium. There are signs that a dual education system is about to be re-established: high-achieving independent schools for the middle class and public problem schools for the less advantaged.

Concern over the UK's poor performance in terms of technical qualifications in comparison with major competitors such as Germany and France has led to efforts to create a new educational culture focused on lifelong learning. In particular, efforts have been made to broaden participation in further and higher education and encourage traditionally underrepresented groups, such as those from unskilled backgrounds and economically disadvantaged areas, to continue their education past secondary level. The establishment of local lifelong learning partnerships and the reforms of post-16 education and training in an effort to expand access to and participation in learning and combat social exclusion can be seen as moves towards a broad based strategy. Nevertheless, despite the Government's rhetoric that policies will benefit the many and not just the few, the introduction of market forces, the encouragement of competition between schools, the pre-eminence given to raising educational standards and achieving excellence has led to a re-emphasis on selection and differentiation. Thus elitism, always stronger than in the Swedish system, has been reinforced through, for example, the growing system of specialist schools able to exercise subtle forms of selection.

Notes

1. The local education committee together with the local government department responsible for education services are referred to as the local education authority. This is part of the local authority and not a separate entity.
2. It must be noted that there also existed, and still exists, an extensive system of private education (so called public schools) for the children of the upper classes, educating in 1996 about 7 per cent of school age children.
3. Previously the 1918 Education Act had set the school-leaving age at 14.
4. Private schools do not need to follow the national curriculum, but most of them do.
5. These were all quasi-governmental bodies independent of LEA control.
6. In September 1999, a revised framework introduced four new categories of state secondary schools: community (largely under the control of the LEA), foundation (replacing grant-maintained and exercising a greater degree of independence, the governing body is the employer and sets admissions policies), voluntary-aided (such as church schools, where the charitable foundation that 'owns' the school makes a financial contribution to its running and the governing body sets admissions policies) and

voluntary-controlled schools (owned by charitable foundations, but the LEA employs staff and sets admissions policies).
7. Compare Chapter 5 in this book.

References

Barber, M. 1994, 'Power and Control in Education 1944–2004', *British Journal of Educational Studies*, 42 (4): 348–62.

Bennett, R.J. 1990. 'Decentralization, Local Government, and Markets: Is There a Post-Welfare Agenda in Planned and Market Economies?', *Policy Studies Journal*, 18 (3): 683–701.

Blackledge, R.C. R. 1994. 'The United Kingdom', in Brock, C. and Tulasiewicz, W. (eds), *Education in a Single Europe*. London: Routledge.

Blair, P. 1991. 'Trends in Local Autonomy and Democracy: Reflections from a European Perspective', in Batley, R. and Stoker, G. (eds), *Local Government in Europe*. London: Macmillan Press – now Palgrave.

Boyd, W.L. 1992. 'Parental Choice of Schools: An International Movement', in Miron, G. (ed.), *Towards Free Choice and Market-Oriented Schools: Problems and Promises*. Stockholm: Institute of International Education/Skolverket.

Burns, D., Hambleton, R. and Hoggett, P. 1994. *The Politics of Decentralisation*. London: Macmillan Press – now Palgrave.

Butcher, T. 1995. *Delivering Welfare; The Governance of the Social Services in the 1990s*. Buckingham: Open University Press.

Chitty, C. 1992. *The Education System Transformed*. Manchester: Baseline Books.

Convey, A. and Merritt, A. 2000, 'The United Kingdom', in Brock, C. and Tulasiewicz (eds), *Education in a Single Europe*, 2nd edn. London: Routledge.

Dale, R. 1989. *The State and Education Policy*. Milton Keynes: Open University Press.

Daun, H. 1993. *Omstrukturering av skolsystemen: Decentralisering, valfrihet och privatisering: En internationell översikt*. Stockholm: Skolverket.

DfEE 1996. *Self-Government for Schools*. White Paper Cm 3315. London: HMSO.

Ds, 1994. *Skolans kostnader, effektivitet och resultat – en branschstudie*. Rapport till Expertgruppen för studier i offentlig ekonomi, Finansdepartementet. Stockholm: Fritzes, 1994: 56.

Falkner, K., 1997. *Lärare och skolans omstrukturering*. Pedagogiska institutionen, Uppsala universitet.

Fägerlind, I. and Saha, L.J. 1989. *Education and National Development: A Comparative Perspective*, 2nd edn. Oxford: Pergamon Press.

Gewirtz, S., Ball, S.J. and Bowe, R., 1995. *Markets, Choice and Equity in Education*. Buckingham, Philadelphia: Open University Press.

Glass, D.V. 1961. 'Education and Social Change in Modern England', in Habey, A.H., Floud, J. and Anderson, C.A. (eds), *Education, Economy & Society*. New York: The Free Press.

Gustafsson, G. and Lidström, A. 1996. 'Redefining the Concept of Educational Equality through Decentralization', in Chapman, J.D., Boyd,

W.L., Lander, R. and Reynolds, D. (eds), *The Reconstruction of Education: Quality, Equality and Control*. London, New York: Cassell.

Heidenheimer, A.J., Heclo, H. and Adams, C.T., 1983. *Comparative Public Policy*. 2nd edn. London: Macmillan Press – now Palgrave.

Hildebrand, S. 1969. *Skola för demokrati*. Stockholm: Sveriges Radio.

Hill, D.M. 1994. *Citizens and Cities*. New York, London: Harvester Wheatsheaf.

Husén, T., Tuijnman, A. and Halls, W. D., 1992. *Schooling in Modern European Society*. Oxford: Pergamon Press.

Isling, Å., 1980. *Kampen för och mot en demokratisk skola. Del 1 – Samhällsstruktur och skolorganisation*. Stockholm: Sober förlags AB.

Isling, Å., 1988. *Kampen för och mot en demokratisk skola. Del 2 – Det pedagogiska arvet*. Stockholm: Sober förlags AB.

John, P. 1991. 'The Restructuring of Local Government in England and Wales', in Batley, R. and Stoker, G. (eds), *Local Government in Europe: Trends and Developments*. Basingstoke: Macmillan Press – now Palgrave.

Kelly, A.V. 1990. *The National Curriculum: A Critical Review*. London: Chapman.

Landell, E. 1996. Skolan och tillväxten, in Svenska Kommunförbundet. *Kommunerna och tillväxten – möjligheter och faror*. Stockholm.

Lindblad, S. 1994. 'Notes on Post-Welfare Education: Towards a New-Liberal Education Reform in Sweden?', in Kallós, D. and Lindblad, S. (eds), *New Policy Contexts for Education: Sweden and United Kingdom*. Umeå universitet: Pedagogiska institutionen.

Lindensjö, B. and Lundgren, U.P. 1986. *Politisk styrning och utbildningsreformer*. Stockholm: Liber.

Lindvall, K. and Ekholm, M. 1997. *Tillsättning av skolledare – rörelser i tiden*. Karlstad: Högskolan i Karlstad.

Marklund, S. 1980. *Skolsverige 1950–1975. Del 1: 1950 års skolbeslut*. Stockholm: Liber Utbildningsförlaget.

Miron, G. 1996. 'Choice and the Quasi-market in Swedish Education', in Walford, G. (ed.), 'School Choice and the Quasi-market', *Oxford Studies in Comparative Education*, 6 (1): 33–47.

Municio-Larsson, I. 1999. 'Rhetoric and Organizational Change', *Statsvetenskaplig tidskrift*, 102 (3): 262–77.

OECD 1994. *School: A Matter of Choice*. Paris.

OECD 1995. *Decision-making in 14 OECD Education Systems*. Paris.

OECD 1997. *Education at a Glance*. Paris.

Peele, G. and Adonis, A. 1990. 'Education and Local Government – Future Prospects', in *New Horizons for Education*. London: Association of District Councils.

Proposition 1997/98:169 (Government bill) *Gymnasieskola i utveckling – kvalitet och likvärdighet*.

Ranson, S. 1994. *Towards the Learning Society*. London: Cassell.

Ranson, S. 1995. 'From Reform to Restructuring of Education' in Stewart, J. and Stoker, G. (eds), *Local Government in the 1990s*. Basingstoke: Macmillan Press – Palgrave.

Ranson, S., Leach, S., Hinings, R. and Skelcher, C. 1986. 'Nationalising the government of education' in Goldsmith, M., (ed.), *New Research in Central – Local Relations*. Aldershot: Gower.

Regeringens skrivelse 1996/97:112. *Utvecklingsplan för förskola, skola och vuxenutbildning.*

Rhodes, R.A.W. and Marsh, D. 1992. 'New Directions in the Study of Policy Networks', *European Journal of Political Research*, 21 (1–2): 181–205.

Richardson, G. 1983. *Drömmen om en ny skola: Idéer och realiteter i svensk skolpolitik 1945–1950.* Stockholm: Liber.

Riley, K. 1990. 'Education and the Role of the District Councils', in *New Horizons for Education*. London: Association of District Councils.

Robins, L. 1987. 'Issues in Education', in Jones, B. (ed.), *Political Issues in Britain Today*. Manchester: Manchester University Press.

Sheldrake, J. 1992. *Modern Local Government*. Aldershot: Dartmouth.

Simon, B. 1974. *Education and the Labour Movement*. London: Lawrence and Wishart.

Skolverket 1996. *Skolan och de ekonomiska resurserna*. Stockholm.

Skolverket 1997. *Ansvaret för skolan – en kommunal utmaning*. Stockholm.

Skolverket 1998. *Skolan: Jämförelsetal för skolhuvudmän. Organisation – Resurser-Resultat. Delrapport mars 1998.*

SOU 1992:94. *Skola för bildning: Betänkande av läroplanskommittén.* Stockholm.

Sullivan, M. 1996. *The Development of the British Welfare State*. Hemel Hempstead: Prentice Hall/Harvester Wheatsheaf.

Svenska Kommunförbundet 1998. *Aktuellt om skolan: Augusti 1998.* Stockholm.

Whitty, G. 1990. 'The Politics of the 1988 Education Reform Act', in Dunleavy, P., Gamble A., and Peele, G. (eds), *Developments in British Politics 3*. London: Macmillan Press – now Palgrave.

Whitty, G., Power, S. and Halpin, S. 1998. *Devolution and Choice in Education: The School, the State and the Market*. Buckingham: Open University Press.

Wolman, H. 1988. 'Understanding Recent Trends in Central–Local Relations: Centralisation in Great Britain and Decentralisation in the United States', *European Journal of Political Research*, 16 (add): 425–35.

Young, K. and Mills, L. 1993. *A Portrait of Change*. London: The Local Government Management Board.

Part II
Choice, Markets and Education

3
Local School Choice Policies in Sweden[1]

Anders Lidström

Introduction

The notion of school choice has entered the Swedish school policy agenda comparatively late. The comprehensive schools, uniformly modelled according to national requirements, were streamlined in order to provide equal education for everyone, but also to facilitate changes of schools as a result of population mobility. However, other reasons for choosing a different school than the one nearby were not recognized. Pupils were expected to attend at the school closest to their homes, and alternative, private schools have always been rare in Sweden. Hence, only in exceptional cases were changes of school a result of parental priorities, rather than family mobility. The opportunities to choose between programmes within schools were greater, but in the main, these occurred at secondary level (Arnman and Jönsson, 1993).

From the end of the 1970s, the question of school choice has gradually emerged on the policy agenda. During the last 15 years, the Moderate (Conservative) Party has consistently argued for greater scope for parental choice of schools, in particular with regard to private or independent schools. The 1980s witnessed gradual changes in the regulation of school choice, aimed at opening up greater opportunities for choice for parents (Skolverket, 1993b). These changes mainly occurred under bourgeois governments, but some were initiated under the Social Democrats, however, with less enthusiasm. Indeed, the Social Democratic position changed considerably during the 1980s (Schüllerqvist, 1995). The differences in views between the two major parliamentary blocs no longer concern whether to allow parents to choose which school their child should attend or if there should be independent schools, but rather how the independent schools should be funded. The bourgeois parties favour a centrally decided guarantee of public funding combined with a right for schools to charge fees. However, the Social Democratic government has implemented a system that leaves decisions about the amount of support to the local authorities. Nevertheless, this is supposed to be set at a level which provides equal conditions for independent and municipal schools, as schools are not allowed to claim fees for their students (Skolverket, 1996). Although only 2.7 per cent of students attended independent schools in 1997, the share has been increasing during the 1990s (Skolverket, 1998). A special feature of Swedish school choice is parents' right to choose at what age their children start school. Normally, children begin school the year they are seven. However, since 1991, local authorities may provide places for six-year-olds if that is the wish of their parents and resources are available. In 1997, parents obtained the right to demand such a place (Skolverket, 1993a).

The more prominent position of school choice on the Swedish school policy agenda corresponds to an international movement. A number of other Western countries have, from the mid-1970s, introduced similar policies, giving parents and pupils greater opportunities for choice (Boyd and Kerchner, 1988; Boyd, 1992; Daun, 1993; OECD, 1994; Boyd, 1996; Walford, 1996; Cohn, 1997). The timing cannot be a coincidence; choice policies are likely to be responses to more general changes taking place in the Western world. These include a general economic restructuring, a better educated population, the spread of Thatcherite and Reaganite ideas and a declining confidence in the ability of the welfare state to provide quality services. Indeed, behind these policies, Brown detects more fundamental transformations in the value orientation of education. An ideology of meritocracy has been replaced by an ideology of parentocracy: There is a 'move towards a system whereby the education a child receives must conform to the wealth and wishes of parents rather than the abilities and efforts of pupils' (Brown, 1994, p. 51).

However, the way these policies have taken shape in each country and each locality varies. In the Swedish case, there is a general national choice policy. For example, from 1989, the School Act gives parents the right to choose which school their child attends, but only if this does not cause unreasonable economic and organizational problems for the local authority. The school may be either public or independent. However, those living closest to a school are always given precedence if the number of available places is limited. Each local authority is free to develop these policies further through its own measures. Indeed, this may be one option open to the local political decision makers to fill the policy vacuum that has emerged in the wake of the decentralization process (Lidström, 1991). Since 1975, powers and responsibilities in school matters have been gradually transferred from national government to the municipalities, giving local authorities greater opportunities to shape more distinctive local school systems (Lidström and Hudson, 1995).

However, central government still retains important functions. It establishes a national curriculum for all public and private education, it sets the legal framework and it provides considerable financial support. Thus, parliament and government specify the main structure and content of the education system, and they also set educational goals for students and schools. The Swedish National Agency for Education evaluates goal-achievements and supports local changes. There is a strong belief in equality and a common national standard in education. In terms of educational achievements, differences between schools are smaller in Sweden than in any other country (Svenska Kommunförbundet, 1998).

Nevertheless, this central regulation should be understood as a frame within which local authorities and schools have considerable freedom to shape the organization and content of schooling. In recent years, local variation has increased. Local authorities now have greater freedom to decide what courses to offer and their content, and it is more common for schools to emphasize a particular profile in terms of subjects or pedagogy. In addition, a general trend is that local authorities increasingly adjust their courses to the needs of local economic interests.[2]

The purpose of this chapter is to analyse how the decisions to introduce local school choice policies at local government level in Sweden can be understood. Which local authorities provide parents with greater opportunities for choice and why? My argument is that the presence of local choice policies is linked to the particular social and political composition of the locality. Among the factors that may make decision-makers more prone to develop such policies, the strength of the middle class is expected to be particularly important.

Local government school choice policies will refer to municipal attempts to facilitate or stimulate parental choice in any of the following fields: selecting an independent instead of a public school, changing from the closest to another public school, and deciding to let one's child start school the year it gets six, which is one year earlier than normally. Local government provision of a more choice-oriented upper secondary school (*kursutformad gymnasieskola*) will also be regarded as a way of increasing choice opportunities.

As a next step, an empirically oriented theory of local government school choice policies is developed. This will be used as a tool in the subsequent analysis. Quantitative data on school policies at local government level and on a number of other variables will be used as a means of empirically testing the theoretical assumptions.

A theory of local government school choice policies

How can local variation in school choice policies be explained? In order to provide a framework for the analysis, we will develop a number of hypotheses on the basis of previous studies in the field. These hypotheses will then be linked into a coherent model. Thus, the theory is not generated according to a deductive format on the basis of overarching axiomatic assumptions. Rather, it has been developed more inductively, based on generalizations from empirical observations and research. An underlying belief is that the local social and political context is crucial for an understanding of the shaping of local choice policies. However, it must be emphasized that while the context provides incentives, the actual decisions are taken by actors. Indeed, this would correspond to the assumption expressed by the Swedish Parliament, that decentralizing powers and responsibilities to local authorities will make them more responsive to local conditions.

Thus, the basic question may be formulated as what conditions are likely to be favorable for the development of local school choice policies? We assume that four conditions are particularly important and these are expressed as four hypotheses. They concern liberal conservatism, the middle class, ethnic diversity and urbanism. To a considerable extent, these are also expected to reflect parents' demands for opportunities for choice.

The liberal conservatism explanation

Extension of individual choice is a classical liberal idea. In their original forms, conservatism and socialism emphasized a view in which the individual was subordinated larger collective entities, for example a nation, a class or a common social cause. Liberalism, however, has from the very beginning stressed the role of the individual. John Stuart Mill emphasized the principle of individual liberty. Society should be constructed to provide the largest possible scope for individual initiatives. The role of the state should be limited to protecting citizens from each other.

The present versions of these ideologies have modified the original assumptions and also borrowed ideas from other thought systems. Not least, modern conservatism has been influenced by the liberal tradition. Indeed, a struggle between traditional conservatism and neo-liberalism has characterized conservative parties in the Western world during the last few decades (Levitas, 1986; Girvin, 1988).

The influence of liberal ideas on conservative parties seems to have been particularly strong at the end of the 1970s and during the 1980s. This may be regarded as a reaction to the continuous growth of welfare states after the Second World War, to an increasing tax burden and to the perception that the freedom of individuals to make decisions about their own lives was narrowing. A large public sector was seen as hampering individual initiatives and thereby reducing the efficiency and effectiveness of the economic system. This was a favourable ground for a re-emergence of the classical liberal ideas of pure market economy, reduced welfare state, and greater individual freedom, expressed by, for example, Hayek (1944) and Nozick (1974).

This tendency towards a liberalization of the conservative parties reached a peak with the heyday of Thatcherism and Reaganism. They represented more classical liberal ideas in the sense described above and managed first to get support from their parties and then to stay in power practically throughout the 1980s. Their policies set an example for conservative parties in other countries, and made a lasting imprint on the ideology of modern conservatism (Levitas, 1986; Girvin, 1988).

In line with these ideological changes, modern conservative parties have become keen advocates of policies that enhance individual choice. Apart from promoting a general reduction of the public welfare commitment, the parties have also favoured the introduction of market-like conditions within the public sector and new means for individual choice. Voucher systems, privatization and outsourcing of public services are just a few examples of new policies.

In Sweden, the Moderate Party changed its ideological emphasis during the 1970s. Freedom of choice and individual independence were new slogans in the 1976 election campaign (Ljunggren, 1992). In 1978, liberalism was for the first time written into the party manifesto, when it was stated that '(M)oderate policies are anchored in conservative ideology and combine this with liberal ideas' (quoted in Ljunggren 1992, p. 286). Gradually, liberalism was established as an ideological source of even greater importance than conservatism (Hylén, 1991). During the 1980s, more radical versions of liberalism influenced sections of the party, in particular the youth and student organizations. This coincided with an increase in electoral support for the party. In the 1970s, the party received 10–15 per cent of the votes, whereas election results below 20 per cent were unusual in the 1980s and early 1990s. The political climate in Sweden in the late 1980s has been labeled *högervågen* (a shift to the right), during which right-wing and neo-liberal ideas not only became more central in the public debate, but also influenced political decision-makers from other parties (Boréus, 1994).

Thus, these ideological shifts within the Moderate Party and its relative increase in strength during this period may be one explanation of the development of school policies that emphasize greater individual choice. The Moderate Party clearly altered its school policies over the last two decades. As late as in the mid-1960s, promoting the establishment of independent schools was not a prominent feature of the Party's education policies (Lundahl, 1989). Now it is the major proponent for support to individual schools and the introduction of voucher systems, permitting parents to choose between independent or public schools (Schüllerqvist, 1995). Major changes were introduced by bourgeois governments, in particular by the four-party coalition between 1991 and 1994, when there were two Moderate Ministers of Education.

We expect these explanations with regard to the ideology of liberal conservatism to be valid also at the local level. When local authorities are given the scope to decide whether and how to establish local choice policies, they are likely to follow the same party political pattern as at national level. Our first hypothesis is that *local government school choice policies are more developed by local authorities with strong Moderate Party representation.*

The middle class explanation

One megatrend in the western world during the last three or four decades is the transformation of the workforce from manual to non-manual. This corresponds to the decline of manufacturing industry and agriculture as employers and the growth of the service sector, including the public welfare sector (OECD, 1992). In essence, the development may be characterized as a growth of a new middle class, which, in particular, has taken place at the expense of the working class.

Class analysis is always controversial. There is no obvious way of distinguishing different classes, and stratification theory repeatedly addresses the question of what to base class identification on (Crompton, 1993; Butler and Savage, 1995). The problems are particularly difficult if the aim is to analyse how classes change over time. Nevertheless, if class is to be a fruitful analytical concept, it is worth making the effort to try to clarify how it can be defined. There are a number of alternatives.

While the classical Marxist definition was based on a dichotomy reflecting the antagonism between labour and capital, modern theories have suggested a more diversified approach, attempting to take into account the more diffuse and fragmented class lines of today. These theories recognize that many individuals occupy middle positions where they may not own capital, but still exert decision making powers in the industrial process and over labor (cp. Wright, 1985). However, these theories share with Marxism the belief that the relationship to the means of production is the major criterion for distinguishing classes.

In recent years, alternative theories have emerged which take into account other sources of power. One example, introduced in particular by Goldthorpe (1982), is the concept of the service class, which consists of white-collar workers with non-routine tasks, such as professionals, managers and administrators. Professionals provide specialized knowledge and managers/administrators possess delegated authority on behalf of the employing class. The underlying formative concept is trust. The employing class – in public or private business – has invested trust in the service class in a way that makes it different from, for example, other white-collar employees and the working class.

Another key notion in the service class concept is the emphasis on cultural capital or education. Other scholars have more explicitly based their class schemes on the possession of educational assets. Giddens (1981) identifies three classes in a capitalist society: one that owns capital, one with educational resources and one that provides labour. The class with educational resources is typically labelled the new middle class. This contrasts to the old middle class, which was much smaller and to a significant extent consisted of middle managers in manufacturing production. The new middle class is not a coherent or stringent actor, and it is not organized in the same way as the working class. As Crompton observes, 'the term encompasses a wide variety of occupational groupings, distinguished only by the fact that they are *not* manual workers' (Crompton, 1993, p. 175). However, a common denominator of the middle class is its educational resources. To a large extent, the middle class has reached its position because of its education.

The middle class has been growing continuously during the last few decades, and this increase is likely to continue in most Western countries. Each year, the new generation that enters the work force is better educated than the generation that retires. This ongoing process is the result of post-war educational reforms, which aimed at giving more people access to higher education. A consequence is the gradual growth of the middle class, which is likely to continue well into the 21st century.

What makes these changes particularly interesting in this context is their value implications. A well-educated middle class, together with the expansion of the service sector and the entry of women into the labour market, are regarded as major features of the post-industrial society (Bell, 1973). In repeated studies in Europe and North America, Inglehart (1977, 1990) has detected a shift in the value pattern. New, post-material values tend to emphasize individualism, freedom and quality of life, participation and influence, sustainability and the preservation of nature. The younger generations, but also the middle class, in terms of the well-educated and the professionals, seem to carry the new values.

Corresponding changes have occurred in Sweden (Lidström and Hudson, 1995). According to data from Swedish election studies, the manual workers' share of the adult population decreased from 51 per cent to 38 per cent between 1960 and 1991, whereas the non-manual workers' (*tjänstemän*) share during the same period increased from 27 per cent to 51 per cent (Oskarson, 1994). Changes in the same direction, although less dramatic, are reported by Ahrne *et al.* (1995). However, compared with other Western nations, the Swedish middle class consists of a larger proportion of economically active women and of public sector employees (Ahrne *et al.*, 1995). Also in Sweden, the middle class is likely to grow further along with a better educated population. In 1970, 8 per cent of the adult population had a post-secondary degree. In 2015, this number is expected to be 29 per cent (Statistiska Centralbyrån, 1994). It should be emphasized that a society dominated by the middle class is not necessarily more equal than the traditional industrial society. On the contrary, during the recent growth of the middle class, there are signs of increasing differences in income and wealth in the Swedish population.

The observation about middle-class individualism mentioned earlier has also been detected in Sweden (Pettersson and Geyer, 1992). In addition, this class exhibits a different form of democratic behaviour than the working class. Instead of utilizing traditional ways of influence through political parties and collective organizations, the middle class favours more individually orientated means, for example, individual contacts with decision-makers and more ad hoc organizing (Petersson *et al.*, 1989).

A point already emphasized is the specific relationship between the middle class and education. Not only have large segments achieved their positions because of their education, but they also tend to take a keen interest in the education of their children (Beare, 1993; cp. also Gewirtz *et al.*, 1995). Therefore, we will expect the more individualistic values of the middle class to make an imprint on the shaping of the local school systems. This adjustment to middle-class preferences may have the effect of reducing the influence of other social strata on education.

Several investigations have shown that well-educated parents are more in favour of choice policies in schools. They know more about choice opportunities, and they are more likely to prefer independent schools for their children (Skolverket, 1993b). However, they are not more prone to choose a different public school than the one closest to their home (Skolverket, 1996).

Thus, it seems likely that the existence of a large middle class in a local community will be favourable for the emergence of local choice policies. Therefore, our second hypothesis is that *local government school choice policies are more developed in local authorities with a larger middle class.*

The ethnic diversity explanation

Not long ago, a common feature of the Swedish society was its ethnic homogeneity. Apart from the Sami minority in Lapland, the Swedes largely consisted of one major ethnic group. As late as the early 1970s, Sweden scored very low on measures of ethnic–linguistic and religious fragmentation (Lane and Ersson, 1987). However, since the 1930s, immigration to Sweden has been greater than emigration. In particular during the 1960s, recruiting labour from other countries was a means of solving domestic problems with workforce shortage. In addition, there has been scope for refugees from war-ridden countries to seek a haven in Sweden.

In a few decades, this has transformed Swedish society (Ålund and Schierup, 1991). Today, one-eighth of the population in Sweden was born abroad or have at least one parent who was. Thus, the Swedish population has become more heterogeneous. It is more common that languages other than Swedish are spoken or that religions other than Protestantism are practiced.

Several more heterogeneous Western countries have school systems that provide considerable scope for ethnic and religious minorities to run their own schools more independently. Schools are a major means in the attempt to preserve sub-cultures (Daun, 1993). In particular, Catholic minorities have been eager to provide their own schools in countries such as the USA and Australia.

There are no data available about how different religious minorities choose schools in Sweden. However, the ethnic factor is obviously important. A survey by the National Agency for Education (*Skolverket*) in 1994/95 shows that parents who are born outside Sweden are more likely to choose a different public or independent school than the one closest to their home. In particular if the parents come from another Nordic country, but also those who are born outside the Nordic countries exert their right to choose more than native Swedes (Skolverket, 1996).

Accordingly, we expect that local authorities with large ethnic or religious minorities will be more in favour of choice policies. This is a way of adjusting the school systems to the specific needs of the local population. Therefore, our third hypothesis is that *local government school choice policies are more developed in local authorities with large ethnic or religious minorities*.

The urbanism explanation

Even if there is strong demand for different choice alternatives, an important requirement is still a certain proximity to alternative schools. Generally, it should be expected that parental choice is exerted to a larger extent if there are reasonable alternatives close by or if there is a transport system that facilitates daily traveling between school and home. Thus, urban settings are likely to promote choice whereas this is probably rare in the countryside. Perhaps not surprisingly, people in the larger Swedish cities are more in favour of choosing a different public or independent school than the one closest to their home (Skolverket, 1993b).

In terms of local government policies, it seems more reasonable for municipalities with large urban populations to develop policies promoting choice. Our fourth hypothesis is that *local government school choice policies are more developed by local authorities in urban settings*.

A combined model

Each of the four hypotheses that have been identified are expected to contribute to explaining why some local authorities develop choice policies and others do not. However, in practice, these likely explanations interact. One possibility is that they overlap and partly cover the same phenomenon. Another is that one variable may exert its influence through another and may, inadvertently, be counted twice. The task in this section is to try to disentangle the specific role of each variable by constructing a combined model which specifies how they are linked theoretically to each other.

We expect urbanism to plays a role as background variable in relation to each of the other likely explanations. The middle class, the strength of liberal conservatism and ethnic diversity are likely to be larger in larger cities and their suburbs, but we also expect urbanism to be important by itself without mediation through other variables.

The middle-class explanation is separate from, but nevertheless closely linked to, the size of the Moderate Party. This party has its stronghold among middle-class voters and leaders of small businesses (Gilljam and Holmberg, 1995). Hence, we expect the size of the middle class to influence the local strength of the Moderate Party. Finally, ethnic diversity is not likely to be directly linked to either middle class or Moderate Party strength. However, an indirect link is likely to exist, since all these variables are expected to be features of urban areas. Figure 3.1 summarizes the model.

An alternative theory has been presented by The Swedish Agency for Education in a study of choice policies during 1992/93 (Skolverket, 1993b). After an investigation of school choices in nine local authorities, more general conclusions were drawn about the relationship between structural factors and the propensity for local authorities to promote parental choice. In essence, three structural

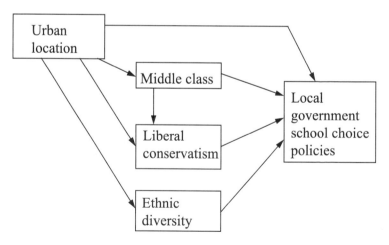

Figure 3.1   Model of analysis

factors, which are positively related to choice policies, were identified: The number of inhabitants per kilometre,[2] geographical proximity to schools and the presence of independent schools in the local area.

For several reasons, this *Skolverket* model seems less appropriate than the one suggested in Figure 3.1. First, the relationship between the different explanatory variables is not discussed. In particular, the first two variables are likely to be highly overlapping. The greater the population density, the closer the schools are. In terms of our model, these two variables correspond to the urbanism explanation. Second, the *Skolverket* model is clearly more limited, as both the role of the middle class and the political context are omitted, and the importance of ethnic diversity is not taken into account. To some extent, but probably not fully, these factors may coincide with presence of independent schools, the third variable in the *Skolverket* model. However, in the subsequent empirical analysis, we will also test the explanatory power of this model.

Measuring school choice policies

The empirical analysis of the theory outlined above is undertaken with the help of quantitative data. A quantitative approach has been chosen, as it permits generalizations from the conditions studied for all Swedish local authorities. The data set consists of information about all 288 Swedish local authorities, although there are some omissions with regard to a few variables. The data base not only contains information about local school policies and practices but it also permits these to be analysed in relation to different social, economic and political characteristics of the local area. The data has been collected from different sources. Two questionnaire surveys of local government chief education officers were undertaken.[3] In addition, the National Agency for Education generously provided us with data collected by its regional officers in October 1995. Finally, publicized statistics from the Swedish Statistical Central Bureau and the National Agency for Education about conditions in local authorities have been included.

Local government school choice policies are the dependent variable in the analysis. As previously mentioned, these refer to attempts to facilitate or stimulate parental choice in the following fields: selecting an independent instead of a public school; changing from the nearest to another public school; and deciding to let one's child start school a year earlier. Local government provision of a more choice-oriented upper secondary school is also included. Introduction of voucher systems and stimulating schools to develop distinct profiles are regarded as additional and supporting ways of promoting choice.

The dependent variable is measured in four different ways. By focusing on assessments of policy as well as what local authorities actually do, the stability of the model can be controlled. Each measure is represented by an index based on a set of variables. These variables are summarized in Table 3.1.

Table 3.1   Variables in indexes of local government school choice policies (%)

Index 1 Perceived local government school choice policy, 1991–94	
stimulating the growth of independent schools	22.0
stimulating parents to actively choose a school	32.0
stimulating schools to develop their own profiles	60.2
Index 2 Perceived local government school choice policy, 1994–98	
stimulating the growth of independent schools	6.1
stimulating parents to actively choose a school	21.3
stimularing schools to develop their own profiles	62.1
Index 3 Local government decisions resulting in wider choice opportunities	
introduced voucher system in the school sector	11.0
implemented/planned a more choice-oriented upper secondary school (*kursutformad gymnasieskola*)	34.0
offering additional local upper secondary study programmes outside those which are nationally prescribed (*specialutformade program*)	33.3
Index 4 Local government provision of information to parents about choice opportunities in primary and lower secondary education	
Informing parents about:	
children starting school as six-year-olds	84.0
the right to choose a different public school	63.1
the right to choose a different independent school	31.5

Note: The figures represent percentages of local authorities pursuing a particular policy. Unless otherwise stated, they refer to conditions in 1995/96.

All indexes represent different ways of operationalizing local government school choice policies and were constructed by adding the values of the relevant variables. They are all ordinal scales where zero indicates no expression of school choice policy whatsoever, and the maximum value represents the presence of all types of choice policies. Indexes 1 and 2 are based on our own questionnaire surveys. The chief education officers were asked to assess how important different school choice policies were for the political majority of the council during the two election periods 1991–94 and 1994–98.[4] This provides an opportunity to analyse changes over time between two very different periods. The 1991 local and national elections resulted in a bourgeois landslide at the same time as the Social Democratic party had its worst election result since 1928. In 1994, however, the pendulum swung back. The bourgeois parties suffered considerable losses, and the Social Democrats regained their majority in many councils.

The figures in Table 3.1 indicate that the importance of choice policies has decreased as the bourgeois parties have lost ground. The only exception concerns the policy to stimulate schools to develop their own profiles, which seems to be regarded as important, regardless of political majority. However, further analyses are required for a more thorough understanding of the relationships.

Indexes 3 and 4 focus on what local authorities actually do in order to promote parental and student choice. They are both based on data collected by the Swedish Agency for Education. Index 3 concerns a number of possible changes, mainly in relation to upper secondary education. Index 4 is about whether local authorities provide information to parents about choice opportunities at primary and lower secondary levels. As the data about the variables included in index 4 illustrate, local authorities are clearly less willing to inform about the right to choose independent schools than about choice opportunities within the public system.

Testing the model

The empirical test of the model has been conducted in several steps. Initially, the bivariate relationships between different indicators of the hypothesized explanations and the indexes were explored. Positive, significant and often strong relationships emerged.

However, the final test required a multivariate approach, since the combined effect of the possible explanations and the relative weight between them are major concerns in the study.

The process of selecting the indicators of the independent variables required careful consideration. Choosing the size of the Moderate Party in local councils as a measure of Liberal Conservatism was fairly obvious. The middle class, on the other hand, is not easily operationalized because of the theoretically unclear status of the concept. Different alternatives were investigated, including level of education of the local population and employment in the service sector, but in the end the share of the population representing intermediate and higher non-manual employment[5] was selected. This measure is more closely linked to Goldthorpe´s concept of the service class. However, all the examined alternatives are highly intercorrelated, with coefficients (r_{xy}) varying between 0.90 and 0.98. Despite the theoretical vagueness of the concept of the middle class, its empirical representation is distinct.

Choosing a measure of ethnic diversity was problematic. There are no data available about the representation of different religious denominations at local level in Sweden. However, different measures of the number of non-Swedish residents were tested in the bivariate analyses. The strongest relationships emerged when the share of non-Nordic residents was correlated with measures of the dependent variable. To some extent, this may also indicate the presence of religious denominations other than Protestantism. The final variable, urban location, is represented by a dummy variable.

Table 3.2 summarizes the multivariate analyses. The relative impacts of the four independent variables have been tested in relation to all four measures of the dependent variable.[6]

A number of observations can be made on the basis of the regression analyses. The variation in the first index, representing perceived local government school choice policy in 1991–94, is to a considerable extent explained by the four independent variables ($R^2 = 0.42$). Also, all four seem to contribute to the explanation, even if middle class appears as the most important of the factors.

This pattern changed during the next election period, represented by index 2. First, the total explained variance decreases radically, suggesting that variables other than the four hypothesized factors

Table 3.2 Multivariate analysis of local government school choice policies: OLS regression estimations

Measures of the independent variables	Measures of the dependent variable			
	Policy 1991–94 (Index 1)	Policy 1994–98 (Index 2)	Decisions (Index 3)	Information (Index 4)
Moderate Party representation in the local council	0.17*	0.19*	0.12	0.08
Percentage with intermediate and higher non-manual employment (1990)	0.23**	0.35***	0.30**	0.13
Percentage non-Nordic residents (1995)	0.21**	-0.03	0.19*	0.16*
Urban location	0.20*	-0.10	0.11	0.20*
R^2	0.42	0.17	0.35	0.21

Note: The coefficients reported are Beta-weights. Significance levels refer to *t*-statistics. Moderate Party representation is represented by the strength of the party 1994–98 in the estimations with index 2 and by the strength of the party in 1991–94 in the other estimations. Urban location is a dummy variable. It selects the 28 largest local authorities and the suburban local authorities around Stockholm, Göteborg and Malmö.

have become more relevant, or that school choice policies no longer follow a clear and identifiable pattern. In particular, ethnic diversity and urban location no longer have the same importance. It should be kept in mind that local government school choice policies have actually decreased in importance after the 1994 elections (cp. Table 3.1). Therefore, we may conclude that the remaining policies are more spread out in different kinds of local authorities in the 1994–98 period than in the beginning of the decade.

However, the second, and our major, conclusion concerns the explanatory role of the middle class which emerges as the major factor behind local government school choice policies. Indeed, its position as an explanatory factor has become stronger than during the previous period. Even if local government school choice policies are less common, those remaining are more closely connected with a strong middle class. The party political variable has also become more prominent, but not to the same extent as the middle class.

The middle class is again the major explanation with regard to the third index, which concerns local government decisions resulting in greater choice opportunities, particularly with regard to upper secondary schools. Basically, the pattern emerging resembles the one behind index 1, even if the coefficients are lower, with the exception of the middle class. This may be regarded as support for the overall model, which is obviously relevant for what local authorities actually do, as well as for perceptions of policies.

The fourth index, which represents information measures undertaken by the local authority about choices available with regard to primary and lower secondary education, exhibits a slightly different pattern. The model seems less appropriate, with an explained variance of 0.20. It emphasizes urban location and non-Nordic citizenship, whereas the other two hypothesized explanations are not significant.

We can now reconnect with the model in Figure 3.1, which also outlined possible relationships between the independent variables in the analysis. Urban location was assumed to have a background function in relation to the other three independent variables, and Moderate Party strength was expected to be associated with the size of the middle class. The path analysis in Figure 3.2 summarizes the disentangling of these relationships with regard to the first index.

As expected in the combined model, urban location is closely associated with the other three independent variables. A strong relationship also exists between the size of the middle class and the strength of the Moderate Party. Urban location appears as more important when its indirect effects through the other variables are taken into account. The path analyses for the other indexes provide fairly similar results, with the exception that the associations between the independent variables and the dependent variable are different, which has already been shown in Table 3.2.

Generally, our theory seems to be able to identify fairly accurately the pattern behind why local government school choice policies emerge in some settings, but not in others. However, there is an alternative. Previously in the article, an explanation, suggested by The Swedish Agency for Education, was reviewed (the *Skolverket* model). This emphasized three factors: number of inhabitants per square kilometre, geographical proximity to schools and presence of independent schools nearby. Data is not available for the second

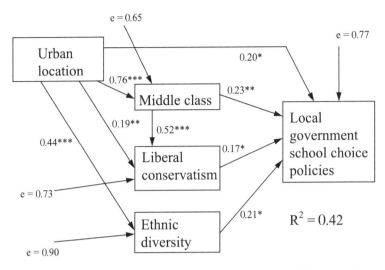

Figure 3.2   Explaining variation in local government school choice policies, 1991–94

factor, but proximity is likely to overlap with population density. The remaining two variables are tested against our measures of school choice policies. As Table 3.3 indicates, the *Skolverket* model is less successful in explaining the variance than our model.[7]

Table 3.3   Testing the *Skolverket* model: OLS regression estimations

	Measures of the dependent variable			
Measures of the independent variables	Policy 1991–94 (Index 1)	Policy 1994–98 (Index 2)	Decisions (Index 3)	Information (Index 4)
Population density (1995)	0.31***	0.16*	0.24***	0.21***
Independent school present in local authority area (1992)	0.29***	0.08	0.39***	0.11
R² (The *Skolverket* model)	0.20	0.03	0.24	0.07
R² (Our model)	0.42	0.17	0.35	0.21

Note: The coefficients reported are Beta-weights. Significance levels refer to *t*-statistics.

Conclusions

On the whole, our theory has been fruitful in explaining why some local authorities develop school choice policies and others do not. Clearly, the size of the middle class is a previously underestimated factor of considerable importance. In the Swedish context, choice policies have mainly been regarded as a result of the 'turn to the right' and the new conservative ambitions to provide greater choice opportunities. However, in the light of this study, this political factor is less important than the extent of middle class domination in the local community. Further, this tends to occur in urban rather than rural locations.

The growth of the middle class is a major contemporary mega-trend. The middle class has specific preferences, not least with regard to education policy. Individualism and greater choice are important components in its value orientation. With time and as more of those entering the work force have a higher education, the middle class will continue to grow. The middle class will come to dominate in more communities and, therefore, it is not unreasonable to expect that this process of adjusting school policies to the needs and preferences of the middle class will continue. Perhaps we are only witnessing the beginning of middle-class influence on local school systems. Such a reinforcement of the position of the middle class may eventually exclude the preferences of other social strata, in particular the working class and the disadvantaged.

The Social Democratic position on these issues has changed in recent decades. Once hostile towards choice policies, the party now accepts and even promotes them. Admittedly, the Social Democratic Party does not exhibit the same enthusiasm as the Moderates. Nevertheless, parents' and students' rights to choose a school and an acceptance of independent schools are now a part of Social Democratic policies. This may be regarded as a move to the right, but a more reasonable interpretation is to see it as an adjustment to the preferences of the growing middle class. Since the traditional working class is slowly but steadily decreasing in number, the electoral basis of the Social Democratic Party is under threat. To compensate for this, the Party has attempted to increase its support in the middle class (Svensson, 1994; Esping-Andersen, 1994). Hence, the adoption of middle-class preferences can be seen as an effort to attract these voters, nationally and locally. School choice policies are parts of a wider strategy by the Social Democratic Party to maintain its position in Swedish politics in a time of major social transformations. These attempts to capture the voters in the middle of the left-right scale may also be seen as an adjustment predicted by the median voter theory (Downs, 1957).

Notes

1. This chapter has previously been published in *Scandinavian Political Studies*, 1999, 22 (2), and is reprinted by the kind permission of the editor.
2. Cp. Chapter 5 in this book.
3. The first, distributed in the spring of 1995, received replies from 75.0 per cent of the local authorities, and the second, undertaken in the beginning of 1996, reached a response rate of 89.2 per cent.
4. Please note that the election period in Swedish local and national elections was extended from three to four years in 1994. Local and national elections are held on the same day.
5. In the official Swedish census statistics, the working population is divided into three major groups: manual workers, non-manual workers and employers. However, in particular the first two have been further divided into sub-categories, mainly on the basis of required education level. Non-manual workers, for example, are divided into four categories: two lower, intermediate and higher (Statistiska Centralbyrån, 1992).
6. In addition to the estimations presented in Table 3.2, possible interaction effects have been examined. In particular, it could have been suspected that the combined presence of a strong Moderate Party and a large middle class would enhance the emergence of local choice policies even further. However, only very marginal effects of this kind were detected. The statistical significance of the coefficients in this chapter is indicated in the following way: Significant at the 0.001-level (***), 0.01 level (**) and 0.05-level (*). Finally, it should be observed that index 3, representing decisions, is only calculated for the 212 local authorities with upper secondary schools.
7. The presence of independent schools was not included among the hypothesized explanations of local government school choice policies. However, adding this to the test of the four variables in Table 3.3 makes little difference. On the whole, its impact is absorbed by other variables. However, it appears important in relation to index 3, which represents decisions by local government in relation to upper secondary education and contributes to an increase in the explained variance from 0.35 to 0.39. The presence of independent schools receives a Beta weight of

0.19**. The Beta weights of the four hypothesized variables decreases slightly.

References

Ahrne, G., Ekerwald, H. and Leiulfsrud, H. 1995. *Klassamhällets förändring*, 4th edn. Lund: Arkiv förlag.

Arnman, G. and Jönsson, I. 1993. *Konkurrens för stimulans*. Stockholm: Skolverket.

Beare, H. 1993. 'Different Ways of Viewing School-site Councils: Whose Paradigm Is in Use Here?', in Beare, H. and Boyd, W.L. (eds), *Restructuring Schools: An International Perspective on the Movements to Transform the Control and Performance of Schools*. London: The Falmer Press.

Bell, D. 1973. *The Coming of the Post-Industrial Society: A Venture in Social Forecasting*. New York: Basic Books.

Boréus, K. 1994. *Högervåg: Nyliberalism och kampen om språket i svensk offentlig debatt 1969–1989*. Stockholm: Tidens förlag.

Boyd, W.L. 1992. 'Parental Choice of Schools: An International Movement', in Miron, G. (ed.), *Towards Free Choice and Market-Oriented Schools: Problems and Promises*. Stockholm: Institute of International Education/Skolverket.

Boyd, W.L. 1996. 'The Politics of Choice and Market-oriented School Reform in Britain and the United States: Explaining the Differences', in Chapman, J.D., Boyd, W. L., Lander R. and Reynolds, D. (eds), *The Reconstruction of Education. Quality, Equality and Control*. London/New York: Cassell.

Boyd, W.L. and Kerchner, C.T. (eds) 1988. *The Politics of Excellence and Choice in Education*. New York: The Falmer Press.

Brown, P. 1994. 'Education and the Ideology of Parentocracy', in Halstead, J. M. (ed.), *Parental Choice and Education: Principles, Policy and Practice*. London: Kogan Page.

Butler, T. and Savage, M. (eds) 1995. *Social Change and the Middle Classes*. London: UCL Press.

Cohn, E. (ed.) 1997. *Market Approaches to Education: Vouchers and School Choice*. Oxford: Pergamon Press.

Crompton, R. 1993. *Class and Stratification: An Introduction to Current Debates*. Cambridge: Polity Press.

Daun, H. 1993. *Omstrukturering av skolsystemen: Decentralisering, valfrihet och privatisering. En internationell översikt*. Stockholm: Skolverket.

Downs, A. 1957. *An Economic Theory of Democracy*. New York: Harper and Row.

Esping-Andersen, G. 1994. 'Jämlikhet, effektivitet och makt', in Thyllberg, P. and Östberg, K. (eds), *Den svenska modellen*. Lund: Studentlitteratur.

Gewirtz, S., Ball, S.J. and Bowe, R. 1995. *Markets, Choice and Equity in Education*. Buckingham and Philadelphia: Open University Press.

Giddens, A. 1981. *The Class Structure of the Advanced Societies*, 2nd edn. London: Hutchinson.

Gilljam, M. and Holmberg, S. 1995. *Väljarnas val.* Stockholm: Fritzes.

Girvin, B. (ed.) 1988. *The Transformation of Contemporary Conservatism.* London: Sage.

Goldthorpe, J. 1982. 'On the Service Class, Its Formation and Future,' in Giddens, A. and MacKenzie, G. (eds), *Classes and the Division of Labor: Essays in Honour of Ilya Neustadt.* Cambridge: Cambridge University Press.

Hayek, F.A. 1944. *The Road to Serfdom.* London: Routledge and Kegan Paul.

Hylén, J. 1991. *Fosterlandet främst?: Konservatism och liberalism inom högerpartiet 1904–1985.* Stockholm: Norstedts Juridikförlag.

Inglehart, R. 1977. *The Silent Revolution.* Princeton: Princeton University Press.

Inglehart, R. 1990. *Culture Shift in Advanced Industrial Society.* Princeton: Princeton University Press.

Lane, J.E. and Ersson, S.O. 1987. *Politics and Society in Western Europe.* London: Sage Publications.

Levitas, R. (ed.) 1986. *The Ideology of the New Right.* Cambridge: Polity Press.

Lidström, A. 1991. *Discretion: An Art of the Possible.* Department of Political Science, Umeå University.

Lidström, A. and Hudson, C. 1995. *Skola i förändring: Decentralisering och lokal variation.* Stockholm. Nerenius & Santérus förlag.

Ljunggren, S.B. 1992. *Folkhemskapitalismen: Högerns programutveckling under efterkrigstiden.* Stockholm: Tidens förlag.

Lundahl, L. 1989. *I moralens, produktionens och det sunda förnuftets namn: Det svenska högerpartiets skolpolitik 1904–1962.* Pedagogiska institutionen, Lunds universitet.

Nozick, R. 1974. *Anarchy, State and Utopia.* Oxford: Basil Blackwell.

OECD 1992. *Historical Statistics 1960–1990.* Paris.

OECD 1994. *School: A Matter of Choice.* Paris.

Oskarson, M. 1994. *Klassröstning i Sverige: Rationalitet, Lojalitet eller bara slentrian.* Stockholm: Nerenius & Santérus förlag.

Petersson, O., Westholm, A. and Blomberg, G. 1989. *Medborgarnas makt.* Stockholm: Carlssons.

Pettersson, T. and Geyer, K. 1992. *Värderingsförändringar i Sverige: Den svenska modellen, individualismen och rättvisan.* Stockholm: Utbildningsförlaget Brevskolan.

Schüllerqvist, U. 1995. 'Förskjutningen av svensk skolpolitisk debatt under det senaste decenniet', in Englund, T. (ed.), *Utbildningspolitiskt systemskifte.* Stockholm: HLS förlag.

Skolverket 1993a. *Tidigare skolstart: Om kommuners möte med en reform.* Skolverkets rapport no. 39.

Skolverket 1993b. *Val av skola: Rapport om valfrihet inom skolpliktens ram läsa[o]ret 1992/93.* Skolverkets rapport no. 40.

Skolverket 1996. *Att välja skola – effekter av valmöjligheter i grundskolan.* Skolverkets rapport no. 109.

Skolverket 1998. *Skolan. Jämförelsetal för skolhuvudmän. Organisation – Resurser – Resultat. Delrapport, mars 1998.* Skolverket rapport nr 146.

Statistiska Centralbyrån. 1992. *Folk- och bostadsräkningen 1990. Del 5: Förvärvsarbetande och yrke.*

Statistiska Centralbyrån 1994. *Trender och prognoser '94. Befolkningen, utbildningen, arbetsmarknaden.*

Svenska Kommunförbundet 1998. *Aktuellt om skolan. Augusti 1998.*

Svensson, T. 1994. *Socialdemokratins dominans. En studie av den svenska socialdemokratins partistrategi.* Stockholm: Almqvist & Wiksell förlag.

Walford, G. 1996. *School Choice and the Quasi-market.* Oxford Studies in Comparative Education 6. Wallingford: Triangle Books.

Wright, E. O. 1985. *Classes.* London: New Left Books.

Ålund, A. and Schierup, C. U. 1991. *Paradoxes of Multiculturalism. Essays on Swedish Society.* Aldershot: Avebury.

4
School Markets and Locality: an Exploration of Difference in the English Education Market Place[1]

Sharon Gewirtz

Over the last two decades there has been a radical restructuring of schooling in Britain. Two key features of these reforms have been the application of market-force principles to the provision of education and the introduction into schools of management practices more usually associated with the private sector. The restructuring, heavily inspired by public choice theory, is based partly upon the contention that giving school managers the freedom to manage and subjecting schools to the disciplines of the market will result in higher standards. Moreover, it is assumed that where schools under-perform in a devolved system of educational governance, this can be attributed to deficient management at the school level. Findings from research into school effectiveness and improvement are used in attempts to lend credibility to this view. In this chapter, I want to suggest that policies that focus on a combination of markets and managerial devices as the route to raising the performance of schools ignore the complex, varied and sometimes subtle interplay between schools and the social, material and discursive environments within which they operate. I will argue that what managers and teachers do, or can do, in schools are necessarily heavily influenced, and constrained, by the nature of the school's locality and by dominant educational discourses. In order to illustrate my argument, I will draw on empirical evidence from two schools that are differently located in the education market place and whose managers are, as a consequence, differently able to exploit the market to their schools' advantages. I want to begin though by describing the policy context within which English schools now operate.

The policy context

Between 1980 and 1997 successive Conservative governments put in place a series of reforms that subjected education provision in England to a regime of organization and funding based on the principles of the market. Taken together, these reforms can be viewed as representing a complex of initiatives, which I have referred to elsewhere as the *post-welfarist education policy complex* (PWEPC) (Gewirtz, 1997). The complex is permeated by a utilitarian discourse of efficiency, effectiveness, performance and productivity and is comprised of a number of disparate elements that initially emerged out of different ideological traditions and pragmatic concerns within the UK Conservative Party. All of these elements combine to constrain schools and teachers while increasing central control over the school system. More specifically:

1. The abolition of secondary picketing and teachers' negotiating rights constituted mechanisms for depressing wages.
2. The PWEPC has given the government an enhanced capacity to define the content and desired outcomes of education through the national curriculum, testing and the standardisation of initial teacher training.
3. Through OFSTED, the market and performance tables, the PWEPC has enabled the government to *attempt* to ensure that those outcomes are attained in the most efficient ways. In this context, the market mechanism is meant to function as a system of resource allocation in which resources flow away from 'low-performance' (unpopular) schools and towards 'high-performance' (popular) ones. The system is designed in part to ensure that only minimal funds are spent on schools which are underperforming, and where schools are seriously under-performing ('failing') OFSTED can set in motion moves to close or amalgamate them.
4. Within schools, the efficient use of resources is encouraged by devolving to headteachers control over their own budgets and by

giving them a financial incentive, through *per capita* funding, to spend resources in ways which will lead to improved performance.

Part of the philosophy underpinning the reforms is summarised in the following way by the US academic duo Chubb and Moe, passionate advocates of choice in education:

> Bureaucracy vitiates the most basic requirements of effective organization. It imposes goals, structures, and requirements that tell principals and teachers what to do and how to do it – denying them not only the discretion they need to exercise their expertise and professional judgement but also the flexibility they need to develop and operate as teams. The key to effective education rests with unleashing the productive potential already present in the schools and their personnel. It rests with granting them the autonomy to do what they do best. ... [T]he freer schools are from external control the more likely they are to have effective organizations.
>
> (Chubb and Moe, 1990, p. 187)

Thus, somewhat paradoxically, given the constraints imposed by the national curriculum, testing and a rigorous inspection regime, the PWEPC was designed, at least in part, to 'unleash the productive potential' of school managers while constraining what was seen as the stultifying bureaucratic procedures and attitudes of local education authorities (LEAs). The idea was that by giving headteachers and governors control over their budgets and by making school income dependent on attracting custom, senior managers in schools would have both the tools and the incentive to behave in more cost-effective, flexible, competitive, consumer-satisfying and innovative ways. One of the key rationales underpinning the reforms, then, was that market forces and more efficient management techniques would help raise standards in schools. The underlying assumption was that if schools were given autonomy to respond to market forces (within the broad constraints set by the national curriculum, national testing and OFSTED's inspection criteria) than any failure to improve and boost recruitment would be due to poor management and teaching.

The election in 1997 of a Labour government led to the introduction of a further series of education reforms. In contrast to

Conservative governments, Labour has emphasized partnership, collaboration, 'joined-up government',[2] the targeting of additional resources on 'disadvantaged' areas and a more humanistic set of values for the curriculum, with a particular emphasis on education for citizenship. However, there has been no attempt to dismantle the main elements of the policy complex put in place by the Conservatives. Crucially, market forces have been preserved, with resources still distributed to schools primarily on a per capita basis. Indeed in some respects marketization has been reinforced, for example, by the creation of more specialist schools to increase the market choice available to (some) parents and children. In addition, the managerialist elements of the policy complex have been formalized and extended. For example, the Labour government is actively promoting performance monitoring and target setting in schools. It has also enthusiastically embraced the use of the contract model of resource allocation. This means that any school or local authority wanting to gain extra funds must compete with other schools or authorities by bidding for money that is attached to particular government initiatives, for example, specialist schools, early excellence centres, family literacy schemes and work-related learning. In addition, the government is trying to encourage a flexibilization of teachers' work and a move away from the existing national framework of teachers' pay and conditions with the introduction of performance related pay. All of these initiatives can be viewed as contributing to a further increase in central control over the school system, or to what Richard Hatcher (1998, p. 493) has called an 'even more authoritarian managerialism' than that of the Conservative era.

As with the Conservative reforms, Labour's policies are underpinned by a belief that the key to raising standards in schools lies with good management operating within the context of a highly regulated market. As David Blunkett, Secretary of State for Education, has written:

> A good head makes a big difference regardless of where a school is located. A strong, dynamic headteacher is vital to success – so is a committed team of teachers with high expectations of what can be achieved.
>
> (Blunkett, 1999, p. 21)

This is a view that is shared by academics in the school effectiveness and improvement tradition, some of whom have had a significant influence on the development of Labour's education policy (Hatcher, 1998). However, unlike the government, much of the school improvement research is careful to emphasize that while schools can and do make a difference, what they can achieve is 'partial and limited, because schools are also part of the wider society, subject to its norms, rules, and influences' (Mortimore, 1997, p. 483). Reynolds and Packer (1992) concluded from their review of school effectiveness research that schools have an independent effect of only 8–15 per cent on student outcomes. But, as Thrupp has noted, while policy-makers and school improvers 'may be aware of the influence of social class on student outcomes', there is nevertheless a tendency for them to 'place faith in formal school management, curricula and assessment reforms to bring about changes to student performance' (Thrupp, 1998, p. 198).

Thrupp's research indicates that such faith may well be misplaced. He argues that the social mix of schools (what he refers to as the student mix) strongly influences 'school organisational and management processes so as to drag down the academic effectiveness of schools in low SES [socio-economic] settings and boost it in middle class settings'. He goes on to conclude that 'schools with differing SES intake compositions will, in fact, not be able to carry out similarly effective school polices and practices even with similar levels of resourcing and after taking account of individual student backgrounds' (Thrupp, 1998, p. 198).

This remainder of this chapter will attempt to shed light on the issues raised in this debate by exploring some of the complexities involved in trying to uncover the determinants of the differential 'success' of schools. It will focus on two inner-London secondary schools, John Ruskin and Beatrice Webb.[3] Both schools are co-educational comprehensive schools but they are very different. John Ruskin is highly regarded within the local community, heavily over-subscribed and performs well in the national league tables of examination results. Beatrice Webb, located within a mile of Ruskin, has a poor reputation, is very under-subscribed and is positioned near to the bottom of the examination league tables. The schools were studied as part of an ESRC-funded project investigating the impact of educational reform on the culture and values of schooling.[4]

I want to briefly introduce the two schools. Then I will explore some of the differences between them in terms of management and teaching, before going on to consider the implications of the schools' social, material and discursive environments for the way in which they operate.

The schools

Ruskin is extremely popular, so much so that students have to live within three-quarters of a mile of the school to gain a place. The intake reflects the social mix of the local area, with approximately a quarter of the children coming from middle-class homes and just over 20 per cent qualifying for free school meals. The intake is mainly white with significant minorities of African–Caribbean, Chinese, Bangladeshi and Indian students. Although 14 per cent come from a home where English is not the first language, the majority of students were born in Britain and only a handful needs extra language support. Of all the students 15 per cent are on the school's register of special educational needs. As is the case with many popular schools, parents have been known to lie about their addresses in order to secure a place for their children at the school. In 1991 Ruskin expanded its Year 7 intake by 20 per cent in order to accommodate growing demand and maximise income. Ruskin's examination results are well above the national average. In 1995, 53 per cent of students got five or more GCSE grades A*–C compared to a national average of 41 per cent. The OFSTED team which inspected Ruskin in spring 1996, while not uncritical of some aspects of the school, was on the whole highly complimentary, describing it as follows:

> The school aims to provide an environment in which its members can contribute and achieve. It is concerned for the development of the whole person, with learning through personal interest and commitment, with social development through collaboration and shared activity, with exercising choice and self-determination, and with acknowledging rights balanced with responsibilities. Raising achievement is a key objective for which there are planned developments and targets in curriculum planning, managing behaviour and assessment and monitoring.

Increased popularity has brought about the opportunity for building development.

Thus, measured against the key public indicators – market performance, examination results and OFSTED Report – Ruskin is an unqualified success.

Beatrice Webb, less than a mile away, is markedly under-subscribed and has a poor local reputation. Very few students choose to go there, the vast majority ending up at the school by default rather than choice. There is a proliferation of short-term accommodation in the area (the chair of governors referred to it as 'bedsit land') and many children enter the school mid-year because their families have been temporarily 'housed' in the area. The school also accepts a significant number of children who have been excluded from other schools. Approximately 30 per cent of the students are refugees, two-thirds are bilingual and 73 per cent are eligible for free school meals. Of all the students 30 per cent are registered as having special educational needs. In 1996 Beatrice Webb had 520 students on roll, although the school is deemed to have a potential capacity of 900 pupils. It consistently performs poorly in the examination league tables, with 10 per cent of students attaining five or more A^*–C grades at GCSE in 1995.

During the course of our research there was a change of headship at Beatrice Webb. OFSTED inspected the school in the spring term of 1996 after the new head had been in post for just a year. They concluded that it was a school 'with major weaknesses' and that, although the new head was beginning to tackle these, a lot of work still needed to be done:

> The headteacher was appointed in September 1995 and faced major problems, which, though diminished, still exist. The school was overstaffed, there were grave financial difficulties, standards were low, and the school was heavily undersubscribed. Since his appointment, many beneficial changes have taken place. Although there are still major problems, the school, though it has a long way to go, is slowly improving.

While the inspectors were complimentary about some aspects of the school, they were highly critical of many, pointing in particular to

low standards of attainment, poor rates of attendance and punctual-
ity and a failure of some staff to rigorously 'implement the measures
recently undertaken by the school to remedy these deficiencies'.

How do we explain why one of these schools is judged a success
and one is considered to be seriously underperforming and in need
of being 'turned around'? Clearly questions need to be asked about
the criteria against which success and failure are measured. Success
and failure are discursively constructed and we cannot simply take
these public discourses at face value. I will return to this issue below,
but for the moment I want to focus on management and teaching
in the schools. As I noted above, it is the current political fashion to
praise or blame school managers and teachers for the success or
failure of schools. This tendency gains its legitimacy in part from
academic discourses provided by the school effectiveness and
improvement lobby. In the following section I want to begin to
examine the validity of such arguments by comparing teaching and
management in Ruskin and Beatrice Webb.

Management and teaching in the two schools

In a review of the school effectiveness literature, Peter Mortimore
identifies two research approaches, the first of which is concerned to
isolate the determinants of *successful* schools. Thus for example,
Maden and Hillman (NCE, 1995):

> emphasize the importance of a cluster of behaviours: a leadership
> stance which builds on and develops a team approach; a vision of
> success which includes a view of how the school can improve
> and which, once it has improved, is replaced by a pride in its
> achievement; school policies and practices which encourage the
> planning and setting up of targets; the improvement of the phys-
> ical environment; common expectations about pupil behaviour
> and success; and an investment in good relations with parents
> and the community.
>
> (Mortimore, 1997, p. 481)

The other approach is to identify the causes of school *failure*. For
instance, Stoll (1995):

has drawn our attention to lack of vision, unfocused leadership, dysfunctional staff relationships, and ineffective classroom practices as mechanisms through which the effectiveness of schools can deteriorate.

(Mortimore, 1997, p. 481).

So to what extent are any of these features apparent in Ruskin and Beatrice Webb and to what extent can such features be said to *explain* the differential performance of the schools?

Ruskin

Ruskin certainly appears to possess all the features that Maden and Hillman (NCE, 1995) associate with successful schools and none of those that Stoll (1995) associates with ineffective schools.

Our study did not set out to evaluate the teaching in the schools, so for the purposes of reporting on the 'effectiveness' of classroom practice in the schools, I will cite OFSTED's judgements (although these do need to be treated with caution). OFSTED's opinion of teaching at Ruskin was formulated on the basis of observing 225 lessons. The OFSTED team was on the whole positive about the teaching in the school, reporting that:

> Teachers work hard to create harmonious relationships in lessons and to provide lessons which contain an interesting variety of activities which largely sustain the interests of students. A good feature of teaching is the way in which subject teachers work with other professionals, parents and outside speakers to provide an interesting and relevant curriculum. ... Lessons are well planned with clear objectives. ... Clear explanations by teachers leave students in no doubt about what they have to do. Teachers are skilful in ascertaining and developing students' understanding through skilful questioning and reformulating their responses.

There were criticisms too, for example, that 'Too often teachers over-direct the thinking of the students' and that 'Occasionally teachers dominate lessons by talking too much.' But, of the teaching time they observed, they concluded that 90 per cent of lessons were satisfactory, very good or better.

With regard to leadership at Ruskin, a number of teachers we interviewed were critical of the head, viewing him as autocratic and sometimes bullying. However, at the same time there was a general feeling amongst staff that they were consulted and listened to, even though they were not always happy with the decisions that are made. While the key decisions were made by the senior management team, there were strong lines of communication between management and staff and a significant degree of what appeared to be constructive debate. Complaints and grievances among staff did well up, but these tended to reach a point at which they were recognized by senior management and dealt with through discussion and compromise. One of the senior management team (SMT), in particular, seemed to have adopted an informal role as conduit between staff and management. He spent more time in the staffroom than the other senior managers and picked up on concerns that were then relayed back to the rest of the SMT, discussed and responded to. Staff meetings were organized by an elected committee of staff and in such a way as to enable teachers to debate issues in the absence of senior management. Teachers were also given the opportunity in these meetings to debate with senior management and a minority of teachers was not afraid to publicly challenge the decisions of the SMT. A committee of staff met regularly with senior management to represent staff concerns and discuss key decisions and policies within the school. While the head clearly saw this group as a useful device for ensuring that management decisions gain legitimacy among staff, the members of the group themselves saw it as a means of influencing management decisions in the interests of staff. And from what I observed, the group appeared to be able to use it quite effectively in this way. I observed a number of occasions in which senior management revised decisions in the light of staff protest. Although the school was not run along democratic lines, it appeared to have enough democratic-like features to ensure that staff morale was kept at relatively healthy levels.

As regards 'vision', the head and senior management team had a very clear view of what the school stands for. While, there were political differences and a range of emphases within the staff, there was a generally agreed commitment to offering students a broad and balanced humanistic curriculum within a relatively relaxed and collaborative atmosphere where children are encouraged to be academically achieving, independent, critical and caring. Target-setting and performance monitoring had become firmly entrenched practices within the school, although many members of staff were opposed to these and critical of their effects on their pedagogical practice (Gewirtz, 1997).

Beatrice Webb

While Ruskin appears to possess the characteristics that are supposed to produce effective schools, Beatrice Webb, seems to have a number of characteristics that are meant to lead to ineffectiveness, although according to OFSTED, the school was showing signs of 'improvement'.

OFSTED concluded that the bulk of teaching at Beatrice Webb was 'satisfactory or better' and a quarter of 'the teaching was good or very good'. However, they also reported, on the basis of the 141 lessons they inspected, that a quarter of the teaching they observed was of poor quality:

> Too many teachers ... have expectations for the pupils that are too low and weak techniques of assessment. In some subjects ... the teaching is flawed by poor subject knowledge, the use of unsuitable methods, and the lack of clear aims for lessons.

There was a significant proportion of teachers who have been in the school a long time, were on relatively high salaries and of whom senior managers were critical in terms of their management and, in some cases, teaching skills. One of the younger teachers described this group as the 'old brigade, middle management, who have been here and are established ... maybe thirteen, fourteen years [and who are] maybe not willing to change their strategies or ideas and costing the school a great deal of money' ('Young' Teacher, February 1996). He compared these teachers to recent appointees who were more open to change. Our interviews revealed many of the staff to be preoccupied with problems of discipline and management, rather than curriculum-related issues.

Webb's leadership changed over the period of the fieldwork, with the appointment of a new head in September 1995. Relationships between the old head, Susanna English and the staff were extremely strained. Using Stoll's (1995) terminology, they could well be described as 'dysfunctional'. A staff that appeared to be dominated by the 'old brigade' of mainly male 'middle managers' blocked any change the head tried to implement. Discussions between staff and management were confrontational and never appeared to contribute to changes in school policies or practices. Many of the staff saw Ms English as a poor manager, and they particularly criticized her for regularly 'taking the side' of children while, often publicly, undermining teachers, and for not excluding students for serious misdemeanours, such as assaulting a teacher. In contrast, at least for a honeymoon period, many believed the new head, Brian Jones, to be a good manager, who was variously described as more honest, open and willing to listen than the previous head. Teachers interviewed in his first term in post argued that he was improving the culture of the school by appearing more appreciative of teachers and imposing a more disciplined regime on students who previously would:

> go running straight to the head and have a shoulder to cry on, whereas now ... hopefully the head won't give them a shoulder to cry on [and] if they've done something serious they'll be booted out for a couple of days. ... If a child needs dealing with, there are now the procedures where you feel comfortable or confident that they will be dealt with in the correct way.
>
> ('Young' Teacher, 1 February 1996)

Certainly, the exclusion rate increased significantly in Brian Jones first term of office. The general feeling amongst staff was that the new head was boosting morale:

> He seems to be able to praise people, boost their confidence a bit more, which is much better. I've had more praise in the past year than I've had in the previous thirteen years, he actually notices where good work is going on, good practice, so he seems to have his finger on the pulse much better.
>
> (Head of Department, 29 January 1996)

However, by his second term in office, the new head had begun to implement redundancies and morale once again began to decline. But the OFSTED team, which inspected Beatrice Webb in 1996, was complimentary about the head. They presented him as someone who had begun to 'turn the school around', by tackling such problems as 'overstaffing' and the budget deficit and by replacing the old, rather vague, one-page development plan with a new one detailing 90 points for action.

Both heads at Beatrice Webb had what Maden and Hillman (NCE, 1995) describe as 'a vision of success' although there were important aspects of these visions that were very different. Ms English wanted the school to focus on the needs of its *current* constituency, on refugees and students with emotional and behavioural difficulties. She was concerned to improve exam results but she also wanted Beatrice Webb to be a school that involved students in decision-making and celebrated difference. Her stance was captured in her vehement opposition to the introduction of school uniform, which she saw as a means of controlling children by:

> taking away a whole area of choice from kids. ... The variety of clothing that you observe when you go there is quite amazing and I think quite delightful, it's part of that general ... sense of difference ... and variety that goes on there.
>
> (29 September 1995)

Brian Jones' vision, which was more popular with the majority of staff, was to make the school into an institution that would attract a different (more middle-class) constituency and make it a success in market terms. His vision was couched in the language of improvement, and emphasised achievement and discipline while downplaying the school's work with refugees. Significantly, his position on uniform was in stark contrast to Ms English's. While she had delighted in the students' varied and expressive responses to the school's liberal dress code, Mr Jones was highly critical. He felt that the lack of uniform contributed to what he described as a holiday camp atmosphere that was simply not appropriate for an institution that needed to establish itself as a place of learning.

One conclusion that could be drawn from much of the preceding description of teaching and management at the two schools is that the school effectiveness researchers are accurate in their analysis of the determinants of school success and failure. After all, Ruskin could well be described as having:

> a leadership stance which builds on and develops a team approach; a vision of success which includes a view of how the school can improve ... school policies and practices which encourage the planning and setting up of targets; the improvement of the physical environment; common expectations about pupil behaviour and success; and an investment in good relations with parents and the community.
>
> (Mortimore, 1997, p. 481)

And all of these things might be said to account for why Ruskin performs so well according to public indicators. Equally, Beatrice Webb's 'underperformance' could be attributed to a number of past failures, in particular: the absence of a team approach to school management; a failure to develop a vision of success couched in the language of improvement; a neglect of planning and target-setting practices; a neglect of the physical environment; 'dysfunctional' staff relationships and a lack of agreement between staff and management around expectations of pupil behaviour; and ineffective classroom practices. If we are to accept OFSTED's assessment, then we might predict that the new head's attempts to try and rectify some of the weaknesses would lead to improved performance at Beatrice Webb.

However, while there may well be a *correlation* between particular features of management and teaching and degrees of school success, we need to be a little wary of concluding that the relationship is *causal*. Or, at least, we should not assume that it is causal in the direction that school effectiveness researchers claim it is. In the next section, I want to delve a little deeper and explore some of the features of the social environments of the two schools that might account for the differences between them in terms of management and teaching.

The impact of 'social environment'

Drawing upon an ethnographic study of four New Zealand schools, Martin Thrupp (1998, p. 216) very convincingly demonstrates the 'stubborn constraints on organizational and management processes in low SES (socio-economic) schools compared to their middle-class counterparts'. In particular he identifies 'intense pressures on teachers and school leaders generated by students in low SES schools' (Thrupp, 1998, p. 214). As a result of these pressures, he concludes, 'time and energy required to consider and implement demands from central agencies will be scarce in low SES schools'. In addition, he argues that 'teachers and principals at (low SES) declining schools are so overwhelmed with pastoral and learning problems that they will be unable to deliver similar academic programmes to those at middle class schools' (Thrupp, 1998, pp. 214–215).

An analysis of the impact of student demands on management and teaching processes at Ruskin and Beatrice Webb would appear to support Thrupp's conclusions about the importance of social mix in determining the 'success' of schools. There are a number of features of Beatrice Webb's intake that create particular demands for the staff, in particular the high proportions of refugee, low income, special needs and bilingual students. Some of the second-language students have poor levels of literacy in their first language. And, as well as the challenge of having to learn a new language, many of the refugee students have emotional difficulties. These are linked to experiences of war in their countries of origin, moving to a strange country, living in bed-and-breakfast accommodation, or arriving without parents and having to settle into local authority care.

In addition, Beatrice Webb has a highly mobile population with an average turn over of approximately 10 children per week. Many of the students who enter the school in Year 7 are on waiting lists for their first choice schools. When a vacancy in one of those schools comes up, the student will leave, and such departures can occur even when a student has reached Year 10. The head of Year 7 at Beatrice Webb noted that many of the students who are offered places at other schools are higher attaining students who would have enhanced the school's league table performance, had they remained in the school until Year 11. At the same time, there are students, across the age spectrum, who join the school regularly throughout the school year, either because they have been excluded from other schools or because they have been moved in to short-term housing of which there is a considerable quantity in the vicinity of the school. One of the younger teachers in the school defined the problem and the difficulties it creates in the following way:

> because we are so skint, we need money and we tend to accept anybody who comes along. So by this stage we lose our best kids

to the other schools, because waiting lists are freed up and they've got spare places ... and in exchange we get kids who have been excluded from those schools who often are the rather unfriendly ones who are aggressive and have been excluded for bad reasons. And we then have to deal with them. So throughout the year ... there is literally a twenty per cent change in pupils in each year. And only about twenty per cent actually manage to make it through the first year to the fifth year. So you've got different faces all the time. Even in Year 11 you are getting different faces, which makes it very difficult to teach and later in the year you get the worst pupils. We start off with some very nice ones but then lose them to other schools, because nobody picks Beatrice Webb as a first choice, which is a shame.

('Young' Teacher, 1 February 1996)

The highly mobile population creates a number of quite difficult challenges for teachers. Teachers have to establish relationships with new students on a weekly basis. They have to settle these students in to their classes, induct them into their particular teaching styles, and assess the students' abilities, learning styles, language skills and what if anything they have already covered in the curriculum. In addition, the composition of classes is constantly changing, which can in itself be disruptive, as one Head of Department explained:

it makes it very difficult, not just for teaching, as in trying to cover all the work that these children should have done in the past, because they arrive with no records, especially if they're refugees, but also in terms of [the] socio dynamics of the group, in that a group can be quite settled and get a new student every fortnight, and it will just disrupt the whole group dynamic ... and a group that would have been settled and working well, can become then a very difficult group to teach, because of shifting pressures within the group.

(Steve Davis, Head of Department, 29 January 1996)

And finally, many of the new arrivals, having been excluded from other schools, exhibit challenging forms of behaviour. According to one of the teachers we interviewed, many of the children excluded from other schools succeed at Beatrice Webb and he put this down to the school ethos:

it's not a regimented strongly disciplinarian place ... there's an atmosphere which is about groups, about caring for each other ... it's a very good atmosphere.

(Language Support Teacher, 29 January 1996)

The OFSTED team made a similar observation about the quality of relationships between staff and students in the school:

Most pupils and teachers like and respect each other. Pupils come from widely differing backgrounds and nationalities, and are tolerant towards each other. No direct evidence of bullying was found. ... Many pupils show concern for other newly arrived pupils or for those whose English is limited. There are many instances of pupils helping others in lessons.

However, it was the general consensus in the school that a small minority of students who had been excluded from at least one other school were an extremely disruptive influence, taking up a disproportionate quantity of teacher and management time. The headteacher has to deal on a daily basis with violent episodes involving these few students. Incidents occurring in the school during a typical two months of the fieldwork period included students attacking each other with a police baton, bottles, a baseball bat and an airgun. One of these episodes was connected to a drug-related dispute. Dealing with such incidents is immensely time-consuming involving liaising variously with teachers, students, and parents (of both perpetrators and victims), the police and social workers. If the head wants to exclude the culprits then he needs to be meticulous in his collection of evidence by interviewing student witnesses and in recording that evidence.

Ruskin is not free of violence and student conflict, but there is not nearly as much of it. As Ruskin is full, it does not need to accept any excluded students. When it has a vacancy, it can take a student from its long waiting list. These students tend to be the ones that Beatrice Webb and other local schools would like to retain. Harvey Smith, a head of year at Ruskin, commented that the students the school accepted when there was a vacancy tended to be very motivated high achievers:

> I could name probably nine or ten kids, we've taken them from Winbrook [nearby school] and every one of them's been a diamond, you know. They've all been really good ... and they've been academic, hardworking kids. We haven't taken any bad kids from Winbrook ... they're all cracking kids. ... And there's probably ten who've come into Year 10, you know, since they've come in perhaps in Year 7 or 8, 9, 10. We take them from other schools as well. ... But we don't take bad kids. ... *And we are doing well at the expense of other schools.*
>
> (Head of Year, Ruskin, 23 November 1995, my emphasis)

Focusing on the impact of student mix should not be seen as an exercise in pathologising the students in low SES schools or of blaming them for the schools' weaknesses, but school populations have different needs and create different demands which need to be acknowledged. Teachers in schools like Beatrice Webb need very special skills to deal with the challenges thrown up by their intakes, and at Beatrice Webb, there simply are not enough specialists. For example, the school had a total of three-and-a-half specialist language support teachers at the time we conducted the fieldwork. These were allocated to different faculties: English was the most 'generously' resourced with 1.5 teachers, science had a full-time teacher and geography and technology shared a support teacher. This left 'history uncovered ... [and] maths gets a raw deal' (language support teacher). One of the science teachers we interviewed did not have any language support teachers in any of the classes he taught. A language support teacher explained the difficulties involved in teaching classes with a high proportion of stage one learners:

> there are subjects which have no support at all, and [it is] very difficult [for one teacher] to organise a classroom when there are perhaps four or five who can't read at all, very difficult, and then all the difficulties of ... if the text is very complicated, how does everyone understand them, how do you access the understanding ... so part of that is to introduce ways of doing that, perhaps providing lists of words, glossaries, cutting up the text into more manageable sections, but ... it takes so long to actually devise stuff, you can't, as a normal mainstream teacher, you can't be

expected to do that. I think you are expected, but in terms of time, you don't have time.

However, it's not just a question of time for curriculum planning and the production of learning support materials. There is also considerable skill involved in making the curriculum accessible to a diverse range of stage one learners. Many of the teachers who have not had specialist training in fact do very well. To take a crude indicator, GCSE results in art and drama were well above the national average for comprehensive schools. However, it is noticeable that the staff and departments that perform particularly well in external examinations, teach those subjects in which students are less dependent on literacy skills for success. This is not to detract from the talent of the teachers in these departments, but it may well be that these subjects are more accessible to students not yet fluent in English.

The pressures generated by the student mix at Beatrice Webb also mean it is much harder for teachers to exert energy into extra curricular activities. And take up of extra curricular opportunities is much lower at Beatrice Webb than at Ruskin, possibly because students have greater domestic responsibilities, for example caring for younger siblings, or helping their parents, for instance as interpreters, in ways which Ruskin students do not have to. OFSTED noted that 'school concerts, performances and musical activities are rare' at Beatrice Webb.

OFSTED were generally positive about the teaching of refugee students and those with special needs at Beatrice Webb, leading them to conclude that:

> Given the very mixed nature of the school's intake, satisfactory progress is being made by about 70 per cent of the pupils. The school has a good and justified reputation for providing well for non-indigenous and refugee children, who generally make satisfactory progress. Such progress is also make by pupils with special educational needs, who are well catered for throughout the school.

They also reported that in three subject areas there was good practice in marking, record keeping and assessment, and they noted 'several examples of first rate team teaching ... with the support and the class teacher each sharing the lead and making full use of their skills'.

However, it is unsurprising that a significant minority of teachers at Beatrice Webb cannot cope with the pressures exerted upon them and can not adequately perform all of the tasks now expected of teachers. A trained observer might well view these teachers as less than competent but it is possible that if these same teachers were teaching in schools with a less challenging student mix, they would be judged satisfactory. Charlene Fraser, a teacher at Ruskin, had previously taught at another local school, Applegate, which was very similar to Beatrice Webb in terms of its intake. She commented that there were many members of staff at Ruskin 'who would not be able to teach at Applegate, and they recognize that and that's why they wouldn't be at that sort of school'. She also described the sheer physicality and emotionality of teaching in a school like Applegate, where behavioural concerns tend to overshadow curricular ones.

> you are not as physically tired at the end of the day working in this sort of school [Ruskin], because ... your classroom doesn't have to be managed in quite such [a] physical way, and the children don't demand as much of you in this sort of school ... because the children [at Applegate] have so little – a lot of the children don't have much input from parents. ... They're very, very demanding.
>
> (6 November 1995)

Charlene went on to argue that at Ruskin, the lack of physicality involved in the work and the fact that the children were less demanding, meant that more emphasis could be placed on reflecting upon and refining the curriculum:

> the emphasis on the curriculum here [at Ruskin] is paramount, because behaviour problems don't get in the way in the same way that they do at Applegate. ... And the importance at Applegate is really to create an atmosphere in which work can be done and in which the children feel safe and secure ... with the curriculum obviously running alongside. And that's what ... makes it very difficult at that school. Whereas here the curriculum is really what ... we're always changing and pushing forward. ... We're really looking at the curriculum all the time. [We] spend very little time, really, worrying about disciplining classes.
>
> (Languages Teacher, Ruskin, 6 November 1995)

Charlene also described how a less demanding intake made the management of a school and the development of constructive and collaborative relationships easier:

> it's easier to make something work, like an ideal plan of manage-
> ment, a structure, if you don't have a lot of other issues that
> really get in the way and hijack agendas ... I feel that at
> Applegate what happened was that there would be issues which
> would hijack agendas constantly. ... And because ... there was
> conflict in the community so therefore there was a certain
> amount of conflict within how we thought it should be managed
> ... [Whereas at Ruskin] where things are seen to work pretty well,
> although we have our gripes and things, there isn't a lot of
> conflict between management and us really.
>
> (6 November 1995)

Charlene makes some important and astute points here and her analysis of the way in which agendas are hijacked at Applegate and of the conflict generated by the social environment of the school applies equally to Beatrice Webb. The head at Ruskin has time to devote himself to strategic issues and the budget. Much of the day-to-day running of the school is delegated to the deputies, senior teachers and heads of department and year. On occasion, the head has to deal with student disciplinary matters and complaining parents but rarely is a whole day taken up with dealing with a crisis caused by say an episode of student violence. And, as Charlene argued, because things are seen to work well at Ruskin, morale is relatively healthy and serious conflict between staff and management doesn't arise. At Beatrice Webb, Brian Jones probably needs more time for strategic planning than the head of Ruskin because the problems the school faces are so much more profound – severe under-recruitment, a poor local reputation, the huge budget deficit, the underfunding of departments, poor relations between management and staff and a highly demanding student population. However, in fact, he has much less time for planning than the head of Ruskin. Both Ms English and Mr Jones invested an enormous amount of energy and time into dealing with violent and/or disruptive students, and, unlike the head of Ruskin, they found it difficult to free themselves from the day-to-day running of the school to focus on strategic planning and to develop initiatives which might have improved recruitment. For example, one of Mr Jones' first initiatives when he joined the school in 1995 was a club for 10–12 year olds, which was designed to try and get more primary age students into the school and cultivate them as potential recruits. But by 1997 this had still not got off the ground, simply because the senior management team's time was taken up with more pressing day-to-day activities. In addition, because the work of teaching is so much more demanding at Beatrice Webb, as a consequence of the intractability of many of the problems the school faces, and because of the budget deficit and the fear of redundancy, morale is extremely low. This undoubtedly creates tension in the school and must exacerbate, if not produce, the bitterly conflictual relationships that exist between managers and the staff in the school.

The relatively harmonious relationships at Ruskin, on the other hand, and the latitude that teachers have to focus on the curriculum and to practice relatively progressive pedagogies, contribute to its reputation as a good school to work in. It is also a growing school and as a result of these things, it is able to attract talented, dynamic and committed teachers. By contrast, Beatrice Webb is a school that is making redundancies, and although it does have its share of highly skilled and imaginative staff, there is, according to some of the more recent recruits, a significant minority of disillusioned and cynical teachers who have lost the energy to be creative. It is much harder to attract 'good' teachers to a school which is conflict-ridden, under-resourced and suffering from low morale.

Another feature of the social environment which makes managing a more middle-class school easier is the higher levels of parental involvement and the fact that parents are more accessible in more middle class schools. Ruskin has an active Parents' Association and the annual governors meeting for parents is well attended. The SMT do not need to invest a lot of energy into developing relationships with parents. If anything, they have the opposite problem – many parents who want to be perhaps over-involved with the nitty gritty of classroom practice, for example, the finer points of teaching grammar in French lessons. In addition, Ruskin has a highly skilled and involved governing body with high levels of cultural capital. For example, one of the parent governors is a very senior civil servant and another the principal of a college of further education.

At Beatrice Webb, attempts were made to develop relations with parents through the appointment, under Ms English, of a deputy head responsible for community relations, but promoting parental and community involvement proved difficult. There is no parent association at Beatrice Webb and very few parents ever attend the governing body's annual meeting for parents. Only the parent governors attended in 1994 and in 1995 only one parent who was not a governor turned up – and the Chair of Governors suspected that this parent only 'came along ... to have something to do, if even to get out of the bloody horrible hotel' where the family had been temporarily housed by the local authority). Only five parents attended the pre-inspection meeting held by the OFSTED Registered Inspector and just seven (1.4 per cent) of the 500 questionnaires for parents that OFSTED sent out were returned. (This compared to a response rate of 29 per cent at Ruskin.) Furthermore, the governors at Beatrice Webb are not skilled at reading and scrutinising budgets like those at Ruskin, and they do not contribute the same levels of support, for example by visiting departments within the school, although strenuous efforts have been made to involve them more.

The material environment

It is not just the social mix but the material environment at Beatrice Webb that makes it a more difficult place than Ruskin to work in. In fact, Beatrice Webb spends more per student, than does Ruskin (£3,400 was spent at Beatrice Webb per student in 1995/96 compared with £2,500 at Ruskin.) However, this is probably mainly because the overheads at Beatrice Webb (costs for heating, maintenance and ensuring adequate curriculum coverage) are a higher proportion of expenditure than at Ruskin because the school has an intake of less than half the size. Yet far more resources are needed for a population of the kind which characterises Beatrice Webb. The school needs more in-class support and more materials to support second language learners and students with special needs. In the 1995–96 school year the language support department at Beatrice Webb spent its entire photocopying budget for the year by Christmas and was forced to resort to getting the old Gestetner machine working again. During the same school year, the science department had a budget of £4.46 per student for the whole year, which was £3.50 less than any other school in the authority. The department had to choose between photocopying differentiated materials, buying chemicals or buying paper or exercise books. There is little scope for eliciting funds from parents, the majority of whom are on income support. One of the teachers we interviewed told us that he often subsidised school trips and other activities 'out of my pocket, rather than the school funds, and I suspect I'm not the only teacher in the school that does this' (Head of Department, 29 January 1996).

One could argue that the insufficiency of resources is the result of a failure of management to bring in more money into the school, and there is some truth to this. Language support money was not part of the school's regular formula-based income and was subject to a separate bidding system within the local authority. One of the support teachers noted that the previous school he worked in, which was in the same authority, had twice as many support teachers although not as many stage one learners. He suggested that the reason for this was that the senior managers at his previous school exhibited more skill in the bidding process. This raises the question of whether the bidding system, which the Labour government has enthusiastically extended to other areas of school funding, is the fairest and most rational way to allocate resources for essential services like language support.

Beatrice Webb is technically overstaffed because it has a higher teacher-student ratio than is deemed appropriate (with 13 students per qualified teacher compared to 15 at Ruskin) and as a result redundancies are being made. At the same time it has larger class sizes, with an average teaching group size of 24, compared with 22 at Ruskin. Now again the larger classes in a school with more teachers could be attributed to poor management of resources. However, not only does Beatrice Webb need to ensure that it covers the same subject areas as Ruskin, but the teachers also need more planning time – for subject teachers to liaise with language and learning support teachers about how best to meet the curriculum needs of the students – and more time to respond to pastoral demands.

The physical condition of the school, also makes a difference in terms of teaching and learning. While Ruskin is not lavishly decorated and furnished, and more improvements are needed, the internal and external environment is pleasant and has been recently subjected to a programme of development. At Beatrice Webb, the situation is very different. OFSTED noted the poor physical condition of the school, commenting (accurately) that:

While the accommodation is adequate overall, much of it is poorly maintained and in need of refurbishment. Classrooms are in need of decoration and much of the furniture, though adequate, is of poor quality. The classroom environment is often uninviting and unconducive to the production of high quality work. Classrooms for English have poor blackboard surfaces, from which it is difficult to read, and the rooms would benefit greatly by the provision of whiteboards. Science laboratories have no blinds, which prevent certain experiments being carried out. Changing rooms for physical education are inadequate and the gyms are often dirty. Corridors are in need of decoration and, where carpets are provided, they are often badly stained.

Performativity and market discourses

A third environmental factor is the discourses of performativity and markets that now surround and permeate education provision (Ball, 1998). It is these discourses that construct Beatrice Webb as a failure and Ruskin as a success. Ruskin is a success because its students are seen to perform well in national tests and examinations, because it is popular with parents and because OFSTED said it was good. Beatrice Webb, on the other hand, is a failure because its students aren't considered to perform well in tests, it is undersubscribed and OFSTED found major weaknesses.

These discourses and the criteria of success/failure embedded within them are internalised within the schools. For example, at Beatrice Webb, some of the governors were critical of the school because of the low per centage of students getting five or more A*–C grades at GCSE. And at both schools, teaching is increasingly focused upon raising levels of performance in GCSEs and SATs, and in particular on those students likely to get C grades and above (Gewirtz, 1997). But the discourses are also challenged in both schools, and particularly at Beatrice Webb where they are viewed as highly inappropriate. For example, one of the science teachers at Beatrice Webb commented:

I know there are some students that I teach in Year 11 who are not going to get graded. It's not because they are not nice kids, it's not because they don't come to school. It's just because their language isn't up to it at present.

(Science Teacher, 26 January 1996)

And one of the language support teacherXs argued:

In the press ... the criteria is A to C and therefore the league tables are weighted against schools which are actually achieving, but is not being recognised as an achievement ... [For] example, someone who comes from Ethiopia in Year 11, say in October, will not have the projects from the first year of the GCSE course and therefore will have to work twice as hard to catch up and also get through the current coursework and then through the exam and learning English at the same time, will have to work so hard to just get, what, an E in the GCSE. ... In geography we're actually thinking that a couple of girls from Ethiopia will get E, maybe even D/Cs. ... It's because they work so hard, they're in local authority homes and therefore for them school is so important, it's the one place which is ... secure, where they know people and people are working, helping them.

(Language Support Teacher, 29 January 1996)

This teacher is making two important points here. One is that in terms of exam performance, Beatrice Webb actually does well for its students, but in a way that is not acknowledged by the public indicators which focus on higher attaining students. Students come in with low levels of prior attainment, and also given that many of the higher attaining students leave before Year 11, 10 per cent of students getting five or more A*–Cs is probably very good on a value-added calculation. In fact, the statistics would appear to indicate that students who've been at the school from Year 7 to Year 11 do well in their GCSEs. But also, simply getting a student who has just come to the country with no prior knowledge of the English language through a GCSE is a major achievement. The language support teacher is also drawing our attention to other aspects of what the school has to offer which are not valued by the discourses of the market and performativity – the provision of a secure and supportive environment for children who are uprooted from their families and countries of origin and living in an unfamiliar country in difficult circumstances.

Conclusion

The analysis presented in this chapter would seem to suggest that poor performance of schools in exams and OFSTED inspections and undersubscription correlates with the kinds of features that the school improvement literature associates with failing schools, and that, conversely school 'success' correlates with 'good' management and 'good' teaching. But the chapter has also indicated that one cannot reasonably conclude from this that good management and teaching are *responsible* for school success. In fact, if the evidence presented here is representative (and obviously more studies of this kind are needed) then it would appear to suggest that the opposite is true: that school 'success' contributes to 'good' management and teaching and school 'failure' contributes to less effective management and teaching. This is because schools deemed to be successful are likely to have a significant proportion (what Thrupp, 1998, refers to as a critical mass) of high attaining and undemanding pupils, they are adequately resourced and can attract talented teachers. As a result of these things morale is relatively high and teachers can focus their attention on developing imaginative curricula. In failing schools, teachers and managers find that, in the words of one of our informants, the agenda tends to get hijacked by behavioural and resource-related issues. In addition, the students demand more of teachers physically, emotionally and intellectually. And as a result of these things morale is likely to be low, relationships conflictual and teachers are left with little energy and insufficient resources to develop appropriate and imaginative schemes of work, classroom materials and pedagogical practices.

In the current system of funding, to bring in more resources, schools need to bring in more students. Research (for example Gewirtz *et al.*, 1995) and the experience of Beatrice Webb indicates that one of the major criteria for parental choice of schools is class based; that is parents choose on the basis of student mix. Beatrice Webb is unlikely ever to be popular with its current intake of mainly working-class students, refugees and bilingual speakers and with its reputation for violence (because of a tiny minority of violent students). Local primary heads told the teacher responsible for primary liaison, that some parents rejected the school precisely because of its 'very good reputation for being welcoming and helping all sorts of refugee kids'. The primary liaison teacher commented that this 'became the overwhelming view of us and some parents thought the kids might suffer'. The general consensus in the school was that for Beatrice Webb to improve:

> what we've got to do is attract some middle-class kids and improve the exam results and improve the image of the school and then through that it's a circle that will attract more. It's getting that first kick start, I think.
>
> (Paul McIntosh, Head of Department, 29 January 1996)

While the head was redistributing resources within the school and targeting them on the needs of the bilingual students, for example, by establishing a reading room and a weekly reading hour for students, he was also exerting energies in trying to change the social mix of the school. In contrast to his predecessor who celebrated and gave a high profile to the school's refugee work, the new head made a conscious decision to play down the work of the school in supporting refugees and he introduced uniform as one strategy for persuading middle-class parents to choose the school. Evidence that his efforts were meeting with some success was a letter circulated by a local group of middle class parents of Year 6 (primary) students appealing to other parents to support and work to improve Beatrice Webb, their local secondary school, by sending their children there.

In the long run this strategy might be successful, transforming the social mix of the school by introducing more middle-class, monolingual students, until it is over-subscribed, enabling it to 'improve' according to official indicators so that it is deemed publicly to be a successful school. But in becoming oversubscribed it will no longer have space for casual entrants – refugees, who had in the past, according to a number of observers, including OFSTED, been so well-served by the school, and students with behavioural difficulties who had been excluded from other schools. It will also be attracting middle-class students who would have attended other local schools, possibly creating vacancies in those schools to be filled by the casual entrants who would previously have gone to Beatrice Webb. There is a possibility, therefore, that while the fortunes of Beatrice Webb may go up, another school may embark on the downward spiral of market failure and reputational decline, and excluded students will continue to be shunted from school to school.

It would, therefore, appear that within the current educational regime governed by the discourses and technologies of the market and performativity, 'good management' is in large part defined as the ability to transform the socio-economic and linguistic make up of a school. Thus within the context of the market and a performance-oriented educational system, management, I would suggest, is severely limited because all it is effectively doing is producing a redistribution of students amongst schools. It cannot address the root causes of educational underachievement.

Acknowledgement

I am most grateful to Alan Cribb, who made some very helpful comments on an earlier version of this chapter.

Notes

1. This is a revised and extended version of 'Can All Schools Be Successful?: An exploration of the determinants of school "success"', published in the *Oxford Review of Education*, 1998, 24 (4).
2. This term is used to refer to cooperation between different sectors of welfare – for example education, housing and health – as well as between different providers (state, voluntary and private).
3. Throughout the chapter pseudonyms are used to protect the anonymity of schools and teachers.
4. ESRC project no. R000235544. I am very grateful to Stephen Ball who co-directed the project with me, to Diane Reay who carried out some of the interviews on which this chapter is based and to Chiz Dubé and Helen Worger who transcribed the interviews.

References

Ball, S.J. 1998. 'Performativity and fragmentation in "post-modern schooling"', in Carter, J. (ed.), *Post-Modernity and Fragmentation of Welfare: A Contemporary Social Policy*. London: Routledge.

Blunkett, D. 1999. 'Do we want to bus the middle class?', *Guardian*. 16 September.

Chubb, J.E. and Moe, T.M. 1990. *Politics, Markets, and America's Schools*. Washington, DC: Brookings Institution.

Gewirtz, S. 1997. 'Post-welfarism and the reconstruction of Teachers' Work in the UK', *Journal of Education Policy*, 12 (4): 217–31.

Gewirtz, S. Ball, S. and Bowe, R. 1995. *Markets, Choice and Equity in Education*. Buckingham: Open University Press.

Hatcher, R. 1998. 'Labour, Official School Improvement and Equality', *Journal of Education Policy*, 13 (4): 485–499.

Mortimore, P. 1997. 'Can Effective Schools Compensate for Society?', in Halsey, A.H. Lauder, H. Brown, P. and Wells, A.S. (eds), *Education: Culture, Economy, Society*. Oxford: Oxford University Press.

NCE (National Commission on Education) 1995. *Success Against the Odds: Effective Schools in Disadvantaged Areas*. London: Routledge.

Reynolds, D. and Packer, A. 1992. 'School Effectiveness and School Improvement in the 1990s', in Reynolds, D. and Cuttance, P. (eds), *School Effectiveness: Research, Policy and Practice*. London: Cassell.

Stoll, L. 1995. 'The Complexity and Challenge of Ineffective Schools', paper presented to the European Conference on Educational Research and the Annual Conference of the Educational Research Association, Bath.

Thrupp, M. 1998. 'The Art of the Possible: Organizing and Managing High and Low Socio-economic Schools'. *Journal of Education Policy*, 13 (2): 197–219.

Part III
Schools and Local Development Policy

5
Education and Local Development Policies in Sweden[1]

Anders Lidström

Stimulating economic growth in the locality is a major policy of contemporary local government (Pickvance and Preteceille, 1991; Waltzer, 1995). Whether the objective is to establish a position in competition with other world cities, to handle the effects of the closure of a major local industry or to alter rural population decline, local authorities in the Western world define as their task to facilitate local economic growth. This is somewhat paradoxical, as in several countries, local economic development policies touch upon, and even exceed the power limits set by central government for local authorities (Hudson, 1993). However, the policies correspond to strong local demands. Public decision-makers, the business community, the media and local voluntary organizations often have common interests in growth (Logan and Molotch, 1987; Logan and Swanstrom, 1990).

For a long time, American local government has regarded the facilitation of local economic growth as a major task (Wolman and Goldsmith, 1992). In Western Europe, where issues of social welfare have been more prominent among local authority functions, economic development has now emerged as increasingly important (Goldsmith, 1992; Keating, 1995; Moulaert and Demazière, 1995; Lidström, 1996). Financial support from the EU to structural development has enhanced this tendency in several countries, as this usually presupposes additional resources from local and regional government (Chapman, 1995). Also Eastern European local authorities are concerned with economic growth (Mitchnek, 1995).

In Sweden, a number of studies have indicated the increasing involvement of local authorities within this policy area (Pierre, 1992; Hudson, 1993; Svenska Kommunförbundet, 1995; Henning, 1996). Not only have local authorities become more eager to facilitate and stimulate the local economy but they are also more interventionist in their approaches and more likely to combine different strategies to enhance local growth (Hudson, 1993). Case studies show that local coalition building and co-operation between local actors is an important component in the development strategies (Olsson, 1995). There is also an increasing tendency for local authorities to co-operate with other municipalities and with different regional actors (Svenska Kommunförbundet, 1995) and across national borders (Östhol, 1996).

Apart from the general increase in these activities, there is also a tendency to subordinate other policy areas under an overaching economic development objective and to broaden the set of instruments used in local development policies (Cp. Friedmann, 1991). The traditional means included advice to businesses and provision of subsidized land and buildings for industry. However, increasingly, other fields of local government activities have been conceived of in terms of whether they can contribute to local growth. Cultural, recreational and environmental policies are used in order to increase the attractivity of the local area (Svenska Kommunförbundet, 1995; Nutek, 1997). But in particular, there is a strong tendency among local authorities in Sweden to make use of municipal education for this purpose. A recent survey of Swedish local government chief education officers indicate the extent of this change (Table 5.1).

The education policy means, which have been used, may include the adjustment of upper secondary and adult education courses to the needs identified by the existing local business community and dominating local industries. They may concern the use of education to develop a knowledge base with relevance for new branches of business, previously not represented in the locality. In small local authorities and in sparsely populated local areas, the most significant means is perhaps to establish an own upper secondary school, often with the purpose of reversing a negative population trend.

From Table 5.1 it can also be concluded that there are differences between local authorities with regard to whether municipal educa-

Table 5.1   The use of schools as a means for local economic development
during the last five years

	%	N
To a larger extent	50.2	112
No change	45.3	101
To a lesser extent	4.5	10
Total	100.0	223

Note: The following question was asked: 'What has the general tendency been during
the last five years: Have schools, to a larger or lesser extent, been used as a means to
make the local area more attractive for business and enterprising?'. The question was
included in a survey of all local government chief education officers in March 1996.
The response rate was 89.2 per cent.

tion increasingly is included within a local economic development
strategy. Half of the local authorities report no or lesser use of
schools as a means to make the local area more attractive for business and enterprising. Why is it such a variation and what characterizes local authorities with different strategies? These questions are
the concern of this chapter, which aims at describing and analysing
the role of municipal education in Swedish local development policies. The empirical analysis is undertaken mainly on the basis of
survey data from the Swedish municipalities.

The broadening of local economic development policies

The previous, narrower, local economic development strategies of
advice and subsidies to land and industrial buildings were aiming
at directly effecting the economic activities in the local area.
The new broader strategies, including recreation, culture and
education, are more indirect means. They are oriented towards
creating a favourable environment for growth (cp. Svenska
Kommunförbundet, 1996). As a consequence, it is more uncertain
whether they bring any positive effects in terms of general
economic development in the local area and if they do, effects are
only likely to appear in the long run. Hence, investing local tax
money in a broader local economic development strategy is a
highly risky project.

The reason why local government, despite this uncertainty and
the attached political risks, still pursue these policies is that growth

in the local economy is regarded as a major asset for the locality. Most policy-makers regard growth – within reasonable environmental and social limits – as the key for the creation of a better community. It makes it more likely that the inhabitants will be able to make a living in the local area and it creates a ground for a greater range of public and private services. Also, the alternative, to do nothing, may make the local area less advantageous in the competition with other authorities.

Since the mid-1980s, a number of national decentralization policies have been introduced within the school sector. By transferring power and responsibilities from central to local level, a more flexible system, better adjusted to specific local needs, was aimed at. In the previous system, central government control of local education was much stricter. After decentralization, local authorities can to a larger extent decide, for example, what courses to offer and their content. They can also decide whether to run upper secondary education and how the local education system should be managed and organized. In addition, the system of central government grants to local schooling has been transformed. Previously, a number of ear-marked specific grants – together providing almost half of the resources to the local school system – were given directly to the schools or the local government Education Committee. Now, central government has lumped together practically all its financial support to local government into one general grant, which is provided to the local council. Thus, the role of local government to make priorities between different policy areas and specific needs has become more pronounced. Several important implications follow from this new power setting (cp. Lidström and Hudson, 1995).

First, a new pattern of interdependence has emerged. Managers and political decision-makers within the local school sector have become more dependent on decisions made by local politicians not directly involved in education matters. However, as the overall amount of resources to local schooling, at the same time, has been reduced (Skolverket, 1996), it has become increasingly important for educationalists to explain for non-educationalists why schools are crucial. Emphasizing what schools can do for the local community and how education can promote the overarching goal of local economic development are frequently used arguments. At the same time, the leading politicians of the local council, with the overall responsibility for the development of the local area, have been given a new means through educational decentralization. The schools used to be difficult to influence by the local politicians as they were heavily controlled by central government regulation. Thus, the recent changes have made it possible to integrate education with other local government services and to use schools for broader purposes. In essence, the new local power setting within education brings together the interests of those local decision-makers who are educationalists with the ones who are non-educationalists into a common interest in using schools for local economic development.

A second major change with consequences for local economic development policies concerns the new role of central government in regional policies (SOU 1997:13). A national policy of regional balance was introduced in Sweden during the 1960s. The purpose was to increase national economic growth by reducing differences between expanding and retarding areas and thus making better use of the resources in the less developed areas. A major feature of the policy was the aim to reallocate resources from the centre to the periphery. For example, central government used investment subsidies to stimulate private industries to move but the state also created new industrial projects of its own. This policy continued during the 1970s. However, at this time, a major industrial restructuring started and the focus of the policy was shifted towards solving suddenly emerging crises in localities hit by industrial closure. Hence, short-term emergencies came to replace long-term development. The redistributive character of the regional policy gave central government a key position but also developed local expectations on state support when industrial crises appeared.

This policy was reconsidered from the end of the 1980s, partly due to the financial problems of central government, but also as a result of the perceived inefficiencies of the policy. However, an additional factor was that problems of unemployment and weak economic activity, which previously was mainly concentrated to the northern and inner parts of the country, now appeared everywhere. Hence, a different strategy was required. The new policy came to emphasize that regions and localities themselves had to identify their comparative advantages and develop their own assets. The industrial crisis emergency room was closed down. The role of the state was reduced to provide financial support to development projects and its redistributive functions were reduced. In addition, the Swedish membership of the EU has further emphasized the role of the regions and also provided new financial resources for economic development. In sum, the state has not only withdrawn but also made clear that development is a matter for localities and regions themselves. The local authorities have been keen to accept this extended responsibility.

However, these changes also have to be understood in a wider context. Neither decentralization policies, nor changes in national regional policy orientations are specific for Sweden. Instead, they reflect fundamental changes, which are common throughout most of the Western world. These were outlined already in the introductory chapter. However, of particular importance here is the globalization of the world economy and its consequences in terms of a changing labour market. Deregulation of world trade and the financial markets, the increasing role of the EU and the development of knowledge-intensive production have put pressure on previously protected traditional industrial economies. The work force is expected to be more flexible, which include demands on higher levels of education and life-long learning.

With tighter competition follows stronger need for the public sector to create favourable conditions for private business. According to one line of thought, this is most efficiently achieved if the public commitment is minimized. However, the question of how the public resources can be used to stimulate business is relevant, independently of the size of the public sector. Direct subsidies are generally not accepted, since these are regarded as hampering efficiency and long-term competition, even if large sectors, in particular agriculture in Europe, is still strongly supported by public means. However, the public sector can provide an infrastructure favourable for growth. Hence, the changing role of municipal education may be regarded as an adjustment at micro-level to these macro-transformations.

Educational resources and strategies

In order for a local authority to make use of education as a part of a local growth strategy, two basic requirements have to be present.

First, there has to be educational resources in the local area, available for such a purpose. Secondly, these resources have to be used strategically towards stimulating growth.

Educational resources may, of course, be defined in different ways. A narrow definition would include only formal education through schools and universities, whereas a broader concept may also encompass all kinds of learning, which takes place in collective or individual forms at the local territory. Admittedly, also learning taking place through for example organizational development, personnel training or individually could be linked to a growth strategy, but we will restrict our use of the concept to the former, more narrow definition, not least since the latter is empirically difficult to handle. Further, the focus will be on formal forms of education within the frame of the local authority.

Primary and lower secondary education (*grundskola*) is present in all Swedish local authorities. In practice, we expect them to play a role as providing basic training and education and not to be directly linked to a growth strategy. However, this is not to say that they are unimportant. There are examples of collaboration between municipalities and industry with the purpose of increasing quality in primary education and good primary schools can be an argument when firms in the local area are trying to recruit specialist personnel. Nevertheless, they are not the key focus of our analysis.

All local authorities also offer municipal adult education courses (*kommunal vuxenutbildning*). These are available to people who have completed their primary and lower secondary education and want to improve or extend their knowledge, perhaps in order to be able to apply to university courses. With just a few exceptions, all local authorities offer adult education courses on upper secondary level (Skolverket, 1995). We expect that some courses of this kind could be linked to a growth strategy. Hence, practically all local authorities have the minimum requirement to include education in such a strategy.

Most local authorities provide upper secondary education (*gymnasium*). This is available for children who have completed their lower secondary courses. The upper secondary schools offer more specialized courses, largely within the frame of one or several of 16 nationally specified programmes. They prepare for work in specific trades as well as provide the basis for further education. In 1995, 74 per cent of the municipalities[2] offered upper secondary education within at least one of the nationally specified education programmes.

Finally, even if this is outside local government control, the presence of higher education in the local area is a highly valued asset in terms of local economic development. At the moment, there are universities, university colleges (*högskolor*) or nursing colleges (*vård-högskolor*) in 35 local authorities in Sweden. Also, higher education courses of varying duration are offered on decentralized basis. In 1995/96 such courses were available in an additional 84 local authorities.[3]

Hence, the different educational resources which may be used in a local growth strategy tends to, on the whole, follow the shape of a ladder (compare Table 5.2). At the bottom of the ladder are local authorities with only primary, lower secondary and adult education. As we move further up, more resources are added to the previous ones. At the top of the ladder are the cities with a permanent institution for higher education.

One way for a local authority to improve its position is to aim at increasing the available educational resources. Generally, this pursuit follows a clear pattern. Municipalities try to reach next step on the ladder. For example, local authorities that already have upper secondary education try to influence neighbouring universities or

Table 5.2   The ladder of educational resources

	Local authorities with specified educational resources within their area 1995.	
	%	N
University, university college or nursing college	12.2	35
Course of higher education offered	41.3	119
Upper secondary school	74.3	214
Primary, lower secondary and adult education	100.0	288

Note: Five local authorities in which courses of higher education are offered are exceptions from the assumption that the ladder is cumulative, as they lack upper secondary school.
Sources: Data from the National Agency for Higher Education and Lärarförbundet, 1995.

university colleges, or perhaps even central government to establish decentralized courses of higher education in their area. In this pursuit, municipal and regional authorities can also contribute with buildings and other study facilities, but the means may also include outright financial assistance (Henning, 1996).

Another example concerns the initiatives by small and medium-sized municipalities to start their own upper secondary school. Before 1992, new upper secondary schools could only be established after decision by a state regional authority, but after this requirement was abolished, and until 1995, a third of the municipalities without upper secondary school have started one.[4] The purpose has been to make young people more prone to stay in the area after they have finished their education, but also to contribute to a general increase of the level of education in the area. In a time when knowledge and education is emphasized as major assets in the modern information society, an upper secondary school is a significant step for many small local authorities, not least since they require considerable municipal funding.

Hence, in order for the local authority to use education as a strategy for local economic development, a first requirement is that there are relevant educational resources in the local area, However, the other prerequisite is that these are being used in order to promote growth. One way of categorizing means, which we will use here, is with regard to the extent to which they are adjusted to the present local business structure.

A first type of means is focused on *adjustments to private business already existing in the locality*. This may include courses and programmes aiming at providing a labour force with skills and knowledge demanded by already established firms. The significance of these means is underlined in a study by Pierre (1995). While the general tendency between 1989 and 1993 was that private firms' demands on the local public sector decreased, at the same time they requested more of special training programmes. In one sense, adjustment to the present structure is a low-risk strategy, as affected firms can be involved as partners and their demands are explicit and concrete. However, there is an element of high risk involved. If these businesses are closed down, students may find their education obsolete. From the local authority's point of view, it also has the disadvantage of binding educational resources, which could be better used for a more long-term strategy.

The second type concerns education aiming at *facilitating the development of new firms or branches in the locality*. The local authority may have a clear idea of what new firms or branches it wants to promote, and can develop courses accordingly. If the local area is characterized by a one-sided labour market, it may want to stimulate the emergence of additional businesses within other sectors. Also, education can be used in order to develop local knowledge and enterprising within sectors that are regarded as future-oriented, such as IT and micro-technology. However, this strategy is more risky, as these courses have to be developed without links to local firms.

Within a third type, finally, the outcomes are even more uncertain. Instead of focusing on specific fields of economic activity, local authorities may want to use education as a means to *establish a more innovative and creative climate in the local area*. This may include courses on innovation and entrepreneurship but may also concern other educational measures that the local authority regard as enhancing citizen creativity.

In our previously mentioned questionnaire to local government chief education officers in March 1996, questions were included corresponding to these three types of educational measures. In addition, a fourth, more general question was asked. The results are reported in Table 5.3.

Among municipalities who use education in order to enhance local growth, the most common strategy is to adjust to needs of already existing firms. Using education in order to develop new firms or branches is the least common of the alternatives, probably since this requires a conscious plan in which alternatives, perhaps not yet present in the local area, are identified. A further analysis of the data which the table is based on indicate that only 16 per cent of the local authorities make no use of education at all in order to improve the attractiveness for business and enterprising. Most local authorities have at least one measure and 41 per cent use at least three; 15 per cent pursue all four measures.

Local variation

From the discussion so far, it is obvious that there is considerable variation between local authorities with regard to the use of education as a part of a local development strategy. Some municipalities

Table 5.3 How do local authorities use education in order to enhance local growth?

	% Agreeing	Total N
Upper secondary or adult education has:		
– been adjusted to needs among businesses already present and active in the local area;	63.8	235
– established new courses with the purpose of contributing to the development new firms or branches in the local area;	39.2	232
– changed in order to contribute to developing a more innovative and creative environment in the local area;	58.4	231
– in other ways been used to make the local area more attractive for business and enterprising.	47.9	219

Note: Local authority chief education officers were asked the following question: 'Has, during recent years, upper secondary or adult education in your municipality been changed in any of the following ways with the purpose of making the local area more attractive for business and enterprising?' The response alternatives at each statement were yes and no.

make no use of it whatsoever, other pursue at least one, and sometimes also a broad range of strategies. Some prefer safe and familiar measures and other are willing to take greater risks. How can this variation be understood? What are the promoting and restraining factors when local authorities make these choices?

Basically, these choices are preferences by actors. Constructing a development strategy is assumed to be a conscious and purposeful undertaking and is not something that is being blindly forced on decision-makers by outside structural conditions. However, even if these decisions must be seen as actors' choices, they, nevertheless, are highly influenced by the particular local setting in which the municipality is situated. Conditions in this setting function as incentives for action, and we will argue that two kinds of conditions are particularly important for whether and how local authorities decide to include education in a local development strategy. One set of incentives are related to the local problems that are present in the area and the other focus on educational resources of the locality, which may be used as a means to solve these problems.

Local problems and educational resources may be seen as two separate categories of incentives. However, they are clearly related to each other in the sense that considerable problems may be regarded as a lack of resources and a resourceful situation may be seen as a lack of problems. At a very general level, one might conceive of problems and resources as end-points on a continuum. Thus, we would claim that local authorities located at the ends of the scale would be more likely to make use of education for local development, than those situated in the middle. However, in practice, problems as well as resources are much more complex categories, and may actually both be found in the same locality.

Local problems concern various disadvantages in the locality that hampers economic development. These disadvantages may be related to, for example, the geographical location of the area, the population density, the particular mix of branches of business in the locality or the characteristics of the local workforce. Problems may appear as high unemployment, strong dependency on traditional manufacturing industry and a low level of education among the population. The final outcome of these local problems may be a population decline. Indeed, previous studies have already established a relationship between local problems and the emergence of local economic development policies (cp. Hudson, 1993, 1995). Hence, we will suggest that in areas where problems are severe, local authorities are more likely to make use of education in order to promote local growth.

We also assume that *the educational resources* of the locality are important. We have already indicated that the presence of these resources is one requirement for the inclusion of education in a local development strategy. Therefore, the extent of these resources, perhaps as indicated by the position on the ladder of educational resources, is likely to be an important explanation for what local authorities do. The higher the position, the more actively is education included in a local development strategy. Attention should also be drawn to the particular content of these resources, as more diversified resources would provide better means for adjustments to specific development needs. Also, upper secondary schools vary with the extent to which they emphasize vocational training. Whereas the theoretical programmes tend to have a more general scope, the vocational ones are often more closely adjusted to specific trades and branches. We will expect that those who mainly offer vocational courses will be more likely to use education as a part of a growth strategy and in particular will focus on the needs of businesses already established in the local area.

Analysing problems and resources

What are the answers to our questions on how the local variation can be understood? The empirical analysis, to which we are now turning, will be undertaken on the basis of information from the Swedish municipalities about conditions between 1994 and 1996. Data on different ways of using education as a part of a local economic development strategy, already reported in Tables 5.1 and 5.3, are included, together with data on local social, economic and political conditions and the local education systems, collected from official statistical and other public sources.[5]

In the analysis, the dependent variable will be represented by five dichotomized variables. The first two concern the overall level of activity whereas the remaining three represent different ways of stimulating local economic development. The explanatory relevance of seven different local problems has been investigated. These are high unemployment, high daily outflow of the working population (which means that a large share of the citizens of the municipality is dependent on employment elsewhere), strong dependency on industry, low level of education, sparse population and a negative population development. In addition, it is examined whether a regional explanation is relevant. Northern Sweden has traditionally been a region with particularly severe problems. The results of the analysis are reported in Table 5.4.

The overall conclusion must be that the existence of local problems, generally, is not a particularly important incentive for municipal decision-makers to use education in a local development strategy. Most bivariate relationships are either unclear, mixed, or negative. Only one problem is consistently linked to the policy in the way we expected, namely unemployment, but also the regional division between the North and the rest of the country follows a similar pattern. However, the explanatory relevance of unemployment is striking. High unemployment, more than other problems, is regarded as such a threat to the local community that triggers political action of the kind investigated here.

Table 5.4   Local problems and the use of education in a local development strategy (%)

	Level of activity		Measures		
	Some activity	High activity	Present firms	New firms	Innovative climate
Unemployment 1995					
High	86.7	51.5	80.0	44.0	64.0
Medium	83.8	38.1	57.1	44.6	58.0
Low	72.6	33.3	55.3	28.4	53.3
Measure of difference	14.1	18.2	24.7	15.6	10.7
Daily labour force outflow/inflow 1994					
Strong net outflow	77.1	21.3	53.5	31.4	57.8
Moderate net outflow	79.0	42.6	65.9	42.0	56.1
Net inflow	89.1	50.8	74.6	46.2	62.1
Measure of difference	– 12.0	– 29.5	– 21.1	– 14.8	– 4.3
Employment in industry 1994					
High	83.8	38.1	71.1	35.8	54.9
Medium	80.2	43.2	64.4	43.7	57.0
Low	79.0	40.4	53.8	37.5	65.1
Measure of difference	4.8	– 2.3	17.3	– 1.7	– 10.2
Upper secondary educated share of the population, 1994					
Low	64.4	29.4	48.0	31.5	46.7
Medium	89.2	46.4	71.6	48.6	62.2
High	88.9	45.3	70.9	37.6	65.9
Measure of difference	– 24.5	– 15.9	– 22.9	– 6.1	– 19.2
Population density 1995					
Sparsely populated	71.4	45.8	52.5	46.2	60.8
Medium populated	87.3	36.0	70.4	38.8	56.3
Densely populated	84.7	40.3	68.9	32.4	58.3
Measure of difference	– 13.3	5.5	– 16.4	13.8	2.5
Population development, 1985–95					
Decreasing	77.9	28.1	51.4	45.6	57.1
Moderately increasing	80.5	40.3	65.9	36.6	58.5
Strongly increasing	84.6	43.3	72.3	36.6	59.5
Measure of difference	– 6.7	– 15.2	– 20.9	9.0	– 2.4
Region: Northern Sweden					
Northern Sweden	90.5	52.6	60.9	47.7	77.3
Rest of Sweden	79.0	38.1	64.6	37.2	54.0
Measure of difference	11.5	14.5	– 3.7	10.5	23.3

Note: A measure of difference is calculated by subtracting the value of the least problematic group from the value of the most problematic.   (*continued*)

Table 5.4   (Continued)

The five measures of the dependent variable represent the following:

Some activity	utilize at least one of the measures listed in Table 5.3;
High activity	utilize three or four of the measures listed in Table 5.3;
Present firms	uses education to meet needs of businesses already present in the locality;
New firms	uses education with the purpose of developing new firms or branches;
Innovative climate	uses education to develop a more innovative and creative environment.

Many other relationships are negative. Municipalities characterized by rapid population increase, a net daily inflow of labour and a well-educated population are more keen to develop these policies than municipalities at the opposite ends of these scales. This seems to support an explanation in terms of resources, rather than problems. However, as all these variables are related to population size, is could be suspected that the relationships are spurious. Therefore, a control for population size was undertaken. It showed that the original relationships remained, even if they were slightly weakened.

On the whole, the choice of different measures follows this overall pattern. However, a number of exceptions are worth noticing. The strength of industry in the locality is clearly related to choice of measure. Perhaps surprisingly, a one-sided local economy, with a dominance of industrial employment, goes with an emphasis on measures supporting business already present in the locality, despite the seeming need to develop new alternatives. Where industry has a weaker position, high-risk, more innovative means are more common. Interestingly, the relationship is the reverse in the Northern Swedish municipalities. It is more common there than in the rest of the country that local authorities emphasize innovation and new alternatives, whereas the regional division does not distinguish with regard to measures adjusted to firms already present in the local area.

What about the second set of explanations, which focus on the educational resources of the locality? We have assumed that the more of such resources, the more will a municipality use education as a means in its local economic development strategy. The previously developed ladder of educational resources will now be used as an indicator of the extent of these resources and we can investigate whether it can explain variations between local authorities. In Table 5.5, where the results of the analysis is reported, we also distinguish between municipalities with upper secondary education established before 1992 and those who have started such a school after deregulation, when these decisions became matters of local government discretion.

The general conclusion is that there is a strong connection between educational resources and the extent to which local authorities make use of municipal education in a local development strategy: Access to more such resources make municipal decision-makers more prone to use municipal education with the purpose of promoting growth.

A number of more specific observations can also be made. Local authorities with newly established upper secondary schools are least likely to make adjustments to firms already present in the local area. Instead, they tend to stress the development of new branches or the improvement of innovation and creativity in the local area. Indeed, a common reason for starting an own upper secondary school has been to support the development of a more diverse local business community. Another conclusion is that even if there is a university

Table 5.5 Educational resources and the use of education in a local development strategy (%)

	Level of activity		Measures		
	Some activity	High activity	Present firms	New firms	Innovative climate
Highest level of educational resources in the local area 1995:					
University/ university college	96.7	55.6	87.1	41.9	70.0
Higher education courses	82.2	52.9	72.6	45.2	60.3
Pre 1992 upper secondary education	92.9	34.6	61.0	47.4	63.8
New upper secondary school	66.7	30.0	40.9	42.9	54.5
Primary and adult education	62.5	25.5	50.0	18.0	43.8
Measure of difference	34.2	30.1	37.1	23.9	26.2

Note: The five measures of the dependent variable are the same as in Table 5.4. The measure of difference has been calculated as the difference between the first and last percentages in each column.

or some other form of higher education in the local area, the municipality does not solely rely on this for creating a good climate for business. Instead, having these facilities tend to make adjustments of municipal education even more common. However, measures aiming at developing new firms or branches appears to be most frequent in areas with well-established upper secondary education. Perhaps this function is performed by higher education in localities where there are such facilities.

Admittedly, drawing too extensive conclusions on the basis of these bivariate relationships may be hazardous. Educational resources are related to population size and hence, to the diversity of courses offered locally. The greater the diversity, the larger is the scope for providing traditional courses as well as those directly adjusted to local economic development needs. In Table 5.6, population size is introduced as a control variable in the relationship.

All indicators representing the dependent variable are dichotomized scales and also, the independent variable is an ordinal scale. This would, at least according to some interpretations, make Pearson's *r* less relevant as a measure of association. However, even if the choice may not be completely accurate from a statistical point of view, it provides a rough estimate and makes it possible to use

Table 5.6   Educational resources and the use of education in a local development strategy, controlling for population size

Pearson correlation coefficients and partial correlation coefficients					
	Level of activity		Measures:		
	Some activity	High activity	Present firms	New firms	Innovative climate
Bivariate relationship with ladder of educational resources	0.26***	0.23***	0.26***	0.17**	0.15*
Remaining relationship after controlling for population size	0.20**	0.18**	0.20**	0.24***	0.11

Note: Levels of significance (one-tailed test) is indicated by the following symbols:
* 0.05–level; ** 0.01–level and *** 0.001-level.

partial correlations as a technique for controlling the impact of other variables. The results indicate that population size is important, but that, nevertheless, the original relationships remain strong. The only exception concerns innovative measures, but these were not particularly closely linked to educational resources at the bivariate level. For one of the measures, the relationship becomes even stronger. Hence, our conclusion is that the amount of local educational resources remains highly relevant for the extent to which local authorities will use education as a part of a local development strategy.

Are other characteristics of the local education system relevant, apart from its position on the ladder of educational resources? As bivariate relationships, also the diversity of the upper secondary courses offered and the relative strength of vocational programmes, are important. However, after controlling for extent of educational resources, these relationships disappear, which further emphasizes the conclusion about the importance of these resources. However, there is one interesting exception. In local areas where a large share of pupils attend vocational courses, municipalities are more likely to use education as a part of a development strategy aiming at stimulating the emergence of new firms and branches. Hence, an emphasis on these, more practically oriented courses does not, as one might have assumed, restrict the focus to already established businesses.

Apart from these explanations, in the literature, reference has also been made to the role of political actors. The political majority of the council emerged as one significant explanation in Hudson's (1993, 1995) study of local economic development policies in Sweden and Britain. In both countries, socialist majority contributed to explain why policies varied. However, later studied have suggested that the party political aspects of local development policies have become less relevant and that there now is local political consensus around the importance for the municipality to stimulate local development (Henning, 1996; Svenska Kommunförbundet, 1996).

As illustrated in Table 5.7, the party political aspect still seem to have some importance, but the level of association is generally low. However, there seem to be a tendency that the highest values are reached where the socialist parties have a medium strength.

Table 5.7 The strength of Socialist parties, the political balance in the council and the use of education in a local development strategy (%)

	Level of activity:		Measures		
	Some activity	High activity	Present firms	New firms	Innovative climate
Socialist parties 1994					
Strong	84.4	41.7	63.3	46.2	56.4
Medium	85.5	43.5	73.8	39.7	61.5
Weak	73.3	37.0	53.9	31.6	57.3
Measure of difference	11.1	4.7	9.4	14.6	− 0.9
Political balance in the council 1994					
Balance between the					
blocks	86.1	44.4	72.3	39.5	63.0
Weak majority	80.8	44.9	62.7	42.7	56.2
Dominating majority	76.3	32.9	55.8	35.5	55.8
Measure of difference	9.8	11.5	16.5	4.0	7.2

Note: The five measures of the dependent variable are the same as in Table 5.4. The Socialist parties refer to the combined strength of the Social Democratic party and the Left party (*Vänsterpartiet*) in the local council. Political balance in council concerns whether the two party political blocks are equally strong, or whether one of them dominates. The measure of difference has been calculated in a similar way as in Table 5.4.

Therefore, it has also been investigated whether it matters if socialists and non-socialists are equally strong. Indeed when this is the case, decision-makers tend to include education in a local development strategy to a larger extent than in a situation when one party block dominates.

Problems or resources

So far, bivariate relationships have been investigated, but in order to be able to draw more general conclusions, the analysis should be carried forward to a multivariate stage. Table 5.8 summarizes an examination of the combined influence of six of the independent variables, used in the bivariate investigations. The dependent variable is the index of level of activity, which also was used in the previous analyses.

Table 5.8 Explaining the use of education in a local development strategy

Multiple regression analyses of all municipalities and of subgroups of municipalities with different population density. Beta weights and significance of t-value.

| | All local authorities | Subgroups of local authorities | | |
		Sparsely populated	Averagely populated	Densely populated
Unemployment 1995	0.1410	0.1033	0.0533	0.2323
	0.049	*0.363*	*0.664*	*0.098*
Upper secondary educated 1994	0.0347	0.2334	– 0.1115	0.1651
	0.630	*0.086*	*0.458*	*0.272*
Northern region	0.0951	0.2172	–0.0905	– 0.1591
	0.186	*0.091*	*0.538*	*0.142*
Educational resources 1995	0.3016	0.3517	0.2526	0.2194
	0.000	*0.004*	*0.084*	*0.110*
Socialist parties' strength 1994	– 0.0213	– 0.1987	0.0402	0.1114
	0.779	*0.130*	*0.765*	*0.460*
Political balance in the council 1994	0.1121	0.0334	0.0137	0.2580
	0.086	*0.778*	*0.916*	*0.032*
R^2	0.1629	0.3299	0.0574	0.3342
Adj. R^2	0.1386	0.2681	–0.0258	0.2676
N	213	71	74	66

Note: The two figures in each cell is the Beta weight and (in italics) the significance of the t-value. The dependent variable is an activity index of the number of different measures undertaken by the local authority (compare Table 5.3). This is an ordinal scale, which can vary between 0 and 4.

In the analysis of all local authorities, which is summarized in the first column, the resource explanation is strikingly dominating. Generally, when explaining why local authorities make use of education in a local development strategy, possession of educational resources is more important than the problems in the locality. The level of unemployment is the only problem that, to some extent, is relevant. Party political balance is also important, but it does nor matter whether the majority is socialist or non-socialist. However, on the whole, the explained variance is low which may indicate that there is a lot to be accounted for by variables not included in the analysis.

Another reason for the low level of explained variance may be that there is an underlying pattern among different subgroups of units, which becomes hidden in the overall analysis. A number of tests of different subdivisions have been undertaken and Table 5.8 also reports on the results from an analysis where the local authorities have been divided into three subgroups according to population density. However, a similar pattern emerges also if the material is divided after population size or population development.

A number of additional conclusions may now be drawn. Our suggested independent variables are relevant among the most and the least densely populated local authorities, but explains very little in the intermediate group. Also, educational resources have a strong position within all subgroups. However, the most interesting conclusion is that the relative importance of the different variables varies between the rural and the urban areas.

In the *retarding, sparsely populated rural areas*, there is an emphasis on the educational resources whereas the unemployment level, in these already problem-burdened areas, is not a significant driving force. However, a well-educated population, a location in the North and a bourgeois council majority also contribute to explain the involvement of education in a local development strategy.

In the *expanding, densely populated urban areas*, on the other hand, the main emphasis is on the party political balance of the council. Where the party blocks are equally strong, the municipality is more likely to use education to promote local growth. The competition for votes seems to enhance this kind of political activity. However, the level of unemployment and the extent of the educational resources are still important explanations. In these areas, which in a sense are more resourceful, the decision-makers seem to be more sensitive for problems of unemployment in the local setting.

Hence, different incentives seem to be important in different types of localities. Somewhat paradoxically, considerable educational resources lead to actions in areas with problems whereas party politics and problems of unemployment are driving forces in resourceful areas.

Conclusions

The analysis in this article detects a general tendency to increasingly involve education in a local government economic development strategy. However, not all municipalities have taken such steps and there are also differences with regard to what set of educational measures they use. Some aim at satisfying needs of firms already established in the locality, others emphasize education as a way of stimulating the growth of new firms or branches. A large proportion of municipalities combines different measures. Explanations to why activity varies are different in rural and urban municipalities. The size of the educational resources is the most important explanation in the sparsely populated municipalities, whereas balance between the party blocks in the council and high unemployment are the two most important factors behind activity in the densely populated areas.

The stronger involvement of education in a local development strategy is clearly linked to more general changes of the focus of Swedish local government. Local authorities remain the major provider of public welfare in Sweden, but this function has become less prominent as financial strain has reduced the generosity of the systems, at the same time as the scope for private alternatives within education, health care and social services has gradually increased. Instead, a growing responsibility has been the task of stimulating the growth of the local economy. This is clearly reflected in new national regional and labour market policies, which to a greater extent emphasizes local responsibility. However, local authorities themselves are also keen to develop local economic development policies and to make use of a wide range of local government services in this pursuit. Even if the focus of Swedish local government is undergoing a change, it must be stressed that welfare and local economic development policies should not be seen as incompatible. At the contrary, future municipal responsibility for welfare requires success in local economic development.

Whether the use of education in a local development strategy really leads to the expected economic results is a matter, which lies outside the scope of this study. Political decision-makers generally have great expectations about the potential of education but it has to be a task for further study to evaluate the impact of these policies. However, it should be emphasized that this assessment is difficult to undertake, since the relationship between policy and impact is indirect. The policy provides an infrastructure, which may or may not work as expected.

Hence, there is an obvious risk for a backlash. The enthusiasm in many local authorities about using education in their development strategy is overwhelming and is usually not balanced by a critical analysis of risks and drawbacks. Under such circumstances, the necessary distance to the projects may be missing. Obviously, some local authorities are better equipped than others, and all are not likely to succeed in their attempt. Only the future will show if this form of municipal policies will be successful or regarded as a major mistake.

Notes

1. A previous version of this chapter has been published as Lidström, Anders, 1998. 'Utbildning och kommunal utvecklingspolitik', *Kommunal ekonomi och politik*, 2 (2): 21–42.
2. The author's calculations on the basis of data from Lärarförbundet 1995.
3. Figures from the National Agency for Higher Education.
4. The system of upper secondary education was reformed in the beginning of the 1990s, which included the replacement of a set of nationally prescribed education lines with a broader set of programmes. The increase reported here represent the proportion of local authorities moving from having no nationally prescribed line to at least one nationally prescribed programme.
5. For further information about the data set, see Chapter 3 in this book.

References

Chapman, M. 1995. 'The Role of the European Union in Local Economic Development', in Demazière, C. and Wilson, P.A. (eds), *Local Economic Development in Europe and the Americas*. London and New York: Mansell.
Friedmann, J. 1991. 'The Industrial Transition: A Comprehensive Approach to Regional Development', in Bergman, E.M., Maier, G. and Tödtling, F. (eds), *Regions Reconsidered*. London and New York: Mansell.
Goldsmith, M. 1992. 'Local Government', *Urban Studies*, 29 (3/4): 393–410.
Henning, R. 1996. *Att följa trenden – aktiva och passiva kommuner*. Stockholm: Nerenius & Santérus förlag
Hudson, C. 1993. *Against All Odds: Local Economic Development Policies and Local Government Autonomy in Sweden and Britain*. Department of Political Science, Umeå University.
Hudson, C. 1995. 'Does the Local Context Matter?: The Extent of Local Government Involvement in Economic Development in Sweden and Britain', in Waltzer, N. (ed.), *Local Economic Development. Incentives and International Trends*. Boulder, Colorado: Westview Press.

Keating, M. 1995. 'Local Economic Development: Policy or Politics', in Waltzer, N. (ed.), *Local Economic Development: Incentives and International Trends*. Boulder, Colorado: Westview Press.

Lidström, A. 1996. *Kommunsystem i Europa*. Stockholm: Publica.

Lidström, A. and Hudson, C. 1995. *Skola i förändring. Decentralisering och lokal variation*. Stockholm: Nerenius & Santérus förlag.

Logan, J. and Molotch, H.L. 1987. *Urban Fortunes: The Political Economy of Place*. Berkeley: University of California Press.

Logan, J. and Swanstrom, T. 1990. *Beyond the City Limits: Urban Policy and Economic Restructuring in Comparative Perspective*. Philadelphia: Temple University Press.

Lärarförbundet 1995. *Årsbok för skolan 95–96*. Stockholm: Lärarförbundet/Lärarförlaget.

Mitchnek, B. 1995. 'An Assessment of the Growing Local Economic Development Function of Local Authorities in Russia', *Economic Geography*, 71 (2): 150–70.

Moulaert, F. and Demazière, C. 1995. 'Local Economic Development in Post-Fordist Europe: Survey and Strategy Reflections', in Demazière, C. and Wilson, P.A. (eds), *Local Economic Development in Europe and the Americas*. London and New York: Mansell.

Nutek 1997. *Kultur som strategi i lokalt och regionalt utvecklingsarbete*. R 1997:25. Stockholm.

Olsson, J. 1995. *Den lokala näringspolitikens politiska ekonomi*. University of Örebro.

Pickvance, C. and Preteceille, E. 1991. *State Restructuring and Local Power: A Comparative Perspective*. London: Pinter.

Pierre, J. 1992. *Kommunerna, näringslivet och näringspolitiken*. Stockholm: SNS förlag.

Pierre, J. 1995. 'When the Going Gets Tough: Changing Local Economic Development Strategies in Sweden', in Waltzer, N. (ed.), *Local Economic Development. Incentives and International Trends*. Boulder, Colorado: Westview Press.

Skolverket 1995. *Skolan: Jämförelsetal för skolhuvudmän*. Skolverkets rapport nor. 76. Stockholm.

Skolverket 1996. *Bilden av skolan 1996*. Skolverkets rapport nor. 100. Stockholm.

SOU 1997:13. *Regionpolitik för hela Sverige*.

Svenska Kommunförbundet 1995. *Kommunal näringslivspolitik under strukturomvandlingen*. Stockholm.

Svenska Kommunförbundet, 1996. *Framgångsrika kommuner – mot en ny näringspolitisk modell?* Stockholm.

Waltzer, N. (ed.), 1995. *Local Economic Development. Incentives and International Trends*. Boulder, Colorado: Westview Press.

Wolman, H. and Goldsmith, M. 1992. *Urban Politics & Policy*. Oxford, UK and Cambridge, USA: Blackwell.

Östhol, A. 1996. *Politisk integration och gränsöverskridande regionbildning i Europa*. Statsvetenskapliga institutionen, Umeå universitet.

6
In the Company of Schools: Schools and Local Development Strategies in Britain

Christine Hudson

> *Education is the best economic policy we have.*
>
> Tony Blair[1]

Introduction

This chapter focuses on the coming together in particular situations of a number of the main trends identified earlier in the book relating to globalization and the growth of the knowledge economy. The interplay of these tendencies is examined within the context of local education policy and local economic development. A weaving together of education and economic development as a consequence of the increasing importance of knowledge in the global competitive economy has been apparent not only at the national but also at the local level. The more traditional definition of local development in terms of economic, technical and physical infrastructure has been challenged by the emergence of a parallel, more holistic development discourse in which education, health, care, culture, environment, and other quality of life issues contribute to an interactive creation of welfare and growth. Social, economic and environmental goals are linked and balanced and the importance of knowledge creation and human resource development in achieving economic development are acknowledged. The attractiveness of an area in terms of its quality of life, the skills of its workforce, its creativity, its

access to knowledge, ideas, new technology, suppliers and customers, its 'soft' enabling infrastructure, are increasingly important.

While globalization has meant a weakening of the nation state in
some respects, the salience of cities and localities as independent
actors has grown and they are increasingly important as arenas of
competitive struggles for economic opportunity. This process is
being reinforced by the promotion of an attitude of self-reliance in
which localities are encouraged to take greater responsibility for
their own well-being and future and find their own solutions or
strategies for dealing with their particular problems. They need to
(re)create their own particular identities and specializations and
develop their comparative advantages in order to be able to survive
and thrive in the global market. More flexible forms of cooperation,
aimed at facilitating development, are emerging between local stakeholders from different sectors. Through these, activities can be co-
ordinated and resources used more effectively, thereby producing
synergy effects. Coupled to the prominence given to knowledge in
attaining economic development has been an increasing emphasis
on the need to make education more relevant to the needs of business and to imbibe in the potential workforce the values of entrepreneurship and the skills required for future economic growth.
Business has been encouraged to take greater responsibility and to
play a more prominent role in the formation and implementation
of public policy. In the sphere of local education policy, these
changes are reflected in the growth of closer relationships, often in
the form of partnerships, between schools and businesses and in the
increasing importance given to education in local development
strategies.

Attention here is mainly on developments in the UK drawing on
case studies of two British local authorities, Birmingham and
Cheshire.[2] Although roughly similar in population terms,[3] the contexts of the local authorities studied are very different. One is a
major city with high unemployment and below average levels of
educational attainment, whereas the other is a relatively affluent,
fairly rural county with below average unemployment and above
average educational achievements. The questions considered here
are whether these differences are reflected in the educational policies and approaches being developed and how they are related to
broader national and international trends.

Globalization as diversity and the importance of the local

Globalization does not simply mean homogenization. Parallel with the assertion of the global is the resurgence in the importance of the local and the particular (this is discussed in more detail in Chapter 1). The globalization of social relations is also contributing to the uniqueness of place. Wider and local forces come together in particular ways in particular places so that each constitutes a distinct mixture of wider and more local social relations and may produce results that would not have happened otherwise (Massey, 1994; Hudson, 1995). Further, it has been seen as the paradox of the nature of the global competitive challenge that its resolution increasingly lies in the local community. This can be linked to the shift from an economic system based on mass production, Keynesianism, macro-economic regulation and the welfare state to a more politically and economically deregulated system and the development of a more decentralized and regionalized form of economic organization. Other developments that are often associated with globalization, such as the increase in the number of supranational organizations, may not only be harbingers of convergence, but may also contribute to divergence. The EU, for example, not only promotes integration. Through its emphasis on subsidiarity and its provision of structural and regional funds (which local government can access) it is also playing an important role in facilitating local action.

Changes in the nature, structure and organization of work, new lifestyles, new social movements, immigration and emigration and so forth have led to greater differentiation, heterogeneity and complexity in society. These developments have challenged national government's monopoly on policy-making, representation, legitimation and questions of identity and a more differentiated polity is appearing (Rhodes, 1997). This is leading to a fundamental change in the state's traditional functions and way of working. Power is increasingly dispersed in networks (both upwards and downwards) and a mode of self-regulation is emerging, in the sense of self-management of society by responsible groups and associations (Cooke *et al.*, 1997). Thus governance, where policy is formulated through interactions between actors in different networks and service provision is shared among a range of agencies, both public and private, is replacing traditional forms of government. In many spheres, national blanket solutions have become less appropriate and responsibilities have been decentralized to the local level.

The (l)earning economy

The growth of the knowledge society has also accentuated the importance of education in economic growth and competition. Access to both theoretical and practical knowledge is playing an increasingly important role in a society that is gradually becoming more based on the production, transfer and sharing of knowledge than on trade in goods. It is no longer possible to think in terms of a *lifelong job* but rather in terms of *lifelong learning*. In many countries, education and training have been seen as playing a key role in stimulating growth, ensuring long-term development, restoring competitiveness and reducing unemployment. For example, the need for a skilled workforce in order to be able to compete in the world economy has been emphasized in recent years (Husèn *et al.*, 1992), as has the importance of education in achieving social cohesion and generating wealth (The Council for Industry and Higher Education, 1997; Närings- och handelsdepartementet, 1997). The British Prime Minister, Tony Blair, has gone as far as to state: 'the successful nations will see education as the key economic and social imperative for us all'.[4] This, coupled with the influence of neo-liberalism during 1980s and 1990s and demands for greater efficiency and effectiveness in the public sector, has led to increased partnerships between public and private actors, particularly in the sphere of local economic development (Syrett, 1997). Local government is becoming less a provider and guarantor of a level of welfare provision and supportive infrastructure for its citizens and more an enabler, intermediary and agent of change (Lloyd and Meegan, 1996). There is an emphasis on entrepreneurship, on working together with others and on economic development.

The importance of education in the post-industrial society has meant that schools have been included in the process of building the knowledge driven economy. However education has been much criticized for acting as a brake on national economic advance; for failing to produce a workforce capable of competing in the global arena; and for lacking the ability to adapt vocational skills to market needs and thereby improve the flexibility of the labour market. The nature of this debate has meant that actors representing different interests (public and private) have been involved in finding ways of rectifying these problems, and making the form and content of education more relevant to the requirements of the 'world of work'. This has led to educational reforms that include a greater involvement on the part of firms and industry. The boundaries between schools (and their staff) and the world of business have become increasingly permeable. Schools are being encouraged to be more market-like in their behaviour (Basini, 1996), to have closer relationships with local businesses so that the potential workforce will acquire the skills required for future economic growth and to promote entrepreneurship from an early age (see, for example, DTI, 1998).

Education has been shifted out of 'its firm location within the sphere of reproduction into a closer relation to the sphere of production' (Ball, 1990:79) and pupils are increasingly regarded as human capital that will eventually fill roles in the economy (Bradford, 1995). The mutual benefits arising from closer relationships between schools and businesses have been strongly emphasized, guides for building more effective links have been produced (jointly sponsored by governmental departments and business consortiums, Miller, 1993) and partnerships between schools and business have flourished in recent years. A survey carried out in Britain in 1992 showed that 92 per cent of secondary and 56 per cent of primary schools had links with business (DfE, 1993). At national level, the Departments of Employment and Education have been amalgamated to form the Department for Education and Employment (DfEE).

Employers' organizations have not confined their interest to the general structure, organization and direction of education, but have also been highly involved in issues concerning the curriculum, syllabi, course literature, and teacher recruitment (Jamieson, 1985). For example, business has been influential in the introduction of more work related learning and qualifications such as the National Vocational Qualifications (NVQs). The new regulatory body, the Qualifications and Curriculum Authority, set up in 1997 was intended to be a close partnership between business and education to ensure that the national curriculum and vocational qualifications meet the needs of a rapidly changing economy.[5]

Institutional context for education–business relationships

Changes that have taken place over the last 20 years have underlined the relationship between education and economic development. National government has introduced measures that have brought local education authorities (LEAs) and schools into closer co-operation with businesses. The latter have been given a key strategic role in local economic development through their influence on policies and planning for the provision of education and training in their communities. Concerns, for example, to tailor the curriculum better to the needs of the labour market led to the introduction, in the mid-1980s, of the Technical and Vocational Education Initiative (TVEI) to improve vocational training for 14–18 year-olds. In order to obtain money under this initiative, the LEAs had to meet a number of criteria including the provision of work-related learning and experience in local enterprises, industry and business within the curricula. Schools were forced to link with businesses. The business-dominated Training and Enterprise Councils (TECs),[6] replaced the TVEI in 1990 and now have the main responsibility for training in relation to vocational education. These have private company status and are producing shared policies and strategies for local government and local businesses. Local authorities, while represented on the boards of TECs, have had their role in relation to training marginalized and many careers services have been privatized or set up as partnerships between the local authority, the TECs and/or private business.

Other developments bringing the worlds of work and education closer together, encouraging business placements in schools and work experience for both teachers and pupils, include Compacts and Education Business Partnerships (EBPs). Compacts are partnerships between pupils, secondary schools, colleges and employers to increase school-leavers' awareness of job opportunities and to equip them with the skills required for the world of work. The Compact employers provide work-related activities and there is work shadowing, in both directions, between teachers and industrialists. EBPs, established through co-operation between Chambers of Commerce and Industry, LEAs and TECs, have as their mission to unite education and business organizations in a common purpose to improve education, personal development and employment opportunities for young people.

The involvement of business in education has continued follow-ing the election of a Labour Government in 1997. The White Paper *Excellence in Schools* (DfEE, 1997) stressed the importance of involv-ing parents and communities (including business) in the education of children and developing effective partnerships at the local level to raise standards in schools. The central role of business in educa-tion has been heavily underlined in the development of the concept of Education Action Zones (EAZs) introduced in the 1998 *School Standards and Framework Act*. The zones are composed of clusters of schools[7] working in partnership with the LEA, parents, businesses, TECs and others and are supposed to be financed partly by govern-ment and partly by other partners, particularly business. High hopes are placed on EAZs as 'standard bearers in the new crusade uniting business, schools, local education authorities and parents to mod-ernize education in areas of social deprivation' and the leading role given to business is expected to 'bring new skills, experience, funding and radical ways of working into education' (DfEE, 1998a).

Education in local development policies

The closer relationship between education and economic develop-ment has also found expression in local development strategies. A highly qualified workforce, research and development, technology transfer, life-long learning and continuous professional develop-ment are important for a city or locality to be able to assert itself in global competition. Many municipalities are emphasizing their attractions as places in which to live and work and thereby retain and/or attract a skilled workforce and encouraged endogenous growth as well as inward investment. They are utilizing education as part of broad development strategies (Hudson, 1996) that include cultural, educational, environmental and human resource develop-ment aspects as well as more traditional economic/industrial initia-tives. For example, a well-educated workforce able to adapt to changing skills required by new developments in technology and the changing demands of the market can attract or facilitate the growth of new industries and sectors. A feature of these strategies is that they stress an interdisciplinary, co-operative, more holistic approach in an interactive process of creating growth and welfare.

As discussed in earlier chapters, global and national processes of change affect places differently, with some advantaged by or able to take advantage of these changes and others disadvantaged by them. While part of a common national context, areas have particular local histories, experiences, cultures, traditions, and political, social and economic relationships. Global changes interact with these local characteristics in differing ways to produce differing effects. Strategies are developed locally in response to particular local needs, even if frameworks are set by national government. The differences between places give rise to variations in emphasis and content, which reflect different local agendas, priorities, problems, needs and opportunities. 'National government produces national solutions. Local government is about producing differentiated solutions – all cities are different and need different solutions.'[8]

Many successful initiatives being taken at the local level have and are informing national policies. In the case of the two local authorities studied here both the forerunner to Compact and to the national system of education–business partnerships were developed in Birmingham at the end of the 1980s. The initiatives the city took concerning setting targets for improving on previous best have also influenced recent national policy and its local learning partnerships have functioned as a prototype for the Learning Partnerships introduced by the government in 1999.[9] Similarly, ideas developed by Cheshire County Council regarding training for the more disadvantaged formed the basis for a government programme introduced in 1996. However, policies and activities developed in particular contexts to meet specific local needs and/or as innovative responses to particular local problems do not necessarily travel well. They may lose their flexibility and appropriateness to meet and/or solve problems if they are implemented as blanket national solutions.

The next section focuses on the two case studies and the particular relationships between education and economic development that are emerging within these specific contexts. It is structured as follows: first, a profile is presented describing the local authority context and the position of education. This is then followed by an analysis of the main thrust of education's role in economic development. Next, given the increasing emphasis, nationally and internationally, on the need for co-operation between different actors in economic development, the role of partnership is examined, and particular attention is paid to the education–business relationship at both local authority and school levels.

Birmingham

Profile of Birmingham

Birmingham is a large, multi-cultural, industrial city, the second largest in Britain (and the largest unitary metropolitan local authority) with a population of over 1 million. It grew rapidly at the beginning of the century as a major centre of manufacturing in Europe. Its wealth was based on metal manufacturing (and later car manufacturing) and craft workshops. It had a thriving economy and relatively low unemployment even in previous periods of economic recession. There was in-migration of people with the necessary skills to support the growth of manufacturing industry. However, the recession in the 1980s and the decline of the traditional manufacturing industries affected the city very adversely. Unemployment rose dramatically, reaching double the national average. Approximately one-third of jobs in the city disappeared over a 30-year period. In 1961 Birmingham supported 685,000 jobs but this had sunk to only 432,000 in 1993. The emergence of a very different kind of manufacturing based on innovative, high-tech industries and demanding new, more qualified skills has left the city with an enormous problem of skills mismatch.[10] In many areas, the living standards and life opportunities of the poorest are low. About half the population is living on or below the official poverty line and there are severe problems of social exclusion.

By the early the 1990s, the city was facing massive structural, social and economic problems. Education had been starved of investment over a long time and there was a record of poor educational attainment and performance was below the national average. However, changes in leadership in education (both political and administrative) at this point appear to have functioned as a catalyst for a fundamental change in the city's *educational culture*. An Education Commission was set up in 1993 to review the present and future needs of the city's education service. It revealed widespread dissatisfaction with education policy in the city, serious problems of under-achievement and under-resourcing. There was a realisation that much of the thrust of the city had gone wrong and that if something were not done about the education system it would have massive kickbacks into Birmingham's long-term economic development. This led not only to specific measures to improve, for example, literacy and numeracy in schools but also to education being put at the centre of the City's long-term economic development strategy.[11] Under the leadership of a highly committed and dynamic chief education officer, it began to develop its image as a *learning city* where education is given an important role in regenerating the city and improving its position in the global economy. A better-educated and appropriately skilled workforce was regarded as a prerequisite for economic growth.

How is education being linked to economic development within the specific Birmingham context? The City has lost its old position as a dynamic, leading manufacturing centre and is searching for a new niche in the global economy. Human resource development, particularly the enhancement of the skills, abilities and confidence of local people has been seen as the key to successful and sustainable regeneration and to achieving competitive advantage. This led Birmingham City Council to establish 'education in the years coming up to the Millennium as paramount to the regeneration of the communities of the City'.[12] Measures such as setting up *Local Learning Partnerships* (which bring together organizations involved in employment, education and training issues), and developing a *Corporate Lifelong Learning Strategy*[13] have been seen as the way to ensure that this is recognized in the development of local and city-wide regeneration strategies.

Reactions on the part of both politicians and city officials to the very tangible negative effects of the development of the knowledge economy have encouraged the development of what can perhaps be described as an egalitarian approach which emphasizes valuing all in the system. Faced with, for example, severe problems relating to the exclusion of large parts of the population (such as the unskilled, the low skilled and even those with traditional skills) from the labour market, a massive push has been taken to raise educational standards right across the board and achieve '*success for everyone*'.[14] This has entailed concentrating on *improving on previous best*, at the level of the individual child,[15] the school and the whole LEA. Although there is a recognition that changes in the education system have meant that schools and other educational institutions are in competition with each other, stress has been laid on the importance of building consensus within and around education.[16] The future of Birmingham is seen as resting not on producing a knowledge elite but on developing the skills and abilities of the population as a whole.

This is reflected in interviews and in documents produced by the City where the emphasis is on both *integration* and *diversity*. This apparent contradiction can be understood in terms of the City 'celebrates difference', that is, it recognizes the contributions made by the particular knowledge, abilities and potential possessed by different groups and individuals but seeks to produce an inclusive development strategy. This is important given that about 25 per cent of the population as a whole and about one-third of children at school are from minority ethnic groups. Exclusion can be costly not only in terms of the social problems it creates but also for the City's image and position if it is to attract, retain and generate investment, competence, knowledge, innovation and compete in the global economy.

The idea of integration is reflected in the regeneration strategy which is seen as involving the whole city, not just the local authority.[17] All the different stakeholders within the city are regarded as having a role to play and a contribution to make – public, private and voluntary; women and men; young and old; and different ethnic groups. There is a strong emphasis on public–private and community partnerships. At city-wide level there has been, since 1994, close co-operation, through the economic development partnership, between the City Council (Economic development), the Training and Enterprise Council and the Chamber of Commerce in the production of the annual economic development strategy. In 1998 the strategy was, for the first time, developed jointly by a partnership of these three bodies.[18] At local level, community involvement in decisions affecting local areas has been fostered through the introduction, in 1997, of Local Involvement, Local Action (LILA). The initiative aims at creating a closer relationship between the City council and local communities. People have an input into local (ward) development plans in which education is given a high profile. The aim is to encourage the engagement of the whole community in local schools and education.

Education's role in economic development

Economic development is no longer seen in terms of simply providing physical infrastructure and/or loans and grants to businesses;

health and welfare are also given a vital part in the economic development process. The need for an integrated approach and to build linkages between different agencies, not only traditional economic actors but also, for example, education, housing and social services is stressed. Actors from both public and private sectors give education a central task as a driving force in economic regeneration and emphasize the need to build closer links between education and work. In the words of the City's Chief Education Officer, Birmingham is determined to make the concept of the 'learning city' a reality and not just rhetoric. He argues that Birmingham is changing from a city that did not need to put a high value on education to one that realizes that its survival depends on improving the educational standards of achievement of all its citizens.[19] This is echoed, for example, in the Economic Development Strategy, which sees people as the local economy's most important asset and argues that a prerequisite for Birmingham to achieve a competitive advantage is a better educated and appropriately skilled workforce.[20]

Given the key role of education in the city's economic development strategy, how is this being expressed in concrete terms? How is it impacting on schools and education in the city? A number of aspects can be identified. A more interactive relationship has developed between education and the local community (particularly business). This is reflected in the growth in the number of partnerships and other forms of co-operation and interchange between education (schools and the LEA) and other actors both from the public and private spheres, particularly local firms. National policies strengthening the role of the market in education have fostered an increase in businesslike behaviour and practices in schools. Schools are in competition with each other even in Birmingham. They need to develop particular profiles, strengths or niches in order to be able to survive. Nevertheless, there is a strong element of egalitarianism in Birmingham's strategy. It places a clear emphasis on improvement for all, on lifting from the bottom. This appears to be tempering some of the thrust of the market-based philosophy in education.

Position of partnership

The idea of partnership particularly between public and private actors has been highly promoted in Britain, as a way of making public services more effective and efficient and saving taxpayers' money. Stakeholders from all sectors in Birmingham have enamoured this concept and it permeates education and economic development strategies and policies. There is considerable emphasis on different actors working together both to improve educational attainment for all and to improve the city's competitiveness in the global economy. Local government officers and politicians stress the importance of partnerships as a way of strengthening the local authority's ability to take responsibility for its citizens despite diminished powers and funding and of delivering better services.

The commitment to partnership figures prominently in the City's official publications and reports. In a situation, where different funding regimes and competition for resources have created a fragmented scene, Birmingham City Council aims to lead in the establishment of a city-wide co-ordinated approach to provision, 'through new models of partnership, both within the City Council itself and with other providers'.[21] This is echoed in Birmingham's educational development strategy which argues that the LEA needs to have partnerships with, for example, schools, community groups, the business community, the media, unions, voluntary bodies and statutory agencies if the strategy's overall aim is to be realized. There has to be 'a sense of shared responsibility and mutual accountability within the overall aim of improvement'.[22]

Partnership is also accorded importance at the individual school level. Head teachers and staff in schools emphasized the importance of partnerships with other actors, including the LEA, other schools, industry, and parents. These were seen not only as improving educational achievements, home–school relationships and the running of the school but also as a means for pupils to acquire the necessary skills for employment. 'It's important that the children acquire the skills relevant to a rapidly changing society. We're trying to achieve this through a partnership between home, school, governors and industry and through a work related curriculum.'[23]

The acknowledgement that schools in more disadvantaged parts of Birmingham cannot, on their own, meet the enormous challenges facing them led to the establishment of the *University of the First Age*[24] in 1995. Working with the local community and linking with all the other agencies that promote learning in an neighbourhood, including business, the *University of the First Age* aims to use the time that young people spend out of school during the evenings, weekends and holidays to help them develop further and enhance their learning experiences.

Stakeholders from the private sector also advocate education--business partnerships as a way of making education more relevant to the needs of the world of work. For example, promotional literature put out on behalf of all the Education Business Partnerships in the West Midlands region stresses the importance of building closer links between work and education under the slogan 'partnership pays, people thrive, businesses profit'. Getting business into schools and schools into the work place is seen as imperative to ensure that what young people learn, and how they learn, are relevant to the world of work. The Birmingham Education Business Partnership (BEBP) regards young people as the City's 'most precious resource' who will help secure the economic well-being of Birmingham. It introduced a Partnership Award scheme in 1993 'to recognize and celebrate established links between schools and companies and to encourage new partnerships'.[25]

Education–business relationship

City level

The crisis in its economic base led Birmingham to invest heavily[26] in education business partnerships since the end of the 1980s. The city established the forerunner to the national system of education--business partnerships in 1988. Much of the impetus for the Birmingham initiative came from industry. A working group, chaired by Sir Adrian Cadbury, a local leading industrialist, identified the need to bring the world of education and business closer together to raise the standard of qualifications and training among young people in Birmingham and thus improve the City's competitive position. The business input into the Birmingham Education–Business Partnership is still strong and its review in 1991 was carried out jointly by the Education Department, the Birmingham Training and Enterprise Council and Birmingham Chamber of Commerce and Industry. The partnership is controlled by a board made up of representatives from industry, education and training. Under this umbrella organization there are 10 autonomous local partnerships that work with pupils/students aged 4–19. Each has its own management board drawn from head teachers and employers. In 1996, in a move to rationalize the network of education–industry links, the

BEBP was merged with the Careers Partnership to form the Birmingham Careers and Education Business Partnership.

School level

Interviews with head or deputy head teachers suggest that the relationship between schools and business is changing and becoming more interactive. 'I think both of us are realizing that we've got points that we can help the other with, whereas before we tended to think we couldn't teach them anything and they couldn't teach us anything. There is so much similarity now at certain levels.'[27] Schools are no longer asking industry 'What can you do for us?', they are also saying 'What can we do for you?',[28] which is leading to a more reciprocal relationship. For example, teachers are becoming more involved in business training programmes, not just learning from them but also teaching on them and helping to develop them.[29] Teacher placements in industry, both in Britain and abroad, are becoming increasingly common and teachers are expected to bring something back that improves the school.[30]

Many considered that the relationship between their school and industry/business had become closer as a result of changes in vocational education, in the curriculum and the introduction of the local management of schools (LMS). The latter, for example, was considered to have provided schools with greater autonomy and more flexibility to decide their own priorities and solutions and respond to local needs. Schools frequently had tutors from industry and local business involved in teaching, syllabus development, pupil assessment and work-related activities. Some schools were trying to develop an entrepreneurial approach in which they work alongside representatives from the business community. This was seen as providing mutual benefits with pupils gaining a better understanding of the world of work and firms benefiting from youngsters who were more self-confidence and better prepared for employment.[31]

Interviews strongly reflected the fact that there are both positive and negative aspects to the closer relationship between education and business. Head teachers frequently expressed the feeling that they were now expected to run their school in a more business-like manner and that their role had changed from educationalist to manager. 'People still see me as a teacher but they also expect me to be a business manager, an entrepreneur, a financial expert and so on.'[32] League tables and other changes emphasized competition between schools, although it was pointed out that this was not necessarily completely negative. It was, for example, suggested that LMS's focus on the competitive aspects of education had improved educational quality, because 'if you are in a competitive situation with other schools, it makes you keener to make sure things are going OK,'[33] and decide priorities.

Schools appear to be acting increasingly like firms, with teachers frequently emphasizing the importance of trying out new ideas and risk-taking, and of becoming more entrepreneurial and innovative in order to survive in a more competitive situation and a global market. They are often working closely with companies and learning from industry. Many are trying out new ideas, teaching children to be innovative and see 'out innovating the competition'[34] as the only way to survive in the increased competition between schools. There was also recognition of the changing nature of the economy and the need to educate children for a global market. For example, in one school, the multi-cultural background of many pupils was seen as something that could be an economic advantage enabling them to move between 'worlds' and lock into specialized niches.[35]

Summary

Birmingham figures clearly as a city which is responding to the growth of the knowledge economy and the increasing importance of education in economic development. Forced to combat the effects of economic restructuring and decline, it is using the concept of a learning city to create an identity more appropriate to the new economic conditions and global competition. The significance accorded to education by the City's leadership (from both public and private sectors), in particular a highly committed and able chief education officer, has led to it being given a central role in the regeneration process. In order for Birmingham to survive and thrive in the global economy, it has been seen as necessary to raise the standard of educational achievement for all. Thus, although many of the changes taking place nationally and locally in education have led to greater competitiveness, in Birmingham this has been tempered by an emphasis on egalitarianism and inclusiveness. There is a strong emphasis on partnerships between the various local stake-holders and closer relationships between education and business are apparent at all levels, as is the introduction of more market-like behaviour and thinking into education and schools. Finally, the city has gone from being a laggard to become a front-runner for developments in education policy and many of its initiatives have become prototypes for national policies.

Cheshire

Profile of Cheshire

The County of Cheshire is situated in North West England. It is a largely rural, fairly affluent, and predominantly 'middle-class' county[36] with a population of roughly 1 million in 1997. The majority of its towns are small- or medium-sized set within attractive countryside and providing a pleasant, high quality living environment. There is a sense of well-being and the vast majority of residents like living in Cheshire and are proud of their county.[37] Despite its prosperous image, there are however some pockets of severe deprivation.[38] Although hit by the economic depression in the early 1990s, the structure of Cheshire's economic base meant that it was less severely affected than many other areas and it now has a relatively strong growth profile with increases in output, employment and in the labour force forecast in the 21st century.[39] There is a diverse local economy with the decline in employment in agriculture replaced by growth in services and manufacturing. Petrochemicals, food and drink processing, instrument engineering and automotive components contribute to a strong manufacturing and industrial base. Financial and business services have continued to grow and the County's historical assets and beautiful countryside have meant that tourism is a major employer. The County has a highly skilled, well-qualified workforce and a strong scientific base and is well represented at the leading edge of technology. This is reflected in the unemployment rate which is below that of the North West and the UK as a whole, in the average gross weekly earnings which are above the national and regional averages and high level of own-occupied housing.

A strong sense of pride in Cheshire's educational achievements and its 'world class workforce' permeates interviews with community leaders from the public and private sectors and policy documents and plans. There is a very widespread and explicit interest in education which is perhaps related to the 'middle-class' character of the county (and reflects the middle-class concern for education, see Chapter 3 in this book). There has been a strong commitment to education, the single biggest service provided by the County Council,[40] on the part of all political parties[41] and efforts made to protect it from cutbacks. However, changes in the national government funding system in recent years have meant that Cheshire is now one of the poorest funded county LEAs in England. Despite this, the County has only small pockets of under-performance and has continued to maintain and improve its traditionally high educational standards. Its pupils perform better than the national average at all levels of education and there is a higher proportion of young people in full-time education post-16.

What are the more specific features of how education is linked to economic development in Cheshire and how are they related to the local context in Cheshire? Its human capital resources give it potential to expand in high tech and other growth sectors requiring high skill levels and innovative capabilities. Thus Cheshire is in a good position to benefit from the development of the knowledge economy and improve its competitive advantage in the global economy. Education and human resource development figure dominantly in the County's development strategy which aims to improve the quality of life of the people of Cheshire. Schooling and training are seen as an integral part of providing opportunities that benefit the entire community and the importance of linking education, industry and the community is stressed. The high standard of Cheshire's schools and level of educational attainment are one of the key features being used to promote the County's image as a place for development and growth for business; to attract and retain highly qualified workers; and to improve its position in the global economy. There is an expressed belief in the importance of the different local stakeholders working together to produce the educational excellence regarded as essential for the future survival and well-being of the individuals and communities in Cheshire. The challenge is seen as creating a 'genuine and down to earth'[42] new learning culture which promotes lifelong learning for all. However, alongside the commitment to consensus and co-operation around education, there is also a recognition of the value of 'healthy competition' between schools and between service providers to ensure that resources are used efficiently and cost-effectively.

The economic development strategy underlines the importance of human resource development and of improving the occupational skills of the existing and potential workforce in achieving regeneration and economic growth within a sustainable and quality environment.[43] It is seen as vital to ensure that the workforce can meet the current and future needs of employers, so that Cheshire can improve its competitive position in the global market. However, the emphasis on excellence is tempered by the inclusion of a social element. Priority is also given to equality of opportunities in education for all regardless of age, ability or background and there is an attempt to balance both business aspects and community services. Thus, although an important part of the training strategy is to match the skill needs of local industries and businesses to help local people get jobs locally, the County also 'tries to act as a catalyst for new developments to broaden choice for disadvantaged groups'[44] so that the good educational opportunities available to most learners will be available to all.

Education's role in economic development

The advantages Cheshire possesses in terms of a well-qualified workforce and the high standard of its schools are being exploited and excellence in education and training are seen as the key to economic development. The importance of workforce development underpins Cheshire's economic development strategy[45] and the excellence of its educational achievement figures prominently in its promotional activities to attract both inward investment and qualified workers. Maintaining an attractive quality of life through all its services and enhancing the quality of the workforce through education and training to ensure the availability of skills, flexibility and enterprise are regarded as critical to the long-term health of the local economy.[46] This is also reflected in policy documents and plans produced by Education Service, where the main purpose underlying the Local Education Authority is given as promoting learning and human development[47] and influencing education and training provision so that they meet the needs of individuals and a modern economy.[48] Further, there is a commitment among local educational officers and politicians to ensuring that the belief in the importance of education for the future is shared as widely as possible and to meeting the learning needs not only of today but also of tomorrow.[49]

Position of partnership

The concept of partnership permeates Cheshire's economic development strategy and its education policies. Joint economic strategies are regarded as essential and partnerships with parents, schools, the local community and business are considered as central to the Education Services Committee's philosophy. It is piloting *Local Learning Plans* as a way to improve learning in local communities. Only a shared commitment to meeting the learning needs of children, young people and adults is seen as capable of producing the educational excellence necessary for the future survival and wellbeing of the individuals and communities in Cheshire. There is widespread agreement among local government staff, politicians and business representatives that the links between business and education have increased in number and importance in recent years. The principle of *Responsible Learning* is emphasised in relation to business, and involves positively promoting 'understanding and collaboration between Education, business and other community services'.[50]

The Economic Development Plan emphasizes the importance of co-ordinated actions and the need for effective partnerships between those interested in Cheshire's regeneration. Partnership working is promoted through the *Cheshire Economic Alliance* involving all key Cheshire public sector agencies and the business community. Joint strategies are seen as essential to successful bids for resources and strategic principles have been developed to form the basis for consensus and partnership actions. Stress is placed on the need for closer co-ordination between education, training and business.[51] The closer relationship with business and the need to keep up with and respond to rapid changes taking place in the economy is also having consequences for traditional local government ways of working and organization. The Economic Development Unit, for example, has adopted a more flexible and organic approach with it acting 'more like a business than a traditional local authority department'.[52]

Education–business relationship

County level

Unlike Birmingham there is not a single TEC or Education–Business Partnership covering the whole of the Cheshire County Council area, instead there are three Training and Enterprise Councils each responsible for an Education Business Partnership. Accordingly, the relationship between education and business is more diffuse at the local authority level, with differences between areas relating to the actors involved and varying problems faced. Nevertheless, there are well developed education–business relationships, possibly encouraged by the importance of research and technological development in Cheshire's local economy and by the high level of educational qualifications and performance amongst the local population.

Both Economic Development and Education services are involved in various types of relationships with the TECs, which have produced shared policies and strategies for the LEA and local businesses. Projects, such as *Pathways Towards Working Life*, aim at providing frameworks for educational/industry activities and involve activities 'to build up progression and introduce economic awareness at primary as well as secondary school level'.[53] Other initiatives focus on helping people from local business and education to make connections and form partnerships (for example, the *Education Business Connection*) or act as catalysts to attract financial support from the public and private sectors to create stronger links between schools and industry (for example '*All change at Crewe*'). The County Council and the TECs are also involved in exchange programmes with major local employers where, for example, teachers have been allowed on to company management courses and company employees have been seconded to local schools. It is considered to be beneficial for both managers and educationalists to gain insights into each other's 'worlds'.[54]

School level

At the school level relationships with business and industry were well developed and generally viewed in a positive light.

Education–business partnerships were seen by teachers and industrialists alike as benefiting both businesses and schools: helping firms to meet their business goals and schools to improve the quality of their education provision. Suggested benefits from employee placements in schools included enabling businesses to become involved in and influence the education process so that pupils obtain relevant skills, experience and qualifications to meet the needs of existing and potential local firms; improving the communication skills of their staff and making them more aware of the changes taking place in education by working alongside teachers; and helping young people to be more personally effective so that they will be able to function and progress at work and in society generally. In turn, it was suggested that teacher placements in industry can help schools enrich and update the curriculum; enable teachers to keep up with new developments in business and technology; and better prepare pupils for working life.

The message concerning the value and benefits of greater co-operation between schools and business was strongly mediated through external organizations involved in education and training such as the TECs. For example, encouraging employers to serve on the governing boards of schools was regarded as an important way of applying business experience to help manage schools effectively, allowing companies to have a direct influence on the running of local schools and enabling schools to develop 'enterprise awareness'.[55] The advantages for businesses of being engaged in education from the 'beginning', from primary school level, was very strongly promoted by the TECs. For example, 'If you want your business to be a long term success, you've got to plan for the future today – which means ensuring that tomorrow's workforce can respond to the demands which will be made of them.'[56]

However, educationalists frequently saw the closer relationships with the business world as more of a 'mixed blessing'. On the one hand, many of the increasingly numerous and extensive links and reciprocal arrangements between schools and industry were advantageous for the schools by, for example, providing extra resources and expertise or even altering the school leaving tradition and encouraging children to stay on after 16.[57] On the other hand, they were seen as signalling a change in educational culture associated with the introduction of a market philosophy and the encouragement of more businesslike behaviour on the part of schools that was not always considered to be appropriate in education. These ideological changes had fostered the development of a strongly market orientated system in which schools have more power but face more competition.[58] The view was expressed that the Local Management of Schools (LMS) had encouraged schools to become more entrepreneurial and changed their position *vis-à-vis* the LEA, leading them to see themselves as the customer with the freedom to go elsewhere if the County did not give them the service they wanted.[59] The role of school leader was also considered to have changed as a consequence of the introduction of market values and ethos into education, with head teachers frequently regarding themselves as more managers than educationalists and hence less attuned to developments in pedagogy. 'I've become more of a manager: a chief executive – responsible for finance and recruitment; a PR man – promoting and selling the school; an accountant and a personnel manager; and less of an educationalist.'[60]

Indeed, as the head teacher of a secondary school located in an area of high long-term unemployment pointed out, it is not always meaningful to talk about improving relationships between education and schools, as there may be very few local firms and technological changes mean that even those may need less workers 'The relationship between school and work is a difficult question in an area like this. We are seeing the emergence of a new underclass. We have youngsters who are becoming the second or even third generation unemployed – half of them won't get a job ... the industries around here are not replacing staff ... '.[61]

Summary

Cheshire's particular local political, social, economic and cultural experiences and relationships mean that it is advantaged by the growth of the knowledge economy. It is making good use of the high standard of skills and education of its population in its development strategy and is emphasising the importance of educational excellence in ensuring the present and achieving the future prosperity of the area. High quality learning is seen as a way of both generating endogenous growth and attracting inward investment as part of a holistic, integrated approach to economic development. There is a strong commitment to and a very positive view of relationships between education and business by stakeholders from both the public and private sectors which is leading to changes in ways of working and behaviour. Some concern was voiced by head teachers and education officers regarding the introduction of a market philosophy into education and the consequences for both pupils and education of increasing competition between schools (and pupils) in the struggle to achieve better results. Cheshire's fairly homogeneous and relatively affluent, 'middle-class' population and the absence of severe problems of social exclusion can probably largely explain its development of a more individualized strategy, with its emphasis on achieving success in competition with others. Nevertheless, there was also a strong commitment on the part of both officers and politicians to helping disadvantaged groups compete in the economy. Thus Cheshire's approach could be summed up as excellence temped by compassion.

Conclusions

The power of education as a force for economic development in the transition to the knowledge society was evident in both Birmingham and Cheshire. This was reflected in the important role education was playing in the local authorities' strategies for regeneration and development of their areas. However, there were differences in emphasis and purpose reflecting different local agendas, circumstances, and resources (both human and financial). For example, Birmingham with its poor record of educational attainment and past history of under financing of education was focusing on 'lifting from the bottom', whereas Cheshire with its high standard of academic achievement and long history of generous commitment to education was directing its efforts towards retaining and extending its standard of excellence. In Birmingham, the diversity of its population and the severe problems of social exclusion were generating a more 'egalitarian' strategy geared towards inclusion and a general improvement of standards of qualifications and skills for all. In Cheshire, on the other hand, the greater homogeneity of the local population and its middle-class characteristics were leading to a more individualized strategy, emphasising competition and achieving individual success.

Both studies exemplify the changing role of local government emerging in Britain and other countries. The local authority is moving from being a direct provider to being a facilitator, working in conjunction with others to achieve change and development. The local authority is not able 'to go it alone' it needs to work with others. This is reflected, for example, in the emphasis on partnerships between local stakeholders figuring in education and economic development in both Cheshire and Birmingham. There was a proliferation of partnerships at all levels ranging from individual to local authority wide. Some of these were intra-sectoral, that is between different public sector actors, for example between education and economic development departments, between the LEA and schools. Other partnerships were inter-sectoral, that is between public and private stakeholders within the local community, for example between the LEA and parents, between the individual school and parents, between the LEA and business, and between schools and local firms.

National policies formed a common context for the local authorities but their introduction and implementation had different consequences and effects in the two authorities. In both Birmingham and Cheshire politicians, education officers and head teachers alike saw one of these policies, the local management of schools (LMS), as leading to fundamental changes in education. Although it was regarded with some apprehension and mistrust when it was first introduced, LMS has been seen as marking a significant change in the relationship between the LEA and the schools. It has given schools greater responsibility and autonomy and is considered by many as marking a *'a change of culture'* in the local education system. This has forced the LEAs to redefine their role in relation to their schools and to find a form and style that fits their particular circumstances. Thus differences in the style and form of the relationships were evident between Birmingham and Cheshire. Nevertheless, there is evidence to suggest that both have been successful in the development of their role, measured in terms of the small number of schools that had chosen to opt out and become Grant Maintained and the very positive comments concerning the LEAs cited in interviews with teachers. Teachers considered that their role with the education authority had become more one of partnership rather than control.

However, some of the changes related to the introduction of a more market-based philosophy into education were regarded with less enthusiasm by educationalists. The negative side of closer relationship between education and business is that values of the market are entering education in ways that were seen as inappropriate or not in keeping with fundamental educational values and principles. Concern was expressed that schools were now in competition with each other, that children were being viewed as 'customers' rather than pupils, that head teachers had become managers rather than pedagogues. Nevertheless, in both cases the effects of the market were being tempered by local authority actions – Birmingham with its egalitarian strategy and emphasis on lifting the base and Cheshire with its own provision for the more vulnerable both in education and employment.

Another aspect of the growing variations in policies and approaches adopted by local education authorities and economic development department is that successful local policies are being used to inform national policies. Birmingham has become model for many of the policies being introduced by the Labour Government since 1997. Similarly, a training policy for the more disadvantaged developed by Cheshire Economic development was prototype for a national policy introduced in 1996. However, as one educationalist in Birmingham pointed out there are dangers inherent in this. Local solutions that have developed as a response to particular local circumstances may not always travel. What works in one area may not work in another. When a policy arises out of particular circumstances it is often characterized by flexibility and dynamism. However, if its reformulated as a blanket national policy and becomes compulsory then there is a risk that it becomes locked at that particular point in its development.

Notes

1. Rt Hon Tony Blair MP, in the introduction to DfEE 1998b.
2. These were qualitative studies based on in-depth interviews and analysis of secondary sources relating to education and economic development/business links. The interviews were carried out with economic development officers, education officers, head teachers and education–business representatives in the period June to October 1996. The documentation studied included published and unpublished

reports, committee minutes, policy documents and other material relating to education and economic development/business partnerships.
3. At the time of the study. Since then the urban areas of Runcorn and Widnes have become unitary authorities and are no longer part of Cheshire County Council.
4. The prime minister's New Year message reported in *Guardian*, 30 December 1999.
5. *The Times Educational Supplement*, 26 June 1998.
6. These are non-elected public bodies. Only one-third of TEC board members are selected from the public sector and voluntary bodies, the rest are from business.
7. Zones typically cover two or three secondary school and their feeder primary schools up to 20 schools in total in areas facing challenging circumstances in terms of underachievement or disadvantage.
8. Interview with Economic Development Officer, Birmingham City Council, 27 September 1996.
9. These were introduced in the Department for Education and Employment White paper *Learning to Succeed – a New Framework for Post-16 Learning*, Cm 4392, 1999.
10. Interview with Economic Development Officer, ibid.
11. Ibid.
12. *An Education Development Strategy for Birmingham Towards the Year 2000*, Birmingham City Council Education Department, October 1995.
13. Report of the Chief Education Officer, Director of Economic Development and Director of Leisure and Community Services to the Joint Economic Development, Education and Leisure Services (Leisure and Training Sub-) Committee, 22 July 1996.
14. Interview with officer responsible for Single Regeneration Budget project, 28 September 1996, and from minutes of Birmingham City Council Education Committee, 11 June 1996. Statement by the Chair of the Education Committee.
15. It is important to note that targets are set for the individual in relation to her/his previous best and not in competition with others.
16. Former Chair of the Education Committee, interview 27 September 1996.
17. Interview with Economic Development Officer, Birmingham City Council, 27 September 1996. This view was also reiterated in interviews with the Chair of Education, the officer responsible for the Single Regeneration Budget project, and the head of the Birmingham Advisory and Support Service.
18. *The Vision*, Birmingham Economic strategy, April 1998, Birmingham City Council, Birmingham TEC & Birmingham Chamber of Commerce and Industry.
19. Discussion with Birmingham's CEO, Professor Tim Brighouse and Stewart Ranson, Professor of Education, School of Education, Birmingham University, July 1996.

20. *Economic Development Strategy for Birmingham 1996–99*, Birmingham City Council, p. 29.
21. Report of Chief Education Officer, Director of Economic Development and Director of Leisure and Community Services to the Joint Economic Development, Education and Leisure Services (Leisure and Learning and Training Sub-) Committee: 22 July 1996.
22. *An Education Development Strategy for Birmingham Towards the Year 2000*, Birmingham City Council, Education Department, October 1995, p. 1.
23. Interview with head teacher, 2 October 1996.
24. Set up as a charitable company limited by guarantee. Interview with officer responsible for Single Regeneration Project, ibid.
25. *BEBP 1995 Partnership Award, Case Studies of Partnerships.* Birmingham Education Business Partnership.
26. In the words of the former chair of the Birmingham Education Committee 'When you talk to people in other parts of the country about the amount of resources we have put behind business-education partnerships, they are staggered.' Interview, 27 September 1996.
27. Interview head teacher, 1 October 1996.
28. Interview head of girls' Technology College, 2 October 1996.
29. Interview head teacher, 26 September 1996.
30. Interview head of girls' Technology College, ibid.
31. Interview head teacher, 1 October 1996.
32. Interview head teacher, 26 September 1996.
33. Interview head teacher, 1 October 1996.
34. Interview head teacher, 1 October 1996.
35. Interview deputy head, 2 October 1996.
36. In 1991 6.3 per cent of workers in Cheshire were professional and 17 per cent had a degree level qualification compared with 4.9 per cent and 13 per cent respectively for England and Wales.
37. Of all Cheshire residents 86 per cent liked where they lived. *Quality of Life Survey 1995/96*, Cheshire County Council.
38. This has been lessened following the restructuring of the county in April 1998 and the transformation of Halton and Warrington into unitary authorities which reduced the County's population by nearly a third.
39. *Cheshire Economic Report 1997 and 1999*, Cheshire County Council.
40. £462,000,000 in 1996/97 – over half the county's total budget.
41. Interview with the Chair of Cheshire County Council's Education Services Committee, 29 May 1996.
42. *Getting Even Better: The Education Development Plan for Cheshire 1999–2002*, Cheshire County Council.
43. *Cheshire Economic Development Statement 1996–1997.*
44. Interview with Economic Development Officer (Training), 29 May 1996.
45. Interview with the Head of the Business Unit, 29 May 1996.
46. *Cheshire Economic Development Statement, 1996–1997.*

47. *Purpose, Values and Principles for the Cheshire Education Service 1995/96: The Cheshire Education Strategy 1998–2001;* and *Getting Even Better,* Cheshire County Council.
48. *Education Services Group Plan, 1995/96,* Cheshire County Council.
49. Interview with the Director of Education Services, Cheshire County Council, 3 June 1996.
50. *Purpose, Values and Principles for the Cheshire Education Service 1995/96.*
51. *Cheshire Economic Development Strategy 1994–95,* Cheshire County Council.
52. Interview with Economic Development Officer (Training), ibid.
53. Interview with the Director of Education Services, ibid.
54. Interview with EBP Co-ordinator, North and Mid Cheshire TEC, 24 March 1997.
55. Interview with EBP, North and Mid Cheshire TEC, 31 May 1996.
56. *Growing Together – a Guide for Employers.* North and Mid Cheshire TEC, Education Business Partnership, 1996.
57. Interview deputy head, 3 June 1996.
58. Interview with the Director of Education Services, ibid.
59. Interview deputy head, 3 June 1996.
60. Interview head, 4 June 1996.
61. Interview head teacher, 31 May 1996.

References

General references

Ball, S. 1990. *Politics and Policy Making in Education.* London: Routledge.
Basini, A. 1996. 'The National Curriculum: Foundation Subjects', in Docking, J. (ed.), *National School Policy: Major Issues in Education Policy for Schools in England and Wales, 1979 onwards.* London: David Fulton Publishers in association with Roehampton Institute.
Bradford, M. 1995. 'Diversification and Division in the English Education System: Towards a Post-Fordist Model?', *Environment and Planning A*, 27: 1595–612.
The Council for Industry and Higher Education 1997. *Widening Participation in Lifelong Learning.* London: CIHE.
Cooke, P., Christiansen, T. and Schienstock, G. 1997. 'Regional Economic Policy & a Europe of the Regions', in Rhodes, M., Heywood, P. and Wright, V. (eds), *Developments in West European Politics.* Basingstoke: Macmillan Press – now Palgrave.
DfE 1993. 'Survey of School/Business Links', *Statistical Bulletin*, 10/93.
DfEE 1997. *Excellence in Schools.* London: The Stationary Office.
DfEE, 1998a. Press release 23 June 1998.
DfEE 1998b. *The Learning Age: A Renaissance for a New Britain*, Green Paper, Cm 3790.

DfEE 1999. *Learning to Succeed – a New Framework for Post-16 Learning*, White Paper, Cm 4392. London: The Stationary Office.

DTI 1998. *Our Competitive Future Building the Knowledge Driven Economy*, Cm 4176. London: The Stationary Office.

Guardian, 30 December 1999.

Hudson, C. 1995. 'Does the Local Context Matter?: The Extent of Local Government Involvement in Economic Development in Sweden and Britain', in Walzer, N. (ed.), *Local Economic Development. Incentives and International Trends*. Boulder; Colorado: Westview Press.

Hudson, C. 1996. 'The Education Business: Education's Role as Part of a City's Development Strategy in Britain and Sweden', paper given at a conference on the City and the Public: the Role of Education, Umeå, 13–14 December, 1996.

Husén, T., Tuijnman, A. and Halls, W.D. 1992. *Schooling in Modern European Society*. Oxford: Pergamon Press.

Jamieson, I. 1985. 'Corporate Hegemony or Pedagogic Liberation?: The Schools–Industry Movement in England and Wales', in Dale, R. (ed.), *Education, Training and Employment: Towards a New Vocationalism?* Milton Keynes: Open University.

Lloyd, P. and Meegan, R. 1996. 'Contested Governance, European Exposure in the English Regions', in Alden, J. and Boland, P. (eds), *Regional Development Strategies*. London: Jessica Kingsley.

Massey, D. 1994. *Space, Place and Gender*. Cambridge: Polity Press.

Miller, A. 1993. *Building Effective School–Business Links: A Practical Guide to Improving Quality*. London: Westex Publications Centre.

Närings-och handelsdepartementet 1997. *Det svenska företagsklimatet*. Stockholm: Närings-och handelsdepartementet.

Rhodes, R.A.W. 1997. *Understanding Governance: Policy Networks, Governance, Reflexivity and Accountability*. Buckingham: Open University Press.

Syrett, S. 1997. 'The Politics of Partnership', *European Urban & Regional Studies*, 4 (2): 99–114.

The Times Educational Supplement, 26 June 1998.

Local authority documentation

Birmingham

An Education Development Strategy for Birmingham Towards the Year 2000. Birmingham City Council, Education Department, October 1995.

BEBP 1995 Partnership Award: Case Studies of Partnerships. Birmingham Education Business Partnership.

Birmingham City Council Education Committee, 11 June 1996, Statement by the Chair of the Education Committee.

Economic Development Strategy for Birmingham 1996–99. Birmingham City Council.

Report of the Chief Education Officer, Director of Economic Development and Director of Leisure and Community Services to the Joint Economic

Development, Education and Leisure Services (Leisure and Training Sub-) Committee, 22 July 1996.

The Vision, Birmingham Economic strategy, April 1998. Birmingham City Council, Birmingham TEC & Birmingham Chamber of Commerce and Industry.

Cheshire

Cheshire Economic Development Statement 1996–1997.Cheshire County Council.

Cheshire Economic Development Strategy 1994–95. Cheshire County Council.

Cheshire Economic Report 1997 and 1999. Cheshire County Council.

The Cheshire Education Strategy 1998–2001. Cheshire County Council.

Education Services Group Plan, 1995/96. Cheshire County Council, Education Services.

Getting Even Better: The Education Development Plan for Cheshire 1999–2002, Parts 1 and 2. Cheshire County Council.

Growing Together – a Guide for Employers. North and Mid Cheshire TEC, Education Business Partnership, 1996.

Purpose, Values and Principles for the Cheshire Education Service 1995/96. Cheshire County Council.

Quality of Life Survey 1995/96, Cheshire County Council.

Part IV
The Governance of Learning

7
Changed Leadership Roles in Swedish Schools

Olof Johansson and Leif Lundberg

Introduction

In the international movement to reform and improve the perform-ance of education systems, various forms of decentralization are among the most popular strategies. Decentralization is thought to provide the means to cure a range of important problems, including bureaucratic rigidity, insensitivity to local needs, and lack of legit-imacy and local democratic control. Even a brief review of such efforts, however, reveals that a wide variety of purposes and mean-ings are attached to decentralization. Indeed, a variety of terms, with varying meanings, are used to label these efforts in the English language – for example, decentralization, deconcentration, deregula-tion, and devolution – and other languages (and nations) have terms and special meanings of their own.

Confusion about the variety of meanings and purposes is far more than just an academic issue. Disputes about the purposes of decen-tralization often become hot political issues, as contending stake-holder groups argue about what is intended by reform policies and what their long-term consequences are likely to be. Policy analysis research designed to clarify the goals and consequences of decen-tralization policies is, therefore, much needed. Examination of the decentralization reforms being adopted in various countries reveals a diverse set of potentially competing goals and rationales advanced to justify policy initiatives. These include the idea of enhancing such goals as: accountability, effectiveness, efficiency, flexibility and diversity, legitimacy and democracy, and empowerment through redistribution of authority and decision-making power.

Most reform endeavours explicitly focus on only a few of these objectives, but critics often see 'hidden agendas' behind the reforms. Cynics frequently contend that decentralization reforms are being adopted to facilitate cutbacks in central funding of government services by disaggregating and devolving decision-making (and related conflict) to regional or local levels of government. The 'good news', in effect, for lower levels of government is that they now control a wider range of policies and decisions; the 'bad news' is that, as part of the bargain, they are given reduced budgets to preside over. The basic idea is that a policy decision leads to implementation and that the outcome of the implementation process is what the policymaker originally intended. This is an idealistic way of looking at political decisions, or what we call, the myth of democratic culture (Johansson and Bredeson, 1999).

Why decentralization?

Why decentralization? There is no easy answer to this question. One answer can be the official one based on knowledge from implementation studies which show that the Swedish state can no longer regulate a school organization in the very strict way intended in the old, highly centralized system. Even with greater control and different steering bodies, it was difficult to uphold the national goals for the system because the conditions in the schools were too different (Lundgren, 1986; Lundgren and Wennås, 1987). The argument put forward for change was that, if the schools had clear goals and could implement these without too many restricting rules, the result would be much better than in a highly regulated system. Decentralization is seen as good for local democracy because important decisions are taken closer to the people involved and sometimes even with their participation.

Another argument, not as often used in the political arena, is that the state could no longer afford a system where the law regulated how much money different schools should be given. The solution to the problem was framelaws and block grants to the municipalities. An unspecified part of the block grant is for the school sector. Through this decision, the state has managed to lower its costs for education and forced the municipalities to take on greater financial responsibility. The problem today is, in many cases, that the municipalities cannot afford to take on the full burden and the result is a large variation in the budgets different schools receive. The amount varies according to geographical location and, of course, the size of the municipality (Riksdagens revisorer, 1999).

A further argument that we would like to put forward is that the state ran out of ideas on how to steer and govern the schools. The national political institutions had no good recipes for how to get the schools to change in accordance with the decisions of the political decision-makers. The learning community, in other words, the local school system, did not respond according to the old hierarchical top-down model for governing. It had become too independent and the goals of the state policies were no longer seen as important. Many of these policies were also challenging the old values of the school – one example is that teachers should work in teams and not alone, and another is that parental involvement should increase in the planning of all education (Skolverket, 1999).

Our purpose

In this chapter we will analyse and discuss what these changes have meant for the positions of principals (*head teachers*) and superintendents (*chief education officers*) in relation to important learning processes in schools. One hypothesis about the results of these reforms is that the greater freedom for local school policy-making is leading to more diversity, but possibly less equality in the provision of schooling. We will also discuss the current situation and the challenge for the future of the principalship and the superintendency. With regard to the latter, we also want to draw some conclusions from an empirical study. Our analysis will focus on the work of superintendents in small and large municipalities in relation to governing schools by goals and objectives. Many of the new demands on the local school board (*the education committee*), introduced when the school system was decentralized, require that the superintendent has a competent support staff – one that can work with evaluations, follow up studies, goal formulation, etc. In small municipalities this kind of support staff is missing. Against this background our hypothesis is that school boards in large municipalities with larger central school offices (*education departments*) will follow the law and it's intentions more closely than those in small municipalities with limited educational support staff.

Our data comes from an empirical study carried out in 1995 of all superintendents in Sweden. A total of 207 superintendents (74.2 per cent of all superintendents in Sweden) replied to the survey. The questionnaire consisted of four types of questions: demographic information, open-ended queries, Likert-scaled items, and rank–order responses.

Decentralization of power in Swedish education – a bird's eye view

Historically, Sweden has been a highly centralized country. The state has controlled most parts of the public sector. Education is probably the example where the state's influence has been greatest. Some examples: until the mid-1980s the allocation of resources for each school, and even each class, was decided by the Regional Board of Education which applied the national laws and rules, and appointed the vice principals of every school in the region. Principals throughout the country were appointed by the National Board of Education in Stockholm.

In every municipality there was a School Board (*education committee*) consisting of appointed local politicians. A superintendent (*chief education officer*) was head of the central school office (*education department*), there were principals (*head teachers*) for every school or school area and, for some larger school areas there were also one or more vice principals (*deputy heads*). Although the School Board was, in some ways, responsible for education in the municipality, the state was unquestionably the responsible authority in this field. Traditionally, the principal's main duty was to interpret the national rules and regulations. He/she was also responsible for planning and administration, finance and student welfare. His/her influence on the teaching and instruction processes in the school was, in general, very low. The reason being mainly that traditionally they were not supposed to direct or interfere with the teachers' work in the classroom. In the late 1970s, a discussion started in official documents about the need for a new role for school leaders.

The state wanted pedagogical leaders, school leaders who took greater responsibility and were more competent in leading the development of the pedagogical activities in their school. Many initiatives have been taken by the state since then to bring about this change. The most concrete example is the National Training Programme for Head Teachers that has been running now for more than 20 years (Ekholm, 1984; Heimer, 1998). Changing the role of the principal has not been an easy task. One important reason for this is the fact that the tradition of the autonomous teacher is very strong in Sweden. The process of acceptance of a new role for school leaders has been very slow (Nygren and Johansson, 2000). The highly centralized school system and the tradition of the autonomous teacher have made it very difficult for parents and other stakeholders to influence the processes of the local school. In the minds of ordinary citizens, the school is 'owned' by the state, and parents and others are not supposed to interfere.

In the 1980s, a process of decentralization started throughout the public sector. In the beginning of 1985, the Riksdag (the Swedish parliament) passed a new School Act. The new law marked a change from a very centralized, detailed and legalistically steered control system to one based on framework laws and governing by goals and objectives. It started a process of decentralization of power over the schools to the municipalities. An example of this decentralization is that the employment of teachers and principals was transferred from the state to the municipality. For principals, this happened in 1991 and somewhat earlier for teachers (Nygren and Johansson, 2000).

In 1991, the old National Board of Education was closed down together with the regional state boards of education making 750 civil servants redundant. It was replaced by a new National Agency for Education employing only about 250 people. Its two main tasks were to evaluate the ways in which the municipalities deal with their schools and help parliament and the government in preparing educational reforms. Under the previous system, the main task of the National School Board had been to help schools interpret the very detailed laws and check that they complied with them. The present National Agency for Education does not have this direct control function. It can still inspect schools but cannot tell them what to do. Recommendations must be given to the municipal council which then has the responsibility to act for change, if this is needed. Thus although the new School Act was introduced in 1985, the process of decentralisation was not complete until the national agency was reformed in 1991. However, there is still a national curriculum. The state makes decisions about the School Act, the national curriculum – the present is from 1994 – with accompanying syllabuses, timetables and grading system (Proposition 1992/93:220). The state also guarantees that international declarations and agreements that Sweden has undertaken to observe in the field of education are applied in the school sector. Nevertheless, after 1991, it is clear that the municipality is the main authority responsible for primary and secondary education in Sweden.

When Leif Moos and Stephen Carney (2000) summarize the tasks of Nordic school leaders they emphasize that the work of schools has become more complex and demanding, as has the nature of school management. There are new forms of public management that have encouraged accountability, effectiveness and competition. In the case of school systems, this has led to a rise in local site-based management where the leader is empowered with direct responsibility for the school processes and performance. Governance structures have been strengthened with the delegation of powers to lay members of governing boards such as parents and community leaders (Lundberg, 1998).

School leaders are now expected to take greater personal responsibility for all school matters. This can be seen in the new curriculum that highlights the role of the principal as the responsible pedagogical leader. It is also demonstrated by the way money for the school is allocated. The principal plays a greater role in financial matters. The new approach to school leadership views the leader as a key resource for building and maintaining teams of educational professionals as well as for achieving change and reform in an effective and efficient way. In this sense, the work of school leaders has become much more dynamic and complex. In the new decentralized structure, they are expected to make use of the formal structures, interpret the goals and objectives, as well as develop the skills and insights necessary to motivate and empower their colleagues (Lundberg, 1996).

In the process of decentralization, new demands and new expectations were put on the principal. Their overall duties are made very clear in the new National Curriculum from 1994 (Lpo 94). First, the principal is the guarantor for a nationally equivalent education.

Every school is required to meet the national standards, regardless of where it is situated geographically and the conditions under which it is working. Secondly, the principal is guarantor for pupils' and parents' rights as laid out in the National Curriculum. Thirdly, the principal is guarantor for education in his/her school meeting the national quality standards. It is also clearly spelled out that the principal is responsible for leading the development of the educational activities at the local school (Nygren, 2000).

Transferring responsibility for primary and secondary education to the municipality has also meant new and different demands on the superintendent. As head of the central municipal school office, the superintendent is, much more clearly than before, a key person in the education system. The position carries with it the responsibility to see to that all the schools in the municipality meet the goals and demands set by the state. The shift of power to the municipality also means that new demands are placed by the local political level. The superintendent, and indeed the principals, are serving two masters – one national and one local. While the decentralization and deregulation of the school system have meant a greater degree of freedom for the superintendent, they have also placed new demands on him/her to take initiatives, make strategic decisions and lead school development in the municipality (Cregård, 1996; Johansson, 2000).

In the recent years there have also been many changes in the way municipalities organize themselves. Nearly all have integrated different boards/departments. As a result the superintendents, as well as the principals, are no longer responsible only for schools (Regeringens skrivelse 1998/99:121). In most cases they are also responsible for day care centres, pre-school for six-year-olds, as well as after school activities for school children. One effect of this amalgamation has been that the policy from the 1980s (SOU 1980:19) of encouraging more women principals has been achieved. Today almost 60 per cent of all principals are women and the figure is even higher for the lower grades (Nygren and Johansson, 2000).

The new roles of principals and superintendents

The fundamental goals of the national school system are set out in chapter 1 of the Swedish School Act of 1985. Education within each type of school is to be equivalent, irrespective of where in the country it is provided. It is, in partnership with the home, to support the harmonious development of children into responsible adults and members of society. Pupils with special needs are to be taken into account. In addition, the School Act contains regulations concerning students' rights and the obligations of municipalities and county councils.

The starting point for conducting a discussion about the new role of principals and superintendents can be taken from the first chapter of the National Curriculum, where it is stated:

> The activity of the local school must be developed so that it corresponds to the goals that have been set. The principal organizer has a clear responsibility in this respect. Both the daily pedagogical leadership as well as the professional responsibility of the teachers are necessary conditions for the qualitative development of the school. This necessitates a constant examination of learning goals, following up and evaluating results, as well as testing and developing new methods. Work of this kind has to be carried out in active co-operation between staff and pupils in close contact with home and with the local community.
>
> (Lpo 94, p. 12)

According to the law and the curriculum, the responsibility of the principal is to safeguard that education in each school is nationally equivalent. For this reason, the principal is a key person and ultimately responsible for the school as a whole and for ensuring that each pupil receives a good education. The state has set up a national training programme for principals to make certain that they have the competence required to fulfil the task of leading the pedagogical development in the school, and to ensure that the rights of pupils and parents are respected. The National Head-Teachers Training Programme is open to all municipal school boards in Sweden to send any principals they wish to the programme. The reason the state has retained the programme is basically that it is viewed as a good way to improve the principal's competence in relation to the goals and structure of the national school system. The National Agency for Education has the overall responsibility for these programmes but they are carried out at six different universities.

In the old school system, it was very clear that the principal in each school was the key person for the protection of the idea of a equivalent school system. He/she was employed by the state and his/her task was highly regulated in laws and formal documents. The decentralization of the school system that has gone on since the mid 1980s has blurred this role. Today, the principal is employed by the municipality and the national school system, for which s/he is responsible, is an obligation that has been transferred to the municipality by the state. The position of the principal has become much more difficult (Johansson and Kallós, 1994). In the old system, s/he could always rely on support from the state for his/her decisions. If, for instance, a principal had to make public that a local political board or the municipal council had made a decision that conflicted with the intentions in the national plan for the schools, s/he was protected by the state because s/he was a state employee. Today, the principal needs to use all his/her professional competence to guide the school board in their decisions but without any real help from the state. If the municipal council, for instance, decides to cut the budget to such an extent that the schools cannot uphold good quality, then the principal is in trouble! The only way out is to try to explain the consequences to the superintendent and, together with other principals in the municipality, describe the effects of the budget cut on the quality of the education. In a situation like this, the new governing system for schools demands a much more political role on the part of the principal than the old system. The only help s/he can get from the National Agency for Education is that it can carry out an inspection, but that is a slow process. Further, educational quality is not a well defined concept, so the Agency will also have problems evaluating whether the cuts in the school budget will have negative effects on the standard of education in the school.

The best way to highlight the change is to present the way in which the 1994 National Curriculum for the schools describes the steering process. The National Curriculum states that the goals and guidelines for education specified in the School Act, the curriculum and the syllabi should be elaborated in the local planning of education. The measures the municipality intends taking in order to attain the national goals should be clearly stated in its Local School Plan. Important here is that the School Plan is approved by the full council, the highest decision-making body in the municipality, and not by the school board. The latter is an appointed body of municipal politicians, but the council is the only elected body at this level.

The Local School Plan is are supposed to describe the measures that the municipality is going to take to implement the national goals. However, these plans generally do not consist of measures to be taken, instead most contain the goals the municipalities have for the local school system. According to the study we carried out in 1995, there is a direct relationship between the school budget and the Local School Plan only in a very few municipalities. We also know that this it is even more so if the Local School Plan has been written by administrators instead of politicians.

One of the principal's responsibilities is to guarantee that the Local School Plan is used in his/her school. There should also be a Local Work Plan for the individual school that describes how the activities as a whole are to be carried out and organized. This document, as well as the Local School Plan, have in many cases not been active and living documents (Lundberg, 1996). Most of the time the teachers do not accept them as steering documents for the school. They only take part in creating them because they are required by law. This is a problem that some municipalities now have recognized and are trying to change. The way they are doing this is by shifting focus from steering and control to school development, follow-up studies and support. This shift in the steering approach on the part of the politicians is based on the research findings from studies of the implementation process.

Finally, in the 1994 National Curriculum, the state gives the teacher the responsibility, together with the pupils, to draw up Learning Goals. These, in combination with the needs and preconditions of different groups of pupils, provide the basis for selecting different working methods. We argue that this is the most important planning being carried out in the school system that has direct effects on what is happening in the classroom. However, the Learning Goals are very seldom documented in a formal way and remain, in most cases, in the form of a private document that the teacher shares with the pupils and their parents when they are visiting the school.

We would also argue that even if the running of the schools is now a municipal responsibility, most teachers still look to the state for guidelines and support (Lundberg, 1998). The municipality's power over the schools is linked to budgets and organization, but not to the basic values and tasks of the school. This might change in the future, but then local politicians would need to move from a traditional form of steering to one based on a dialogue with the schools around the Local School Plan and the Local Work Plans.

Some theoretical implications

As argued in an earlier study (Johansson and Bredeson, 1999), it is a myth that the political decision-makers have the capacity to govern the learning community. Effective policies that influence the values of educational leaders and the educational process are those created within the educational community and subsequently transferred to the political decision-makers. Considering these complexities, new policies will always be in great need of a democratic leadership that holds the same values as the political community.

Policy decisions tend to be value-based, and this makes educational reform initiatives difficult to implement. The myth of democratic culture can be described as an ideal situation in which the school political decision-makers and the learning community share the same values and culture. There is much empirical evidence that demonstrates that this is not the case. In reality, what occurs is illustrated in Figure 7.1: the political community makes a policy decision, in the next step, the decision is then passed on to the school learning community. If the learning community has a different set of values and culture, it views the original policy through a different set of lenses. These lenses change the substance and perhaps even the intent of the original policy (Begley and Johansson, 1998). Figure 7.1 represents this transformation in terms of white to grey. What is clearly a white policy from the perspective of the political decision-makers becomes varying shades of grey for professionals in the school community. The effect of the grey learning community culture is that the decision is implemented as grey, not as white as originally intended by the political community (Johansson and Bredeson, 1999).

Certain decisions made by the political community are least likely to be implemented in the intended way. These are decisions that

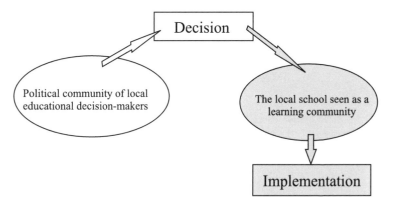

Figure 7.1   Value orchestration of the learning community by the political community

challenge existing values and norms of the school learning community and its culture (Johansson and Kallós, 1994) and policy decisions that are very political in nature. New policies can, of course, sometimes be varying shades of white because they are the result of political compromises. Principals are frequently confronted with this situation. They are also often faced with a situation which is problematic because the political majority has made an ideological decision which principals know will not be accepted by the majority of the learning community. These two types of decisions can be seen as extremes on a continuum, where the middle type of decisions could be seen as 'real' (this is explained below) decisions (see Johansson, 2000). These can sometimes be as problematic as the other two types if they are in conflict with the prevailing culture.

To be a leader in a public sector activity such as a school is, in some respects, very different from being a leader in a private sector company. In public schools, the role of the principal is to implement the goals and objectives set by the political community; to explain and motivate staff to follow political decisions, to implement policies, to handle resources (both money and personnel) carefully, to develop and expand activities within given political boarders and, while doing all this, still keep students, parents and staff in a good mood, that is, to be a democratic leader! Obviously, it would be much easier to do this if the political decisions the principal has to implement were clear and concise and accepted by all the political decision-makers. However, this is very seldom the case.

In Figure 7.2, we talk about three types of decisions: compromises, 'real'decisions and ideological decisions. With compromises, we mean decisions that have no real character because the intent of the decision has been blurred by all the changes that have been made to get a majority for the decision. By 'real' decisions, we mean decisions that most politicians, even if they represent different parties, want to see implemented and fulfilled (Gustafsson, 1983). Finally, by ideological decisions, we refer to decisions made by a single party

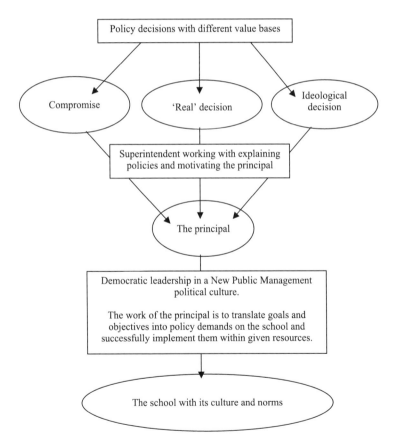

Figure 7.2 The principal in the policy stream

or groups of parties that have a similar understanding on an ideo-logical aspect of education. All these forms of decision put new demands on the principal in a decentralized system. In the old system, the principal could always turn to the state for help, but in the new system he or she is alone and has to both follow the national school laws and try to implement local policies within given resources – in a new public management environment (Hagström, 1990). The principal frequently finds him/herself in a situation where most of the politicians have different opinions about the content of the decisions taken and, even more problem-atic, they all too often believe that when the decision is taken it is also implemented. Another difficult aspect of the implementation process is that the principal also needs to try to keep everyone happy! By everyone we mean; politicians, members of the local community, the media, parents, students and staff.

We would like to argue that what is required of the principal in this situation is to apply the goals of the National curriculum, to be a democratic leader and, at the same time, work in a New Public Management culture (Hughes, 1998). The role of the principal in such surroundings is to translate goals and objectives into policy demands on the school and successfully implement them within the given resources.

Parents' interest in their children's well-being and academic train-ing in schools has always been a part of the principal's workday. However, we now increasingly see parents coming together as a pressure group in, for example, informal groups, in groups called upon by the teacher or principal and even in formal bodies – advi-sory school boards. If the school has a tradition of parents being active collectively and teachers and principals in the school value interaction with parents, then research has shown that these advi-sory school boards are more likely to be successful. However, if there is a silent contract, a pact between the teachers and the principal that the school should not engage in processes of change, then it is more likely that the prevailing school culture will dominate over external pressure for change. This can be done by employing delay-ing tactics or showing no interest or trying to find different obsta-cles or using value arguments to oppose suggested changes (Parker, 1998).

We think that, in the years to come, more and more interest in schools will come from agencies outside the school – parents, local community members, community organizations and the political parties. Different stakeholders will probably from time to time disagree about what is desirable in policies, procedures and outcomes. There can also frequently be an important difference between the values articulated by a group and the values to which the group is actually committed. The pressure on the school will be greater and the demands and expectations on superintendents, principals and staff to provide good education and excellent results will continually make itself felt (Fullan, 1998, 1999).

To illustrate this pressure from different stakeholders, we would like to look at school leaders and their two different roles as manager and leader. We will argue that a successful superintendent or principal must relate to and understand the importance of his/her school board's political decisions concerning the school, but s/he must also be a leader for the staff – democratic leadership – and motivate them to understand what the politicians want for the school. If the principal can manage this balancing act, we will have an ideal situation. If neither the staff nor the politicians are satisfied with the performance of the school leader, then we have a person who is a disaster in his/her role!

Our interviews with superintendents and principals in Sweden have pointed to the fact that they often operate in another way. They all dream of being able to work in such a way that both politicians and staff are satisfied, but they find this difficult to achieve in reality. Frequently the reasons given are differing opinions/values about what is good for the children and the school. However, it is often also reported that it is difficult to distinguish between personal, professional, organizational and social values in these situations. For school leaders, it is very important to be able to use educational arguments that are grounded in the value system of good democratic education in their discussions with politicians and staff. They must know which values are appropriate and justifiable in a given situation. Education leaders are agents of society accountable to an established system of educational governance, to the teaching professional, and to the members of the local community served by the educational system.

The theoretical base for all administrative decision-making is objectivity and rationality. Administrative decisions very often also can be characterized as 'ritual rationality', which occurs when the decision-maker hides the real intention or disguises unintentional effects of the decision by highlighting values acceptable to the stakeholders. This is frequently done in relation to economic cut backs and it is important for the school leader to be able to analyse this kind of decision from a value perspective.

In all the situations discussed above, it is very important that the principal realizes that the only way to successful implementation is through insightful and open communication. A communication that finds its strength in educational arguments for the proposed policy. Whilst it might be considered natural in theory that principals and leaders of schools should use arguments from their own field of expertise – education – this not always the case in practice. Begley and Johansson have shown that principals, both in Canada and Sweden, when confronted with critical decision-making situations that involve value conflicts tend to use the ratio of six managerial arguments, to three leadership arguments to only one educational argument to solve their problem (Johansson, 2000). We would argue that the reverse should be the case.

To summarize, there have been many changes going on at the same time in the Swedish education system. One very important change has been the implementation of a new steering system. The motives behind the reform were mainly two. First, there was a desire for decentralisation and simplification. Secondly, there was a need to devise new and more effective forms for supporting school development at the local level. As a result of the reform, the responsibilities of the different levels in the system were made much clearer. Particular responsibilities were articulated for three levels/actors in the system. First, there is the municipality, which has been given the overall responsibility for the prerequisites, processes and development of the local education system. Secondly, there is the principal, who is responsible for meeting the educational goals and standards at the level of the individual school, as well as for the pedagogical development. The third level of responsibility is accorded to the individual teacher.

Some empirical observations on the role of the superintendents

How then, is this new steering system, in which the superintendents are supposed to perform a new role, forming itself? Steering systems are, in themselves, complex and difficult to describe. Our intention here is to focus on the aspects of control that have the closest relationship with the development of the core processes in schools, the meeting between teachers and students in the learning situations; namely the introduction of governing by goals and objectives.

The School Act and the national curriculum are valid for all municipalities in Sweden irrespectively of their size. However, it is reasonable to assume that conditions for governance are different in small and large municipalities. Therefore, we will use the size of the municipality as an explanatory factor when analysing the superintendents answers to questions related to governing by goals and objectives. In order to emphasize differences, we have excluded middle-size municipalities from the analysis. Our hypothesis is that larger municipalities will have adjusted more to the new form of governing than smaller municipalities.

Table 7.1 summarizes the replies from several questions about the implementation of steering by goals and objectives and about how

Table 7.1 Establishing and evaluating local school plans: differences between large and small municipalities (%)

Question/reply	Large municipalities	Small municipalities
1. Is steering by goals and objectives implemented in the municipality?		
Yes	65	34
No	35	66
2. Does your municipality have a Local School Plan decided by the municipal council?		
Yes	80	57
No	20	43
3. Has your Local School Plan been evaluated?		
Yes	35	46
Yes, partly	53	41
No	12	13
4. Has your Local School Plan been changed after the evaluation?		
Yes	31	12
No	69	88
N	96	96

Note: The data on which the table is based was collected through a postal survey in 1995 of municipal superintendents in Sweden.

local school plans are established and evaluated. There is a clear pattern distinguishing large from small municipalities. Governing by goals and objectives has been implemented to a much greater extent in the larger municipalities. Local school plans, established by the municipal councils, are an important part of the new steering system, and are more common in large municipalities.

Evaluations are a very important tool for securing standards and national equivalence in the new Swedish system for governing schools. Politicians often see them as a means for securing political decisions (Johansson and Kallós, 1994). However, evaluations can export, to the principals and teachers, the insecurity felt by the politicians concerning what is happening in the schools, especially if the results are negative with regard to what the schools are doing. A small study, we carried out with 50 Swedish principals, reveals that despite the fact that 75 per cent of all school boards conducted written evaluations, only 4 per cent of them reported back to the schools in a written form or through meetings. The schools were not informed about the findings or what the board expected from the individual school with regard to its results (Johansson, 2000).

As Table 7.1 indicates, evaluations of School Plans are not commoner in large than small municipalities. However, it is more likely that evaluations bring about changes in the School Plan in the larger municipalities, which would seem to suggest that it is used as a more active document in these settings. Nevertheless, the figures also reveal that most of the municipalities have made no alterations at all in their local school plans. Perhaps evaluation has become more a ritual than part of a real process of change geared towards school improvement.

Control of this kind has little to do with school improvement. If the role of the political decision-makers and the educational leaders in the educational community has shifted from top-down control to providing support to enhance local success, the possibilities are greater that the work of school leaders will effect the goal fulfilment of the educational process. We would argue that too much emphasis has been put on the control side and too little discussion has concentrated on what kind of support processes are needed for the successful implementation of different educational reforms or decisions (Johansson, 2000).

To what extent is the Local School Plan an important document and does this distinguish large municipalities from small? Earlier in this chapter, we reported that if the local school politicians have been involved in the planning and writing of the Local School Plan, there is more likely to be a link between the amount of resources allocated and the goals and objectives of the Local School Plan.

As shown in Table 7.2, a link between budget decisions and the decision about the local school plan is unusual. However, as hypothesized, such a link is commoner in large municipalities. Further, in these municipalities, the Local School Plan more frequently describes the organizational and economic conditions for

Table 7.2   The importance of the Local School Plan: differences between large and small municipalities (%)

Question/reply	Large municipalities	Small municipalities
1. Have financial resources been allocated to cover important priorities in the Local School Plan?		
Yes, for three priorities	21	9
Yes, for two priorities	6	8
Yes, for one priority	8	4
No	65	79
2. Does the Local School Plan describe the organizational and economic conditions for the schools?		
Yes	57	37
No	43	63
3. Does the Local School Plan describe how the municipality is to work with the goals of the National Curriculum?		
Yes	90	56
No	10	44
4. Does the Local School Plan govern planning at the school level?		
Yes, for all schools	65	34
Yes, for about half of the schools	19	7
Yes, but only for a few schools	8	7
No	27	45
5. Do the teachers view the vision, goals and objectives of the Local School Plan as important for their work?		
Yes	58	37
No	42	63
N	96	96

Note: The data on which the table is based was collected through a postal survey in 1995 of municipal superintendents in Sweden.

the schools. The school gets to know how it should be organised and the amount of resources allocated to it. It is then a task for the principal and his/her staff to use the money to reach all the goals in the national curriculum and the local school plan – a new public management approach. Every year the national and local politicians decide which questions and priorities will be given particular focus in evaluation and these are set out in the annually revised Local School Plan.

One direct effect of this arrangement is a lack of resources. There are never enough resources to fulfil all the goals to the desired standard. It may also be the case that there is insufficient time to work with all goals contained in the different political steering documents. It is very clear that since the mid-1980s there has been a considerable increase in the number of goals and objectives for schools, whilst, during the same period, there has been a decrease in their budget allocations. Schools have been required to do more with less money. Within such a fiscally constrained environment, teachers are being asked to improve pedagogical methods and pupil performance (Johansson and Bredeson, 1999). This overload leads to a situation in which goals are regarded as visions that do not necessarily need to be achieved by the learning community.

Large municipalities seem to use the Local School Plan very much to describe the school board's intentions in relation to the national goals, as shown in Table 7.2. Only half of the Local School Plans in small municipalities have this clear connection to the national curriculum. Further, the Local School Plan appears to govern planning at the school level to a greater extent in large than in small municipalities. Again, this supports our hypothesis that the larger municipalities have adjusted more to the new forms of governing than the smaller ones. Not surprisingly, whether teachers regard the visions, goals and objectives of the Local School Plan as important also varies according to municipal population size.

Conclusions

Let us return to our research questions. Our intention was to focus on the aspect of steering, the introduction of governing by goals and objectives, that has the closest relationship with the development of the core processes in schools – the meeting between teach-

ers and students in learning situations. We have found great variation between large and small municipalities in relation to the new
steering system as perceived by the superintendents. Large school
boards are much more in line with the national regulations as set
out in the School Act and the national curriculum, but on the other
hand, their teachers are only slightly better at following these regulations than their counterparts in small communities.

The role of the educational leaders in implementation processes is
not only to apply formal power to bring about changes in education, it must also focus on the reform itself. We can conclude that
the new steering system is still not working and that its implementation is moving slowly. Further, there is a need for a better understanding in the school culture of the relationship between the
steering system, resources and school improvement. The roles of
superintendents and principals have, because of the new governing
system, become more complex and difficult. We argue that the
school leaders are now required to apply the goals of the National
curriculum, to be democratic leaders and, at the same time, work
within a New Public Management culture. The role of the school
leader in such surroundings is to translate the educational goals and
objectives into policy demands on the school, and to successfully
implement these within the given resources.

We would like to underline the fact that, in Sweden today, a great
many changes are taking place in the school sector that are a direct
effect of the decentralisation of power over the schools from the
state to the municipality. Many of the questions we would like to
address are impossible to answer from a bird's eye view. They have
to be answered in relation to different types of municipalities, even
subtypes, and also sometimes in relation to different schools.
Decentralization has initiated a great many different processes so
that, even if schools are still recognizable as schools from the
outside, they differ considerably from each other on the inside. This
uncontrolled development will be an eldorado for future research!

References

Begley, P. and Johansson, O. 1998. 'The Values of School Administration:
Preferences, Ethics and Conflicts', *The Journal of School Leadership*, 8 (4):
399–422.

202   *The Governance of Learning*

Bredesen, P. and Johansson, O. 1998. 'Leadership for Learning: A Study of the Instructual Leadership Roles of Superintendents in Sweden and Wisconsin', in *Toward The Year 2000: Leadership for Quality Schools*, The Sixth Yearbook of The National Council of Professors of Educational Administration. Lancaster, Pa: Thechnomic Publishing.

Cregård, A. 1996. *Skolchefers arbete: Om chefsuppdrag och styrning inom skolsektorn*. Skrifter från Centrum för forskning om offentlig sektor. Göteborg: CEFOS.

Ekholm, H. 1984. *Skolledarskapets rötter: Historien om folkskolan och dess ledning 1842–1962*. Skrifter från Skolledarutbildningen, 1984:10. Linköping.

Fullan, M. 1998. 'The Three Stories of Educational Reform: Inside, Inside-out, Outside-In', unpublished paper. University of Toronto: Ontario Institution for Studies in Education.

Fullan, M. 1999. *Change Forces – The Sequel*. London: Falmer Press.

Gustafsson, G. 1983 'Symbolic and Pseudo Policies as Responses to Diffusion of Power', *Policy Science*, 15: 269–87.

Hagström, B. 1990. *Chef i offentlig verksamhet: Forskning kring offentligt ledarskap*. Lund: Studentlitteratur.

Heimer, J. 1998. 'Rektorsutbildningens historia och morgondagens krav', in Johansson, O. och Lundberg, L. (eds), *Rektor en språngbräda för utveckling – om rektor i skärningspunkten mellan erfarenhet och utmaningar*. Skrifter från Centrum för skolledarutveckling, 1998:2, Umeå universitet.

Hughes, O.E. 1998. *Public management & Administration*, 2nd edn. Basingstoke: Macmillan Press – now Palgrave.

Johansson, O. 2000. 'Om rektors demokratiskt reflekterande ledarskap', in Lundberg, L. (ed.). *Görandets lov – Lova att göra*. Skrifter från Centrum för skolledarutveckling, 2000:1, Umeå universitet.

Johansson, O. and Bredeson, P. V. 1999. 'Value Orchestration by the Policy Community for the Learning Community: Reality and Myth', in Begley, P. (eds), *Values and Educational Leadership*. Albany: State University of New York Press.

Johansson, O. och Kallós, D. 1994. 'Om rektorsrollen vid målstyrning av skolan', in Hård af Segerstad, A. (ed.), *Skola med styrfart*. Rektorsutbildningens skriftserie 1994:1. Uppsala universitet.

Lundberg, L. 1996. 'En skola som lär för livet' in Johansson, O. and Kallós, D. (eds), *Tänk utveckling*. Rektorsutbildningens skriftserie nor. 3. Umeå universitet.

Lundberg, L. 1998. 'Behöver skolan omvärlden', in Johansson, O. and Lundberg, L. (eds), *Rektor en språngbräda för utveckling*. Skrifter från Centrum för Skolledarutveckling 1998:2, Umeå universitet.

Lundgren, U. 1986. *Att organisera omvärlden: Om grundskolans organisation och ledning*. Stockholm: Liber.

Lundgren, U. och Wennås, O. 1987. 'Framväxten av nuvarande ansvarsfördelning och styrsystem', in Du Rietz, L., Lundgren, U. and Wennås, O., *Ansvarsfördelning och styrning på skolområdet: Ett beredningsunderlag*. DsU: 1987:1.

Lpo 94. *Läroplaner för det obligatoriska skolväsendet och de frivilliga skol-formerna*, Utbildningsdepartementet 1994.

Moos, L. and Carney, S. 2000. 'Ledelse i den nordiske kontext: Realiteter, muligheter og begränsninger', in Moos, L., Carney, S., Johansson, O. and Mehlbye, J., *Skolledelse i Norden*. Kobenhavn: Nordisk Ministerråd.

Nygren, A.M. 2000. 'Rektors görande utifrån målkrav', in Lundberg, L., (ed.) *Görandet lov – Lov att göra*. Skrifter från Centrum för skolledarutveckling, 2000:1, Umeå universitet.

Nygren, A.M. and Johansson, O., 2000. 'Den svenske rektorn efter 1945 – Kvalifikationer, arbetsuppgifter och utmaningar', in Moos, L., Carney, S., Johansson, O. and Mehlbye, J. (eds), *Skolledelse i Norden*. Kobenhavn: Nordisk Ministerråd.

Parker, K.1998. 'School Councils and Classroom Change', Doctoral thesis. Ontario Institute for Studies in Education/University of Toronto, Canada.

Proposition 1992/93:220. *En ny läroplan för grundskola och ett nytt betygssystem för grundskola, sameskola, specialskola och den obligatoriska särskolan.*

Regeringens skrivelse 1998/99:121. *Samverkan, ansvar och utveckling: Utvecklingsplan för förskola, skola och vuxenutbildning.*

Riksdagens revisorer 1999. *Skolverket och skolans utveckling.* Rapport, 1998/99:3.

Skolverket 1999. *Nationella kvalitetsgranskningar 1998.* Skolverkets rapport nor. 160. Stockholm: Liber.

SOU 1980:19. *Fler kvinnor som skolledare: Betänkande.*

8
Learning Cities for the Learning Society[1]

Sue Cara, Charles Landry and Stewart Ranson

Introduction

Education and learning need to move centre-stage to secure our future well-being – and especially so in periods of rapid, yet consistent social transformation (Ranson, 1998). Only if learning is placed at the centre of our daily experience can:

1. individuals continue to develop their skills and capacities;
2. organizations and institutions recognize how to harness the potential of their workforce and be able to respond flexibly and imaginatively to the opportunities and difficulties to this paradigmatic period of change we are living through;
3. cities act responsively and adapt flexibly to emerging needs;
4. societies understand that the diversity and differences between communities can become a source of enrichment, understanding and potential.

The challenge for policy makers then is to promote the conditions in which a 'learning society' or 'learning city' can unfold. A learning society is much more than a society whose members are simply well educated; it goes well beyond merely learning in the classroom. It is a place or a society where the idea of learning infuses every tissue of its being: a place where individuals and organizations are encouraged to learn about the dynamics of where they live and how it is changing; a place which on that basis changes the way it learns whether through schools or any other institution that can help foster understanding and knowledge; a place in which all its members are encouraged to learn; finally and perhaps most importantly a place that can learn to change the conditions of its learning, democratically.

The lineages of the learning city

The idea of a 'learning society' has become enormously influential during the 1990s. It has provided one of the guiding assumptions for the renewal of the economy and society for national politicians, the National Commission on Education, the European Commission White Paper on education and training, city policy makers, corporate strategists and industrial trainers. Within the academic community the Economic and Social Research Council has identified the learning society as one of its key issues and set up a special programme of research projects to assess what it is and how it works.

The vision, which informs the idea of learning societies or communities, has in particular become central to creative strategies for regenerating cities, towns and regions. The ideas and concepts have inspired the formation of the Learning Cities Network in the UK which has grown rapidly over the last three years, and now includes a number of cities, including Derby, Hull, Liverpool, Milton Keynes, Norwich, Nottingham, Sheffield and Stockton, as well places with Learning City Initiatives including Birmingham, Brighton, Co Durham and Darlington, Gloucester, Greenwich, Tyneside and York. Cities and communities are increasingly understanding that the mutual learning processes unleashed, and the potential uncovered, by involving the various publics in cities is immense, as is the power of synergy through building partnerships of traditional and non-traditional, organizations concerned with learning. This enhances the capacity for economic and social renewal in a period of global change. In Europe too there is a similar interest in taking forward this set of ideas.

The concept of the Learning Community, as it has developed in Britain has drawn upon a rich vein of ideas about learning. The concept of the *learning city* was promoted initially by an OECD/CERI study in 1992 (Hirsch, 1993) and this became a major influence upon the development of the Learning City Network in the UK. Ideas in relation to how *individuals best learn*, and how *the learning organization* learns as well as historical connections to the idea of *the village college* have also contributed to our understanding of the different aspects and levels of learning in the learning community.

Learning thus needs to be understood at different levels:

1. how individuals can continue to develop their skills and capacities throughout their fives;
2. how the 'learning institution', be that a school, a TEC (Training and Enterprise Council) or a company with nothing specifically to do with learning, is enabled to respond openly and imaginatively;
3. how the 'learning city and town' can provide for itself the preconditions to develop a sense of direction for its future;
4. how the 'learning region' can understand the resources and cultural traditions it has to tap into in order to enable it to support economic and social development.

The learning city or the educated city?

The terms 'learning' and 'learning city' are used rather than 'education', 'educating' or 'educated city'. Why do we wish to distinguish these terms? We do so because the concept of 'education' is restrictive, leading to a focus on a particular institutional system. Learning is a more overarching process that embodies education. Learning is both concerned with the way educational and learning processes proceed as well as with a whole raft of skills and core competencies well beyond the satisfaction of immediate vocational needs, or indeed those traditionally considered as educational. The capacity for learning, and thus enrichment and understanding of the place one lives in and how one relates to it, includes as preconditions a strong focus on human and social capital development.

It is easy to envisage the learning city merely as a place which both enables and encourages its citizens to educate themselves as they have greater 'leisure' time while simultaneously being increasingly responsible for their own education and development. Yet in that model of the learning city, the defining characteristics are the nature and extent of educational investment and its take up by citizens. Thus the city with a high number of university and college places, extensive investment in apprenticeships and vocational training and an active adult education sector may be described as a learning city. It would have comprehensive ladders of educational opportunity at the formal and informal level.

But this is a very limited definition. It could be argued that it does no more than state the obvious fact that cities with a high proportion of students are better educated than those which, for reasons of poverty or short-sightedness, have failed to invest in higher education. Critically, as a concept, it fails to deal with issues of collective learning, of quality or to present a developmental challenge. There are towns which can demonstrate a high degree of success in some respects such as Kirklees, which do not have highly ranked universities. So a definition of a learning city that considers only the extent of its educational sector, even with some qualitative measures, may be inadequate.

The other danger is that it offers little guidance to cities beyond the suggestion that they should invest in educational infrastructure. The UK, for example, has seen an explosion of further and higher education in the past 10 years (a growth whose financing has, it may be remembered, recently forced the introduction of tuition fees), with cities like Derby and Portsmouth witnessing a huge expansion. Eight years ago, Derby College of Further Education had fewer than 1,500 students: today it has 14,000 and is still expanding. It now has a very big 'learning factory' yet the impact of this on the city remains to be seen. A definition of the learning city which restricts itself to easily identifiable and measurable areas such as the formal and informal education sectors, vocational and in-service training and similar activity is entirely feasible. But, just as there is a difference between knowledge and understanding, we would argue that this is an unnecessarily limited concept of the learning city.

A learning city is a reflexive city

There is another way of envisaging the learning city. A true learning city is one that develops by learning from its experiences and those of others. It is constantly on the lookout, searching out examples of success and failure and always asking why is this so. It benchmarks itself to appropriate other cities to get a grip on how well it is developing. It is thus a place that understands itself and reflects upon that understanding – it is a 'reflexive city'. It is a place where individuals feel they can become empowered, where organizations – public, private and voluntary – are open-minded and most difficulty a place where this amalgam of various actors with differing cultures coalesce to work together towards an agreed set of objectives for its city. The key characteristic of the learning city is its ability to develop successfully in a rapidly changing socio-economic environment. In order to do this it nurtures the potential of all, because it understands that in the emerging knowledge based economy it is the capacity to learn and reflect in all its facets, in responding to urban challenges that will largely determine success or failure. It knows that knowledge is more than information. Today cities have one crucial resource – their people. It is their cleverness, ingenuity, aspirations, motivations, imagination and creativity which are today of crucial economic significance, as the old Vocational factors – raw materials, market access – diminish to the point of insignificance. Thus the objective of farsighted urban leaders should be to *'embed a culture of learning into the deep codes of their city'*.

Where the unreflective city flounders by trying to repeat past success for far too long, the learning city is creative in its understanding of its own situation and wider relationships, developing new solutions to new problems. The essential point here is that any city can be a learning city. It is not a factor of size, geography, resources, economic infrastructure or even educational investment (though this will play an increasingly important role if a city is to sustain itself as a learning organism in the emerging knowledge economy). To some extent, it might be argued that the fewer natural or historical advantages a city enjoys, the more important it is that it should re-think itself as a learning city.

The learning city is thus strategic, creative, imaginative and intelligent – it looks at its potential resources in a far more comprehensive way. It sees competitive edge in the seemingly insignificant; it can even turn weakness into strength. An example from Huddersfield might suffice. The town not particularly renowned for its creativity drew up a strategic programme called the Creative Town Initiative made up of 20 projects based on the idea of the cycle of urban creativity. Some projects actively encourage individuals and groups to have ideas and generate projects such as their 'creativity forum'; others are concerned with turning ideas into practice such as the 'advisory service for inventors' or the 'creativity investment services'; then products and services need to be circulated and here the Northern Creative Alliance is an example; then there are projects for people to work on ideas and showcase them and finally to disseminate them. This idea seemed so unusual coming from

Huddersfield that the European Commission funded it as part of their Urban Pilot Projects scheme in order to find what could be learnt form the experiment.

By this definition the learning city is both richer and more complex than the educated city, though it encompasses it. It requires investigation not only of a city's educational inputs, but also issues such as the open-mindedness and flexibility of city institutions, the quality of partnerships, the track record of innovation, vitality of democratic and political activity, questions of empowerment and so on. But this very richness does make both definition and evaluation of the learning city more complex. The learning city society concept is thus a multi-faceted idea. Just remember the range of learning environments as one instance (devised by R. Balsam, Kent County Council):

1. *Obvious*: Pre-school groups; nurseries; schools; colleges; universities; adult learners' centres, homes; libraries; television.
2. *Less obvious*: Businesses; community centres; arts centres; museums and attractions; health centres; post offices; citizens advice bureaux; cities; towns; villages; the Internet; nature reserves; the outdoors; newspapers; bookshops.
3. *Surprising*: Old peoples' homes; homeless shelters; refuges; prisons; shopping malls; hospitals; churches; trains; stations; football stadia; service stations; restaurants; hotels; cafés; nightclubs; local parks.

Key moments of the learning city movement

The concept of the 'Learning' or 'Educating City' has been current as an idea since the early 1970s but it developed real momentum after a report of a conference organized by Barcelona City Council in 1990 – The First International Congress on Educating Cities. The report of this conference contains the beginnings of the ideas incorporated in the concept of the Learning City. These include the need:

1. To have a vision of the city as a place which contains a diversity of educational institutions, but also as a city which sees itself as a transmitter of learning and within which the city itself is an 'object of learning', and thus the city can be learnt about and changed.

2. To understand the complexity of educational processes and the wider environment within which learning relationships both designed and accidental are produced. Thus to truly appreciate that learning goes beyond the classroom.
3. To develop more possibilities for integrated planning for learning, to create relationships between formal and non-formal systems of education and a desire for equity.

The interest that has led to the development of a number of Learning Cities in Britain in the mid-1990s evolved from two main sources. First, the general context of thinking about education and training in Britain and then from reports of two different but related European events which both discussed the idea of the Learning City.

The first was a Conference in Gothenburg in Sweden in 1992 where a study from m CERI/OECD by Donald Hirsch was presented which was intended to explore through examples the degree to which cities might encourage a culture of lifelong learning. The cities studied were: Bologna, Adelaide; Edmonton; Vienna; Pittsburgh; Gothenburg. The second was a Conference organised by the European Lifelong Learning Initiative (ELLI) in Rome in late 1994 where the concept of the Communities of Learning, cities, towns or villages was discussed and the creation of a network of 20 cities of Learning in Europe was included in ELLI's targets for the year 2000.

In spite of their later influence neither of these two events lay behind the development of the first 'City of Learning' initiative in Britain. In June of 1992 the Council of Local Education Authorities annual conference was hosted in Liverpool under the banner 'Liverpool City of Learning' at the same time as John Moore's University in the city published major research on the economic effects of higher education institutions on the local economy. The initial phase of the Liverpool initiative began based on the assessment of the contribution of the education sector to economic development.

The second British initiative grew directly from the Gothenburg Conference. Edinburgh was represented at the conference and follow up activity by the District Council's Economic Development Section and the University Centre for Continuing Education resulted in a group of educational providers, private interests and the District Council commissioning a development plan and launching a learning city initiative with a conference in 1994. Sheffield too began an initiative as a direct result of the Donald Hirsh's work with a series of seminars in the city linked to themes identified in the OECD report.

The early 1990s importantly saw a change in the context within which education and training operated in Great Britain. Analysis of competitor nations identified increasing educational achievement as a key indicator for economic success. The 1992 Further Education Act signalled an expansion of the Further Education Sector to complement the earlier expansion of Higher Education. It was appreciated that this expansion would not be achieved solely or even mainly by the engagement of more young people in education and training, but would mean a massive growth in learning by adults – lifelong learners. Traditionally, the involvement of adults in education and training had been regarded as concerned with individual development and fulfilment, perhaps doing a painting class, learning a language or a craft skill, but this needed to change.

Lifelong learning

Those thinking about the economy, the effects of globalization on the UK and the changing face of industry began to articulate more clearly a view that the skills needs of the nation could not be met by the compulsory education sector alone and that the new patterns of industry would have to rely on a flexible workforce willing and able to learn new skills and acquire new knowledge. The increasing importance of technology both as a tool for work and as an example of the pace of world transformation emphasized the need for all to continue to learn and change through a life with changing demands. Thus the National Education and Training Targets included not only foundation targets for young people but also targets for the whole workforce.

The European Year of Lifelong Learning in 1996 saw the publication of major reports on the need for lifelong learning for economic competitiveness not only by the EU and the British Government but also by the CBI and the TUC. The Government funded a national 'Campaign for Learning' led by Sir Christopher Ball whose slogan 'Learning Pays' summarized the connections being made between economic development and education and training. The government's amalgamation of the Departments of Education and

Employment into a single department has encapsulated the connections being made.

Within local economic development there were also considerable changes. A number of diverse funding streams for local economic development were amalgamated into a single source, the Single Regeneration Budget, which was allocated regionally and which required partnership for funding success. Within economic development there was a change of focus from infrastructural development to a recognition of the role of skills, education and training on economic success and inward investment opportunities. SRB applications began to include substantial education and training components and partnerships of providers grew in response to funding requirements. The requirement upon local Training and Enterprise Councils to draw together a local Forum for the development of strategies to achieve National Education and Training Targets also acted towards the development of partnerships between local authorities, the private sector and further and higher education interests.

The early 1990 also saw moves to reorganize local government in Great Britain, last reorganised in 1974. Scotland and Wales were reorganized first and this was a wholesale reorganization to unitary local government. This process resulted in a number of new Unitary Authorities which were either completely new entities or which had been old County Boroughs prior to 1974 and were re-emerging in some form or another.

It was against this background that some of the ideas and concepts encapsulated in the work by Donald Hirsch began to appear relevant to individuals working to develop learning within specific communities and localities and the idea of the 'Learning City' began to attract attention. At the same time, work being carried out in Birmingham in relation to school improvement and the publicity being given to the City of Learning initiative all contributed to a context where the idea of focusing effort in securing lifelong learning became both powerful and attractive.

The importance of the city unit

The CERI/OECD report concentrates its attention specifically on cities pointing out that the majority of people in OECD countries five in cities or urban areas with populations greater than 100,000.

While recognizing that the city is not the only geographical area on which to base education and training – accepting for example that national and regional governments may be best placed to initiate broad policy changes – it argues that the city unit in particular is capable of making a significant difference in terms of advancing life-long learning.

The city provides an area of a size which offers scope for collaboration and a sizeable learning infrastructure but Hirsch also identifies a sense of urban identity as being important and indicates the difficulty in some conurbations of using the concept of the 'Learning City' because a strong sense of self-identity may not exist. Within the range of British places that call themselves 'Learning Cities' there are places which are either too small or too diverse to fit the pattern but which have nevertheless found value in either the concept or the way of working which underlies it. However, in terms of the development of lifelong learning other sizes and kinds of community have felt that they could use similar strategies and need similar kinds of initiative.

What seems to have attracted a number of British towns and cities about the ideas in the CERI/OECD report were the 'ideas for action' and in the reports of what cities had been doing. These included Norwich, Nottingham, Hull and Derby. Thus by the end of 1996 about 20 British Cities had either adopted a title reflecting the idea of a Learning City or were considering doing so and a network of Learning Cities was meeting on a regular basis to exchange good practice and to promote and build on the kinds of activity which Hirsch felt to be useful in developing lifelong learning with a focus on a particular city community.

Part of the attraction of the concept of a Lifelong Learning Strategy which focuses on the local is that it allows for variation according to the needs and aspirations of the community concerned. This is apparent in the international examples given in the CERI/OECD report but even given the shared national context of the British examples there are differences of emphasis which reflect the priorities of those involved. However, there are common themes which run through the concept as developed both in the OECD work and also through the thinking of European and World Lifelong Learning Initiatives.

The now many examples of practice show what has actually been done have varied and continues to vary from community to community. Thus Sheffield has been seriously concerned to involve communities in decision-making on learning within the city, Hull has been concerned to build the education and training work of the City of Learning into the economic development plan for the city as a whole and Norwich has marketed and promoted learning through a guidance shop and a festival. In Derby the Learning City has been promoted by the Training & Enterprise Council and in Milton Keynes the focus of a multi-agency forum.

Hull – the learning chapter

Hull has a vision of becoming a new successful maritime city and City Vision Ltd is the public/private partnership charged with taking this ambition forward. It sets out its tasks as being preparation and delivery of the City Regeneration Strategy, managing the Single Regeneration Budget, Challenge Fund Programmes, co-ordinating partnership bids for additional funds from appropriate sources.

When City Vision drew up its economic development strategy it formed four task groups for each of four key activity areas – economy, people and communities, essence and fabric and lifetime learning. Initially the lifetime learning plan was in the hands of an Education Forum but Hull City Learning offered to take on and was given the task of improving on a first draft of a learning plan.

Hull City Learning is a forum involving partners from the Universities, TEC, City Vision itself, College of Further Education, City Council, Private Sector, Media and Voluntary Sector. The result of the efforts of the group was 'The Learning Chapter'. This provides a comprehensive vision of how partners wish to see lifelong learning develop within the city. It has formed the backdrop for a large city wide bid for regeneration funding in Single Regeneration Budget Round four. It is a framework within which individuals and institutions can locate their activities. The document has been widely distributed and consulted upon throughout the city.

The key regeneration strategies which the City Learning Group has been addressing have been enhancing skill levels, improving the learning infrastructure, raising achievement and staying on rates and pursuing lifelong learning.

The partnership between providers enables a more powerful and less sectoral voice to be heard and the inclusion of learning elements in city centre regeneration activities evidences this. Although very many communities are conscious of the need to increase skills, few have articulated this so clearly through their economic development and regeneration planning as in Hull.

Norwich – the learning shop

Educational Guidance in Norwich has a history of collaboration but has consisted of a number of short-term initiatives which have revealed substantial need with periods when little has been possible in terms of provision other than that provided in connection with Government Training Schemes. None of the major providers of post school learning in the City has premises that are in the City Centre and though all offered guidance its very location tended tie it to particular institutions.

Norwich is the only major City within a 45–mile radius and large numbers of people come in each day to shop and work. The city centre is compact with the city hall and market providing a key landmark in the shopping centre. The group which meets to drive forward the Learning City has representatives from the TEC, all post school educational providers, city council, employers, media, the LEA, voluntary sector and careers service. The partnership had attracted a limited amount of funding from the DfEE to take forward the Learning City Initiative.

Two major providers, the College of Further Education and the University of East Anglia had been having joint discussions on funding a city centre learning shop which would give information on educational opportunities on their provision and would also carry information on other local providers. The Learning City Group discussed and supported the initiative assisting joint working between institutions. Applying some of the DfEE funding to the project providing advice on the development of the project to its individual member organizations who 'own' the shop embedding the shop in the Learning City Initiative and using the shop as the public face of the Learning City.

Norwich City College and the University of East Anglia are the main funders and jointly planned and set up the initiative. Additional funding for premises and start up costs came from Bull International, Norwich City Council and the DfEE funding. Additional partners, also contributing funding include the

Norfolk Adult Education Service, Norwich School of Art and Design, Open University and Easton College (Agriculture and Horticulture).

The shop is in a prime central location in the market area and opposite the Norwich Advice Arcade, which houses organizations such as the CAB. It has large shop widows with displays from providers and has a high standard of decoration and furnishing. It is permanently staffed with trained advisers and open six days per week. As well as information on formal learning it carries the Norfolk Library Service database on local dubs and societies.

In its first six months of operation 12,000 people have visited the shop from all sectors of the population from those with basic skills needs to post graduates. Take up of learning opportunities is being monitored. At least one provider believes that they have seen increased numbers through referrals. Callers are often referred to other agencies for specialist advice and support.

Without the Learning City initiative the College and the University might well – in time – provided a city centre guidance facility. What adds value in terms of what has happened is the involvement of all the publicly funded adult learning organiza-tions in the City in a joint project that markets learning opportu-nities to all prospective learners. Each provider is getting a six-day a week information outlet in the middle of the city; for their con-tribution no single provider could do this alone and if they did the information to the public would be the poorer. The interest and involvement of the City Council, employer interests or the voluntary sector might not have accompanied a single provider initiative. A facility which did not involve negotiation with the Careers Service would not have received the support of the TEC or the DfEE.

The Learning Shop is a public face for the Learning City and also a public demonstration of the value of collaboration over competition.

Besides the Cities which have declared themselves to be 'Learning Cities' are others which have serious city wide agendas for learning, and are used as examples of good practice but which have not using 'The Learning City' as their banner. The work of Professor Tim Brighouse, the Chief Education Officer of Birmingham, in connec-tion with the advancement of educational standards in this City being just such an example.

Glasgow's Education Business Partnership

The Education Business Partnership was established to ensure, for Glasgow, a skilled and motivated workforce able to meet the economic and social challenges that face the city. The partnership has been running – 'Aim High in Glasgow' and intends to incorporate a 'Local Learning Strategy'. These strategies are designed to help schools, colleges, businesses and other organisations to raise standards and levels of achievement. The programmes are based on a programme of 'pathways' to support individual development. The 'pathways' are set up so that schools can select their own priorities and a package of projects that benefit young people, teachers and employers. The projects and activities are delivered by Education Support Services, the Careers Service, Local Development Companies, Community Education and Business. They include:

- Curriculum Enhancement, Teacher and Employee Development
- Enterprise Education and Entrepreneurship
- Economic Awareness and Work Related Experience
- Personal Skills Development and Access

Detailed targets have been set for each programme.

The Education Business Partnership was founded by Glasgow City Council and the Glasgow Development Agency. It now has representation from Further Education, training organizations and business.

A change of government in May 1997 and the publication of a number of key educational reports have put partnership back into focus as a means for using the limited resources available for education and training seriously. Such reports have also strongly advanced the arguments for the widening of participation and the prioritizing of funds to forward this aim. At the heart of the Kennedy Report 'Learning Works' (Kennedy, 1997) is the idea of strategic partnerships which will do just that, in the report of the National Advisory Group for Continuing Education and Lifelong Learning (NAGCELL) partnerships, and among them Learning City Partnerships are seen as the means by which coherent local learning opportunities can be secured and the concept of learning being secured outside the domain of the Department for Education and Employment is discussed. A community is key to the Health of the

Nation Report as is a partnership between employers, individuals, the government; and partnership is inherent in childcare strategy, the prospectus for the University of Industry and proposals for regional government.

The Green Paper, *The Learning Age* (DfEE, 1998) takes the idea of learning communities into Government Policy:

The learning age

Our vision of the learning Age is about more than employment. The development of a culture of learning will help to build a united society, assist the creation of personal independence and encourage our creativity and innovation. Learning encompasses basic literacy to advanced scholarship. We learn in many different ways through study, reading, watching television, going on a training course, taking an evening class, at work and from family and friends ...

This country has a great learning tradition ... . We want more people to have the chance to experience the richness of this tradition by participating in learning. We want all to benefit from the opportunities learning brings and to make them more widely available by building on this foundation of high standards and excellence.

For individuals: learning offers excitement and the opportunity for discovery ... it takes us in directions we never expected, sometimes changing our lives. Learning helps create and sustain our culture. It helps all of us to improve our chances of getting a job and of getting on. Learning ... helps older people stay active and healthy, strengthens families and the wider community, and encourages independence. There are many people for whom learning has opened up, for the first time in their lives, the chance to explore art, music, literature, film and the theatre, or to become creative themselves. Learning has enabled many people to help others to experience these joys too.

For intellectual capital: learning helps business to be more successful by adding value and keeping them up-to-date. Learning develops the intellectual capital which is now at the centre of a nation's competitive strength. It provides the tools to manage industrial and technological change, and helps generate ideas, research and innovation. Because productivity depends upon the whole workforce we must invest in everyone.

For cohesive communities learning contributes to social cohesion and fosters a sense of belonging, responsibility and identity. In communities affected by rapid economic change and industrial restructuring, learning builds local capacity to respond to this change.

For an inclusive society: learning is essential to a strong economy and an inclusive society. In offering a way out of dependency and low expectation, it lies at the heart of the Government's welfare reform programme. We must bridge the "learning divide" – between those who have benefited from education and training and those who have not – which blights so many communities and widens income inequality. The results are seen in the second and third generation of the same family being unemployed, and in the potential talent of young people wasted in a vicious circle of under-achievement, self deprecation) and petty crime. Learning can overcome this by building self-confidence and independence.

(DfEE, 1998, p. 00)

Learning is at the centre of regeneration

The capacity of learning and for learning to assist in economic revitalization, and its capacity to engender social capital development and its role in democratic renewal, is now at the centre of regeneration.

A better trained and more knowledgeable and intelligent workforce clearly helps in developing economic prosperity. Building social capital is a means of addressing social exclusion, which not the same as dealing with poverty, as not all poor people are socially excluded. As Ralf Dahrendorf notes it can be defined as 'a loss of access to the most important life chances that a modern society offers, where those chances connect individuals to the mainstream of that society'. And as Perri 6 (1997) notes: 'because social exclusion is a multifaceted phenomenon there is no single indicator that captures it like income does with poverty'. It can be best measured he goes on 'by looking at how many people are cut off from work. learning and other forms of participation'. This involves looking both at measures 'concerned with the processes that cause social exclusion such as mobility, educational failure or family breakdown as well as the conditions of social exclusion such as ... worklessness ... lack of effective social contacts lack of a car or a telephone'. As he further notes: 'the most valuable form of capital today is arguably human capital – not just formal qualifications and skills, but subtler ones: knowing how to behave at work, knowing how to please a customer, knowing how to work in a team ... being able to spot an unexploited opportunity'.

In order to deal with these types of problem government itself needs to become more holistic, cross departmental and concerned with creating the administrative conditions to achieve multifaceted outcomes of which skills development may only be a part. Thus the need for partnership at every level.

Learning in the community

In education the interpretation given to learning cities typically focuses upon developing the opportunities for individuals to develop education and training throughout their lives. The learning city movement by contrast argues that the city, and the strategies it adopts, can make a difference to life long learning. This is for several reasons, because:

1. People relate their participation in learning activities to their immediate environment as a lifelong learning culture is hard to achieve through national initiatives alone;
2. The importance of creating coherence among a very large number of actors now involved in the planning and delivery of education and training. Beyond initial schooling, there is no single 'system' conveniently managed by a centralised public structure. Here, again the city can be a useful focus, as illustrated by the 'Further Education Council' developed in Edmonton, which acts as co-ordinator and policy forum for the many providers of adult learning. In Norwich and in Sheffield 'Learning City' initiatives develop from post 16 provider partnerships.
3. The community based nature of much adult learning. This makes it possible to build learning elements into city-led community activity – from health awareness campaigns to support for small enterprises. Conversely, learning in a city can be seen as a means of community action. In Kakegawa, Japan, lifelong learning has

been a way of involving citizens in the revitalisation of their city (Hirsch, 1993, p. 9).

Birmingham – networks of learning

Birmingham, has been enjoying a renaissance as a result of these types of strategies which have been developed in the city. The Chief Education Officer, Professor Tim Brighouse, has been a particular source of inspiration who recognises the urgency of creating highly educated citizens who are fitted for the new age of information technology. The challenge for learning cities is 'to transform attitudes towards and achievement from education: How do you help a population, old and young alike, which is used to seeing school as 'a once and for all' activity, not especially important, to acquire the habits not merely of taking school seriously but of sustaining life-long habits of learning' (Brighouse, 1996, p. 3). The prospect of failure in this agenda, it is argued, does not bear contemplation if cities turn into divided enclaves of the educated and the deprived of learning. The task, Brighouse advocates is to promote networks of learning across the city:

> Ideally in a 'learning city' there would be readily available and accessible local learning networks for all people of all ages. These networks or partnerships would involve providers – whether in colleges, schools, libraries, business shops or local amenities – in facilitating access to learning resources for all the population so that the advantages of information technology are available irrespective of wealth
>
> (Brighouse, 1996, p. 3).

In Birmingham strategies have worked to create such partnerships. The Training and Enterprise Council, Education Business Partnership, the Chamber of Commerce, employers organisations and particular businesses, with the Local Education Authority, have all played a vital role in working towards local economic and social regeneration through providing, stimulating and developing education and training opportunities. Thus, a Learning City has a thriving learning culture which builds organic links to wealth development and economic innovation.[2]

The strategies of partnership – inside and outside local authorities and in and outside 'classic' educational institutions – and the more holistic, cross departmental governance implied throughout the 'Learning City' discussion is promoted strongly by the European Learning Cities movement, which argues that:

1. the development of city-wide coalitions co-ordinating all relevant actors in both public and private sectors of education is necessary;
2. the co-ordination of work-oriented and general leisure-oriented education and training, in a way that allows all citizens easily to relate their development as individuals to their development as workers, exemplified in Unison's Return to Work scheme;
3. the co-ordination of learning at different stages, for example by encouraging different generations to learn together and to learn from each other; whether this be in a library, the workplace or a school, or as shown by family literacy initiatives;
4. the use of local media both as teaching tools in themselves and to raise awareness of learning opportunities, such as Eastern Counties Newspapers' supplement for the Norwich Learning Festival;
5. the promotion of the concept of the 'learning city', in which communities attempt to learn collectively through public dialogue as a means of changing their own futures (Hirsch, 1993, p. 10).

Regenerating the city through public dialogue

Michael Piore (1995) brings out the need for public dialogue in local regeneration brilliantly in a study of the significance of dialogue for local development: whereby a form of double loop learning is instigated as the key to regeneration. This involves going beneath the surface of a problem to locate its source in underlying differences of interests and values and recognizing that shared understanding and agreement can only grow out of a dialogue which addresses these difficult differences.

In traditional economic development the nation state and the large corporation were the central change agents when it was been driven by the logic of mass production. Then growth was perceived to depend upon highly specialized resources, dedicated capital equipment and narrowly trained semi-skilled workers, but now in the context of globalization, roles are changing. Subnational communities become more dependent on their own initiative and this requires them to become clear about who they are and how their traditions and resources can be developed for world markets:

> In the new environment, development is about the community finding a place for itself in world markets and thinking about how to turn its particular cultural heritage into an asset in that endeavour. It is no longer a question simply of negotiating among local interests to obtain resources ... it is more a question of purposeful reflection and debate within the local community.
>
> (Piore, 1995, p. 80).

This is where the learning city or community comes in as it needs to deliberate both upon the nature of its own community and how it can adapt to the changing outside world in which it must live. Many examples reinforce the notion of groups, businesses, communities 'learning to support each other' and develop the 'capacity for co-operation'. The role of government in this new world is 'to catalyse that learning process', enable the creation of a denser network of collaborative relationships.

Cities learning together

In one example, given by Michael Piore, small teams of community leaders drawn from different economic and social groups in the city were sent overseas to visit areas which might serve as models for economic regeneration. Piore describes how these visits served a number of purposes including enlarging the vision of team members, and providing materials to catalyse the *debate* at home. However the most significant benefit is the experience of travelling together in a foreign environment helps people from different, often antagonistic segments of the local community get to know each other: it breaks down the barriers among them and provides a common set of experiences and shared knowledge base upon which to build a more co-operative relationship (Piore, 1995, p. 81).

Similar evidence of the centrality of this type of learning comes from two other sources. In the first, a study of how the Swedish public library system was innovating itself it assessed how different forms of communications assisted learning and innovation, whether this be through reading books; talking to friends; television; conferences; seminars, the internet and so on. It found that the most profound learning experiences came from librarians jointly visiting another place, preferably another country, to see a best practice example, but to use this opportunity for discussing their own new ideas or innovations which they were trying out at home.

The other example comes from the work of the Washington based Partners for Liveable Communities described in 'The State of the American Community: Empowerment for Local Action'. It notes:

> A representative group must find pleasure in the association and profit in learning together. One way is shared experience, retreats, study trips, seminars that build first name familiarity and personal bonds that foster collaboration. For example 60 people from all walks of life in Chattanooga visited Indianapolis for days. Those 60 people discussed Indianapolis proposals to improve how the city worked, how Indianapolis has been able to depoliticize issues too important for political division. But in the process of learning about Indianapolis they learnt about one another. They travelled by bus returned home then created Chattanooga Venturer a vision for the city; now 10 years later they have completed Re-vision 2000, an encore of their original vision. Indeed the example was so successful that it won one of the Habitat best practice awards.

In Britain urban regeneration projects increasingly provide illustrations of Piore's theme of dialogue being central to learning for community development. Initiatives include the setting up of local forums, or citizens' panels, Planning for Real sessions; developing joint Parish Maps; Community Appraisals; Action Planning techniques to promote effective dialogue between different interest groups as well as between the community or local economic developers about the key local issues of poverty, unemployment, and social exclusion.

Planning partnerships are formed, or coalitions built, between local developers, voluntary associations and local communities to support credit unions, access courses, or new jobs because there is recognition that economic access of excluded groups (for example, the young black unemployed, or single mothers) to training and jobs develops the social and economic wealth of the community. The social capacity (and thus wealth) of disadvantaged communities has also been enhanced through organized action of local 'user groups' seeking to identify gaps in services that are vital to support women if they are to contribute to the labour market or take up learning opportunities, as well as support young children.

Dialogue, learning and planning

The recognized need for an urban vision and forward plan are key opportunities to develop and create momentum for a learning city notion. Below we list some examples taken form the extremely useful *Participation Works!: 21 Techniques of Community Participation for the 21st Century*, published in June 1998 by the New Economics Foundation.

Action Planning: The Greater Shankhill Planning Weekend was held in Belfast 1995. A five-day event attended by 600 people including representatives from 62 community organizations and 45 public, statutory and private agencies to prepare a £3.2 million lottery bid.
Citizens' Jury: The Lewisham Citizens' Jury met for four days in April 1996 to consider the question 'What can we do to reduce harm from drugs?' Sixteen members of the jury were selected at random form the population to represent fairly the community. The report was sent to over 100 opinion formers in politics, the civil service, research organizations and the media.
Community Indicators: The development of indicators by local communities of issues that really matter to them. Merton identified equal access as a key indicator . Volunteers from Merton Association for Independent Access (MAFIA), whose mobility is restricted visited shops, banks, churches, post offices to see how accessible they were. With a long term target of 100 per cent they found only 49 per cent of places were accessible. On this basis the local community and authority agreed that 60 per cent was an achievable interim target.
Future Search: Generates action by building a shared vision among a diverse group of people. Hitchin in Hertfordshire created a 'Whole Settlement Strategy' through Future Search. Sixty people spent two days start the process. Subsequently specialist groups have worked

on particular projects including some the projects they have since achieved such as finding a building for the Bancroft Youth Centre, developing a one-stop shop for council services or installing a town centre manager.

The unfolding local discourse or dialogue can clarify or recreate a local identity which grows naturally out of the history of the local community and 'the materials through which its people have traditionally expressed themselves' and serves as 'the fulcrum for a development strategy, fostering internal coherence and giving it direction in the world market place'.

Network organizations which depend for their effectiveness not upon autonomous economic actors but upon the interaction of individuals embedded in their social context provide, for Piore, a deeper vision of a progressive democracy. Individuals realize themselves in their social settings, through interaction with other people. The formation of the identity of the individual and that of the community grow out of the same processes: 'the pre-eminently human capacity from this point of view is speech, the essential human creation is language, and the prototypical human activity is *conversation*' (Piori, 1995, p.81). As Perri 6 argues: 'Even if learning were better organised and measured, the best training and schools could still leave people effectively excluded and liable to be poor. One of the recent lessons of social research is that human capital needs to be matched by social capital ... the quality of contacts people have and networks they plug into.' 'The best kind of social network for finding work is rich in "weak ties" to a wide range of people who are unlike oneself.' People with strong ties have less chance for mobility 'many long term unemployed people only know other unemployed people' (Perri 6, 1997).

We have learnt many lessons about regeneration in the last two decades. As Landry notes:

Significantly regeneration and renewal, it is now increasingly understood, is a much more subtle and over-arching process than previously appreciated, it is more than simply technological innovation, it is more than physical improvements on their own and involves in particular innovation at every level of decision making. For this reason organisational capacity, governance and appropriate organisational structure in itself has also been acknowledged as a tool for urban competitive advantage and thus needs to be creatively developed.

(Landry, 1998)

He continues:

Physical changes assist in regeneration, it can help build confidence and provide visible markers of progress. Yet if renewal is to be self-sustaining people need to feel engaged, involved and have the opportunity to give of their best and be empowered. This means finding opportunities to give vent to peoples' creativity and harnessing their capacity to solve their own problems. Urban reinvention and renewal is essentially a holistic process embracing economic, social, political, environmental and cultural factors.

And as Perri 6 adds:

We have learnt that we need to act on several fronts at once ... we have learnt people need to build on the own capacity, rather than depending on outside experts. We have learnt that communities need to "own" their strategies for renewal. And we have learnt that the public sector can't work alone ...

(Perri 6, 1997: 6)

In this analysis of the learning city we end up at the same point as in the discussion of learning organizations and learning societies – with an understanding that effective learning and its conditions rest upon the quality of democratic dialogue to realise the identities of individuals and communities alike.

Notes

1. This chapter is Part One of a longer report: Cara, S., Landry, C. and Ranson, S., 1998. *The Learning City in the Learning Age*, Working Paper 10 of series *The Richness of Cities, Urban Policy in a NewLandscape*, Leicester, Commedia/Demos.
2. See further Chapter 6 in this book.

References

Brighouse, T. 1996. 'The Birmingham Governor', Autumn 1996.

DfEE 1998. *The Learning Age: A Renaissance for a New Britain*, Cm 3790. London, HMSO.

Hirsch, D. 1993. *City Strategies for Lifelong Learning*. Gothenburg, CERI/OECD.

Kennedy, H. 1997. *Learning Works: Widening Participation in Further Education*. Coventry: The Further Education Founding Council.

Landry, C. 1998. *Helsinki: Towards a Creative City*. Helsinki: City of Helsinki Urban Facts.

New Economic Foundation 1998. *Participation Works!: 21 Techniques of Community Particaption for the 21st century*.

Perri 6 1997. 'Social Exclusion: Time To Be Optimistic', in Perri 6 (ed.), *The Wealth and Poverty of Networks*. London: Demos Collection, issue 12.

Piore, M. 1995. 'Local Development on the Progressive Political Agenda', in C. Crouch and D. Marquand (eds), *Reinventing Collective Action: From the Global to the Local*. Oxford: Blackwell.

Ranson, S. (ed.) 1998. *Inside the Learning Society*. London: Cassell.

Part V
Concluding Section

9
Conclusions

Anders Lidström and Christine Hudson

A recurring theme throughout this book has been the interplay between general tendencies of change and specific local adjustments and responses. At the outset, we asked ourselves how education policies, which are increasingly established at the local level, could be understood in relation to global transforming forces and specific local conditions. It was recognized that contemporary societal change includes tendencies towards both homogenization and fragmentation. Economic, cultural and political globalization, the further development of a knowledge society, challenges to the polity and new demographical changes, were identified as major ongoing transformations. At the same time, there are strong diversifying tendencies, which emphasize the local and the specific. These may concern establishing business profiles in a competitive world economy, stressing cultural identity and developing stronger local and regional units of governance.

Education is in the midst of these seemingly contradictory processes. Globalization and the knowledge society may partly have a streamlining effect, but there are also strong diversifying tendencies, emphasizing decentralized decision-making and education adjusted to specific local needs. The question we have asked ourselves is how local education policies are created in this intersection between the general and the locally specific?

The contributions in this volume provide analyses of different local education policies in Britain and Sweden. Focus has been on three areas – choice and market policies, the role of education in local development strategies and the governance of learning.

Together, these have provided a picture of diversity, both between and within countries, but they have also illustrated commonalties. In this chapter, we pull the threads together by extracting some of the conclusions that have emerged.

Common influences of change

According to the chapters presented in this book, contemporary local education policies are shaped within a common context of global or, at least, Western tendencies of change. Local decision-makers cannot avoid or isolate themselves from the influences of these broader changes. However, because there are differences between localities in terms, for example, of their economic base and their social and political structures and cultures, they can have differing relationships with this common context. Some areas may be favourably affected by global trends whereas others may experience more adverse effects. Further, as we have shown in this book, local decision-makers themselves are not simply helpless prisoners of fate, they can choose different strategies or approaches to meet these changes.

In the framework presented in the introductory chapter, a number of general changes were discussed. Most of these have also been referred to in the other chapters in the book, but some seem to stand out as particularly significant. Changes linked to *economic globalization* emerge as a common feature of most chapters. World-scale economic competition and the removal of trade barriers have created incentives for national decision-makers in both Britain and Sweden to emphasize economic instrumentality in their education policies. Increasingly, the usefulness of education is measured in terms of its ability to contribute to economic growth. Even at the local level, education is seen as a means for enhancing the competitiveness of the area. As reported by Anders Lidström in Chapter 5 and Christine Hudson in Chapter 6, there are strong tendencies for local decision-makers to use education as a means for improving the relative position of the local economy in both countries. This is achieved, for example, by a better adjustment of the content of education to the needs of local firms and by establishing partnerships between schools and businesses. Sue Cara *et al.* show, in Chapter 8, how the concept of learning is important for a city or a region aiming at improving its dynamism and economic competitiveness. Closely linked to economic globalization and ideas of the economic instrumentality of education is another general tendency of change – the increasing importance of *the knowledge society*. One result of the greater emphasis on knowledge, research and education is that the population is gradually becoming better educated and that educational institutions, such as universities and research centres, have gained a stronger position in society. However, the quality and content of primary, secondary and adult education are also regarded as important. Again, this is enhanced through national policies in both Sweden and Britain.

The emphasis on the knowledge society is also reflected in local policies. In Chapter 5, for example, it was shown that many Swedish local authorities have tried to improve their educational resources by establishing sixth-form colleges and other more advanced educational institutions in their area. Chapter 6, together with Chapter 8, illustrate how British local authorities are involved in strengthening formal educational institutions but also underline how education is linked to the broader concept of learning as a strategy for developing the local community. In both countries, there is a general awareness among local policy-makers that success in the knowledge society requires constant training and re-training – lifelong learning.

One consequence of the gradual increase in the level of education among the population is *the growth of the middle class*. As a social force, this well-educated class is becoming increasingly significant, despite its fragmented character. Its members take a keen interest in the quality and content of education, in particular when it affects the schooling of their own children, and this reinforces the focus on education in the knowledge society. The importance of this class for the emergence of local choice policies was explored in Chapter 3 with regard to Sweden.

Contemporary general change also includes an *ideological transformation*. In both Sweden and Britain, there is a move towards a stronger position for a market agenda in education, with an emphasis on parental choice, competition between schools, and the further growth of the independent schools sector. Both public sector and private schools are encouraged to establish their own particular profiles in order to attract pupils with special interests. Market-like conditions are created, for example through the use of vouchers. These changes are linked to the spread of neo-liberal ideas throughout the world, but can also be regarded as a result of the stronger influence of the growing middle class and its more individualistic values.

The local consequences of this ideological transformation are analysed in the book. In Chapter 4, Sharon Gewirtz shows how two British schools, in different environments, have responded to this general change. The increasing acceptance of market ideas is also evident in Sweden, a country where the values of comprehensiveness and equality dominated for so long, and they have been enamoured even by political parties that previously strove to counteract them. In Chapter 3, Anders Lidström analyses these choice and market policies in relation to Swedish municipalities.

Educational transformation in the Western world also emerges as *new ways of governing education*. Nowadays, the previously mentioned use of market type measures is a common way of achieving an adjustment between parental demands and schools' provision of education. However, traditional political ways of governing have also developed further in a way that is similar between countries. Decentralization, governing by goals and objectives and, to some extent, even evaluations of outputs and results are often based on traditional notions of hierarchy and political control. In Chapter 7, Olof Johansson and Leif Lundberg discuss how this has affected the role and position of school leaders in Sweden, who have to combine their traditional role as pedagogical leaders with a New Public Management style of leadership. In the British context, these conflicts are analysed in Chapter 4, where leadership functions in different social and material environments are explored. Matters of governance are also discussed in Chapter 8, with specific focus on how the learning city can be governed and how it can involve people in the process of decision-making.

A final observation concerns *the intensity of change* that characterizes contemporary Western societies. Structures, previously taken for granted, are reconsidered. New ideas and technologies challenge established patterns of living and working. As argued by Sue Cara *et al.* in Chapter 8, a rapidly changing society is an argument for the dynamism inherent in the learning city. By learning, individuals as well as organizations become more aware of changes, but are also better equipped to reap the benefits from them and to avoid pitfalls.

In sum, the contributions in this book have illustrated how the general tendencies of change exert an influence over education in contemporary society, and how they impact on countries, in our case Sweden and Britain, and at the local level. However, this is only a part of the picture. Even if some trends are common, they emerge in differing ways in different countries and localities. Apart from these common traits, but to some extent linked to them, there are a multitude of varying responses and solutions. This becomes obvious when we take a closer look at the mosaic of local education policy-making.

Specific local responses

In the framework presented in Chapter 1, it was emphasized that contemporary education policy at the local level has to be understood also in terms of particular national and local contexts. Some conditions may be common for a nation as a whole whereas others are local in the sense that they characterize a specific sub-national territory. Indeed, every locality is unique. Local education policy is not only a question of implementing national policies or reacting to overarching trends, but it is also a response to particular local circumstances. National decentralization policies have extended the scope for local decision-makers to adjust education to local requirements. In addition, some of the general trends, mentioned earlier, in themselves promote fragmentation and disintegration. These dialectic, and seemingly contradictory tendencies, are captured by concepts such as 'glocalization' and 'fragmegration'. A practical consequence is that distinctive education systems can be identified at the local level. Together, these represent extensive variation in terms of educational provision, content and governance.

The various chapters in the book emphasize this feature of contemporary education policies. Differences in *national contexts* were investigated in Chapter 2. It was observed that education in Britain has a deeper tradition of elitism, which is still reflected in recent education policies. Sweden, on the other hand, has relied more on comprehensive values of education, even if these are being eroded by present changes. The British tradition of élitism has made the system more prone to accept market policies and competition between schools. These changes have occurred also in Sweden, but in milder versions.

Nevertheless, the most significant variations can be detected at the *local level*. As mentioned previously, each locality is unique. This is reflected in the culture and the historical and institutional legacy of a place. Some of these characteristics are peculiar to specific places and cannot be generalized, but other features may lend themselves to capture within more general categories. Throughout the book, a number of such local characteristics have been identified as being important for the shaping of local education policies.

It should also be emphasized that there is no direct link between certain kinds of local features and particular types of local policies. Local conditions are always mediated trough the perceptions, values and beliefs of local policy-makers. Actors, not structural preconditions, make the decisions, even if structures provide both limits and opportunities. Bearing this in mind, we can, nevertheless, offer a few examples of factors, which appear to bring out certain patterns in the mosaic of local education systems.

Several contributions emphasize how *the urban–rural divide* represents different preconditions for local education. A school system in an urban location is faced with other challenges than one located in the rural countryside. Problems may be different, but also, there are more schools, and hence more choice alternatives, at a close distance in the city. Therefore, it is not surprising that local authorities are more prone to develop local school choice policies in urban settings in Sweden (Chapter 3) and education policies are shaped differently in rural Cheshire than urban Birmingham (Chapter 6). Further, the size of municipalities (terms of their population) is highly significant with regard to how Swedish education administrators and school leaders respond to new ways of governing by goals and objectives (Chapter 7).

The existence of major *local problems* is also important for how different local education systems take shape. Education can be used as a way of responding to or counteracting such problems. This can be exemplified by the results presented in Chapter 5, where it was shown that Swedish local authorities with high unemployment problems tend to adjust courses to the needs of local business. Again, this is particularly relevant in the densely populated municipalities. It is also illustrated in a more qualitative way with regard to Birmingham's response to its problems of severe unemployment and low educational achievements discussed in Chapter 6. However, as shown in Chapter 4, a social environment with high mobility and where students are disruptive requires other kinds of responses from the school and puts different pressures on teachers and school leaders, than an environment characterized by limited problems and more extensive parental involvement.

An important feature of the social environment is the strength of *the middle class*. Even if the growth of the middle class, as previously mentioned, is a general tendency of change, its strength varies between municipalities. In middle-class communities, parents tend to be more involved in their local schools. However, this also puts pressures on local education policy-makers. The analysis in Chapter 3 showed how Swedish municipalities that are dominated by the middle class are more likely to develop choice policies. Indeed, this appeared to be the single most important explanation of the pattern behind school choice policies. Middle-class influence over schooling is also reported in Chapters 4 and 6, which deal with British conditions.

The *ethnic composition* of a locality may also be reflected in how local education policies are shaped. It may manifest itself in adjustments of educational content, extensive provision of home language education and religious education. Indeed, the ethnic diversity of a municipality appeared to be an important explanation of why some Swedish local authorities develop choice policies, as was shown in Chapter 3.

Several of the factors that have been mentioned reflect differences in value orientations between communities. However, and not surprisingly, local education policies also mirror *the political composition of the council*. This is most clearly brought out in two of the chapters that deal with local education policies in Sweden. In Chapter 3, the strength of liberal conservatism in the local council was an important explanation to why some councils aim at facilitating school choice. Chapter 5 illustrated how a competitive situation between the two major party blocks was conducive for local authorities' use of education in their local economic development strategy, particularly in urban areas.

Are local education policies different in localities with different *resources*? Chapter 5 illustrated that the extent of local educational resources was important for whether Swedish municipalities incorporated education into a local economic development strategy. In

Chapter 8, on the other hand, we learned that a lack of resources could be an important reason for cities to establish themselves as learning cities. The fever historical and natural advantages a city enjoys, the more important it is that it adopts the notion of a learning city.

Finally, as Sharon Gewirtz underlined in Chapter 4, differences between local education policies may be seen in terms of *discourses* or dominating assumptions. The way schools were assumed to be in terms of failures or successes appeared to be important for what actually could be done. The discourses of failure/success, together with various social and material differences, created differing scopes for action on the school market.

These examples of factors, which distinguish between different aspects of local education systems, are by no means exhaustive. Neither are they general, as they have been identified in relation to specific features of local education policies. In addition, as was emphasized previously, some local characteristics can never be captured in general categories, since they represent unique phenomena, such as the particular culture or historical legacy of a place. Nevertheless, through this overview, a few important patterns have been distinguished in the seeming disorder of the mosaic of local education systems.

Final remarks

The study of local education systems is a challenging research agenda. This book represents an exploration of a field which has become increasingly relevant and important, but which still remains under-researched. The studies collected in the volume have provided a number of answers and insights. However, in the same way as many other explorative studies, these tend to provide more questions than they do answers.

On one of the first pages of the book, the question was posed as to whether there is a general tendency towards convergence arising from the impact of general trends or whether we can expect increasing differences. If we were to attempt to summarize an answer to this question on the basis of the experiences from the studies in this book, it would be – both. Global changes interact with specific local conditions in varying (and sometimes unexpected) ways to produce particular local responses. Thus while there are strong influences of a general kind that affect local education systems throughout the Western world, there are also distinctive features of each and every local education system. Some of these features have been identified, at least tentatively, but others remain to be explored. Further comparative analyses are required in order to reach a fuller understanding of the rich variety of local education in different settings. This is a challenging task for education policy researchers in the future.

Index